The social history of Canada

MICHAEL BLISS, GENERAL EDITOR

Report on social security for Canada

LEONARD MARSH

WITH A NEW INTRODUCTION BY THE AUTHOR
AND A PREFACE BY MICHAEL BLISS

UNIVERSITY OF TORONTO PRESS
Toronto and Buffalo

© University of Toronto Press 1975

Toronto and Buffalo

Printed in Canada

Library of Congress Cataloging in Publication Data

Marsh, Leonard Charles, 1905-
Report on social security for Canada

(The Social History of Canada; 24 ISSN 0085-6207)
Includes bibliographical references.
1. Insurance, Social — Canada. I. Title.
II. Series: The Social History of Canada; 24.
HD7129.M3 1975   368.4'00971   74-82286
ISBN 0-8020-2168-9
ISBN 0-8020-6250-4 pbk.

This Report on Social Security for Canada was originally published in
1943 by the King's Printer (Ottawa).

This book has been published with the assistance of a grant from
the Canada Council.

Contents

A Preface

BY MICHAEL BLISS

PERHAPS IT IS BECAUSE the most far-reaching changes in Canadian society have been so recent that they are still so neglected in the study of Canadian history. Canada has only become a modern welfare state since the end of the 1930s, a development which has barely begun to be appreciated as a major event in the society's history. No one can minimize the importance of our transition from a society in which provision for destitution was largely an individual responsibility to one in which a variety of programs guarantees a level of social and economic security to all citizens. At the same time very little has been written about the nature of this transition, the concepts underlying it, the social, economic, and political environment in which it took place, or the men involved. The most important single document in the history of the development of the welfare state in Canada is Leonard Marsh's *Report on Social Security of Canada,* presented to the House of Commons Special Committee on Social Security in 1943. The Marsh Report was a pivotal document in the development of war and post-war social security programs, the equivalent in Canada of the Beveridge Report in Great Britain. It is being republished in the Social History of Canada series to make its contents more widely available to those already concerned with the history of Canadian social policy and in the hope of drawing the attention of other students of Canadian society to this vital theme of our social development.

We are particularly fortunate that Dr Marsh has written a new introduction for this edition of his report. His comprehensive and succinct discussion of the circumstances in which the report was written, as well as his afterthoughts on the reception it received, are in themselves another important contribution to our understanding of the development of social security in Canada. But there is one weakness in the introduction, Leonard Marsh's reluctance to tell us more about himself.

Leonard Marsh was still in his thirties when he wrote the *Report on Social Security for Canada.* But he was already one of the most experienced, prolific, and versatile social scientists in the country. He had received his early training in economics at London University, in the course of which he had participated in research for Sir William Beveridge and Sir Llewelyn Smith. In 1931 he was appointed Director of Social Research at McGill University, where for the next ten years he directed a pioneering program of co-ordinated social science research on employment and related topics, financed by grants from the Rockefeller Foundation. The McGill program produced several major studies of Canadian social conditions, the most important of which was Leonard Marsh's own *Canadians In and Out of Work* (1940), the most comprehensive study of employment and the Canadian social structure before John Porter's *The Vertical Mosaic.* While also managing a teaching load in McGill's Department of Political Economy, Leonard Marsh found spare time to offer extension courses on social problems, travel widely in North America to appear at conferences, serve on occasion as an advisor to the Dominion Bureau of Statistics, the Canadian Federation of Mayors, and various Montreal social agencies, conduct a study tour of Scandinavia and the USSR in 1937, and appear frequently on CBC radio forums. He contributed to the League for Social Reconstruction's program of democratic socialism for Canada, *Social Planning for Canada,* besides submitting briefs and reports to the Canadian Welfare Council, the Quebec Social Insurance Commission, and the Royal Commission on Dominion-Provincial Relations. Along with Harry Cassidy, Charlotte Whitton, and others in that first generation of Canadian social workers and researchers, Leonard Marsh was fully employed, indeed over-employed, in the desperate struggle to develop the specialized understanding of Canadian society and its problems that would be essential to the development of modern social welfare legislation.

After his wartime service in Ottawa, Leonard Marsh worked in Washington, London, and Geneva for the first UN agency, the United Nations Relief and Rehabilitation Administration (UNRRA), first as a welfare advisor and later as Information Officer. From 1948 to 1960 he co-ordinated over a hundred Master of Social Work dissertations as director of research at the School of Social Work of the University of British Columbia. In 1965 he became Professor of Educational Sociology in the Faculty of Education of UBC, and since 1973 has been Professor Emeritus of Education. Through these years he continued to give a wide variety of auxiliary lectures and courses, and published books and articles on topics ranging from slum clearance and community colleges to the appreciation of music. In his forty years of research, teaching, and public service in Canada, Leonard Marsh has made an unparalleled contribution to the development of Canadian social science, social policy, and social justice.

An Introduction

BY LEONARD MARSH

THE SOCIO-HISTORICAL PERSPECTIVE of welfare legislation is very different from the bursts of publicity and news headlines that characterize signal events – such as the Social Security Report seemed in April 1943. It has to be related to the depression of the 1930s which preceded it; the war years (at first sight surprising); and the immediate post-war period, when 'reconstruction' was in the air, nationally and internationally. The War, whatever it was in death and destruction, was a vortex in terms of social ideas and political ferment. To understand the Social Security Report, it is necessary to recall the epoch-making events of the 1940s, both internationally and specifically in Canada.

In Britain, the depression did not start in the 1930s: it was persistent in the older industrial areas in the late 1920s. Unemployment Insurance in the form in which it was launched in 1911[1] – not without considerable opposition – was intended for the most seasonal occupations, and therefore for short-term periods of need. Chronic unemployment led to prolonged extensions to the periods for which benefits would be payable, as well as to the coverage of the labour force; and to those who did not understand this small bulwark between joblessness and destitution, it was in disrepute on this side of the Atlantic as 'the dole.' It was widely alleged, before depression produced the mounting totals of people on relief in Canada and the United States, that the dole *prevented* men from finding jobs. In Britain, demands for a complete overhaul of all the social insurances – which had grown up piecemeal and with many gaps and anomalies since Old Age Pensions had started provisions, in 1908 – had mounted. When the Labour party entered the Cabinet at the onset of World War II, it was with the understanding that this reform would be worked on during the war; as one of the guarantees, indeed, that the war must have a democratic purpose. The Committee was set up (June 1941) under one of the Ministers, the Honourable Arthur Greenwood, and a key advisor, Sir William Beveridge, was appointed as activator. What was eventually to be the 'Beveridge Report' was thus several years in the making; it was a joint analysis by a range of Department heads and advisors (some of whom might not have met but for the Greenwood Commission); and it dealt to a considerable degree with *existing* provisions and pieces of legislation. These points are important for a proper understanding of the Canadian report, as will be seen below.

Canada and the United States suffered the depression of the 1930s together, but there were significant differences. The financial crisis was precipitated by the stock market crash in New York, and there were no bank failures in Canada, although trade and business connections were too intimate for Canada to profit by insulation. But the prairie droughts, though equalled in the Dakotas and other sections of the middle west, were an altogether special catastrophe adding to the unemployment and relief burdens of the 'Dirty Thirties.' By 1933, the low point, fifteen to twenty per cent of the *population* (depending on how the counts were made, and there were no adequate statistics until about 1937) were dependent on municipal social assistance; more than twenty-five per cent of the normal male *working force* were unemployed; and most of the young men had not found their first jobs after leaving school. For a while the only expedient for them was the relief camps set up under the Department of National Defence. From the onset these were an unpopular resort; growing resentment culminated in the March to Ottawa, and the confrontation with the police in Regina, in 1935.[2] Following a change of (federal) government in that year, they were discontinued. More adequate arrangements were worked out to share relief costs with the municipalities (who, under the BNA Act, were primarily, if not solely, responsible for aid to people in need, but many of whom were bankrupt by the middle thirties); a number of surveys, both public and private, began to inject their information into policy-making;[3] and the first halting steps in 'welfare state' legislation began to be taken. Unemployment insurance was non-existent. It was regarded in conservative, political, and business quarters as unsuitable to North American conditions, where men could move around to find work. The decision of the Bennett government to legislate an unemployment insurance scheme in 1935 – by now widely advocated because 'the emergency' did not disappear – was so desperate that it ignored the obstacles of federal-provincial division of jurisdictions. It was declared unconstitutional in 1937; and the Liberal government's subsequent bill in 1940 was empowered by a specific BNA Act amendment. Medical care, housing, improvements to mothers' allowances, and pensions for the aged, all merited attention; but so much hinged on the need for a complete overhaul of fiscal arrangements between the Dominion government and the provinces that social welfare measures received

only piecemeal attention at best. 'Medical relief' for the unemployed
was instituted in some provinces, and in Ontario the medical profession launched OMS (Ontario Medical Services) as a private, pre-paid
scheme.[4] Health insurance had been projected in two provinces,
British Columbia and Saskatchewan, without achieving implementation. The surveys essential for policy-making came in the complementary reports of the Royal Commission on Dominion-Provincial
Relations, appointed in 1937. Its work was still proceeding when
World War II engulfed Canada, and the federal-provincial Conference
which might have permitted many agreements and new legislation
was overshadowed by the urgencies of the war. Interim fiscal procedures were negotiated, giving large responsibilities and fiscal
powers to the Dominion government with grants-in-aid for the provinces, which were also understood to be subject to revision at the
end of the war.[5] Even so, the Rowell-Sirois reports (as they were
known after their respective chairmen) were a landmark in Canadian
social history. The 'red books' – supplementary reports – reviewed
all the social services, including municipal responsibilities, in great
detail; old age pensions, widows' pensions, and mothers' allowances;
'state medicine' and public health; social insurance and contributory
social services; and education. The subsequent 'green books,' the
complementary documents of the Dominion-Provincial Conference
on Reconstruction (1945), also dealt separately with the subjects of
health, social assistance, education, and related social services.

In the United States, provisions for unemployment and farm
relief were in the first four years even more delayed than in Canada.
Until mid-1933, indeed, federal aid was confined to Red Cross distributions of wheat and cotton, and the unemployed sold apples in the
streets. With Roosevelt and the New Deal, however, a series of
expedients were embarked upon, aimed at business recovery, agricultural aid, and state provision of employment. Many Canadians in
those years advocated study and suitable emulation of the Federal
Emergency Relief Administration (May 1938), the Civil Works
Administration (November 1933), the Arts Program and the
National Youth Administration which evolved out of the Works
Progress Administration, and the Civilian Conservation Corps.[6]

But the New Deal also launched the first Social Security administration to use this title. By present standards it was elementary. It
had two main branches: (a) aid to the aged, blind persons, and

dependent children; (b) the first 'unemployment compensation' system, with contributions from employers and employees, and graduated benefits. Many occupations, such as domestics and farm labourers on the one hand and civil servants and railway workers on the other, were excluded; and each state was left to frame its own variations of the plan. The first part of the program provided only grants-in-aid (federal standards came later), but at least social assistance was lifted from solely municipal shoulders. It is fair to mention that unemployment insurance and developed employment exchanges had long been advocated by persons of the stature of Francis Perkins, Paul Kellogg, and Professor (later Senator) Paul Douglas. A completely definitive study was published by Paul Douglas and Aaron Director (from the University of Chicago, with the sponsorship of President Aydelotte of Swarthmore College) under the title *The Problem of Unemployment*) (Macmillan) as early as 1931.[7]

Thus events in both the countries which have most influenced Canada were moving to the acceptance of social security legislation. But the War brought British and Canadian contacts particularly close. Canadian troops were in Britain before the Dieppe raids and in preparation for D-Day; British and other Commonwealth air-force personnel trained in Manitoba. Canadian personnel abroad were much interested in post-war re-establishment prospects (and education services for the forces included pamphlets and discussion material on the subject). They were able to sense the dynamic which produced a Labour government in Britain in 1945, in spite of the oratory of Churchill which had buttressed the efforts and deprivations of the years of war.

But the psychology of the times cannot be fully assessed without remembering the Atlantic Charter. The historic meeting of Churchill and Roosevelt, at sea, took place in August 1941 – before the Pearl Harbor attack brought the United States into the war against Japan. President Roosevelt's 'four freedoms' included 'freedom from want.' The Atlantic Charter included 'social security' and 'fair labour standards' among its aims. The Allied declaration after Pearl Harbor, the first Declaration of the United Nations, proclaimed as the basic goal of victory 'the preservation of human rights and justice in their own lands as well as in other lands.'

⎦ By the 1940s, therefore, social security had become not only an avowed national aim, but an international idea⸝ The term 'social security' itself was significantly American, replacing 'social welfare,' reflected in the Canadian Welfare Council and its several publications, and the 'social insurances' favoured in Britain and retained in the title of the Beveridge Report.[8] But the force of the idea was clear. The Ottawa correspondent of the *Montreal Gazette,* Canada's leading conservative newspaper, wrote in March 1943 just before the Canadian report was released:

... more significant than the probable monetary costs and estimated domestic benefits of such a plan to any of the democracies are the international aspects of this widespread interest in and demand for greater social security. They are inseparably related to the aims expressed in the Atlantic Charter and that document is as essentially global as the war which produced it.

By 1943, social security was in the air as never before. It was the mid-point of the war, though nobody was sure of that; but there was at last evidence that the Allies would win out. The International Labour Office (ILO) had been issuing reports on social insurance components for many years, but comprehensive co-ordination had not been tackled, or perhaps even envisaged, till the work of the Greenwood Committee culminated in Beveridge's masterly systhesis. This Plan, as it was quite properly called, differed from all others in that Britain already had a widespread basis of actual pieces of legislation.[4] The American contribution to this 'year of synthesis' was the magnificent report of the National Resources Planning Board (NRPB), which had been started as early as 1939 and was soon to be known as the Burns Report, after the Board's director of research, Evelyn M. Burns. Its title was significant – Security, Work and Relief Policies:[10] it was much more influenced by the experience of the depression than the immediate stress of war; it put primary emphasis on employment (though public and private welfare agencies were an integral part of its many consultations); it emphasized long-range policy as much as immediate administrative changes. Of its nineteen chapters, a majority dealt with the past, present, and recommended future of 'public aid.'[11] Even the summary of the report required more than fifty pages. As a product of the New Deal, it deserves to rank not with the many improvisations (whose collective impact undoubtedly eased the situation substantially by 1937), but with the Tennessee Valley Authority, one of the world's contributions to long-range planning, co-ordinated protection and development of resources, and fundamental amelioration of rural, agricultural, and community life.

CANADIAN POST-WAR PLANNING

In Canada, post-war planning began with provisions for discharged soldiers, sailors, and airmen (including training grants as well as medical care benefits, etc.), for these began to appear, of course, long before the end of the war. Moreover, a Department of Veterans Affairs was already in existence, and one of its first moves was to improve on the experience of World War I by anticipating a complete system for the thousands of young men (and a greatly increased proportion of young women) who would be the veterans of World War II. An Advisory Committee on demobilization and re-establishment was set up as early as August 1940. It reported to the Minister of Pensions and National Health, the Honourable Ian Mackenzie, and through him to the Cabinet Committee which was set up at the onset of the war. It soon became apparent that the problems of demobilization could not be assessed without reference to the total post-war economic situation, especially if employment opportunities for returned men were the issue, and a separate Advisory Committee, on post-war reconstruction, was discussed in Ottawa in February 1941 and formally established the following September. Dr Cyril James, then president of McGill University, was recruited to chair this body, and a representative group of members was invited to join. It included Dr R.C. Wallace, president of Queen's University, Mr Tom Moore (labour; succeeded by Mr Percy Bengough), Mr J.S. McLean (business), Mr Donald McKenzie (agriculture), Dr Edouard Montpetit (Université de Montréal; succeeded by M. Arthur Surveyer, a professional engineer from Quebec). There were also liaison members including Mr K.M. Cameron and Mr W.S. Woods, deputy ministers from Public Works and Veterans Affairs, respectively. Early in 1945 it was arranged for the Committee to report directly to the Privy Council (in effect, to the Prime Minister). On its termination, its activities were merged and co-ordinated with the Advisory

Committee on Economic Policy which had been established immediately at the outbreak of war and was reconstituted in 1943.

The Advisory Committee on Reconstruction set up six Subcommittees – on Post-War Employment Opportunities; on Agriculture, Conservation and Natural Resources, and Construction; on Housing and Community Planning; and on the Special Post-War Problems of Women. The Committee set up eighteen research projects contributory to all these branches of the task and found qualified people with the time and willingness to undertake them – no easy matter in that period of manifold recruitment to wartime tasks. One of these was a 'type study' of conservation (the Ganaraska Watershed Survey, largely the work of A.H. Richardson of the Ontario Department of Lands and Forests) which anticipated the type of work nowadays recognized as ecology-directed.[12] Another was a type study of regional planning based on the St Lawrence Waterways International Section. Two studies related to social security: one undertaken by the Research Advisor himself, on 'Social Security Legislation: A Survey of the Prerequisites for Post-War Planning'; the other, a survey of existing social welfare legislation, in which Dr Stuart Jaffary was a collaborator, was only partially completed, but incorporated into what later became the published Social Security Report. With the exception noted below (note 12), the contributory studies were mimeographed, made available to the Cabinet, senior civil servants, and the Parliamentary Committees, but otherwise incorporated into the published reports of the Advisory Committee on Reconstruction and its Subcommittees.

Both the House of Commons and the Senate set up Committees of their own, which on various occasions heard submissions from members of the advisory committees. The House committee adopted 'Reconstruction and Re-Establishment' as its title, the Senate opted for 'Economic Re-Establishment and Social Security'; but the House of Commons struck a Special Committee on Social Security in 1943, and it was to this committee that the Social Security Report was formally presented.

In the flood of publicity and comment which followed the release of the 'Marsh Report,' two misapprehensions persisted for a considerable time. One was that the 'plan' was a hasty document, put together under pressure because the government, or particular politicians, decided it had become timely. The other, of more consequence, was that too much emphasis was placed on providing a vast scheme of monetary benefits 'from cradle to grave' and not enough on the importance of providing employment – and in the process, of course, preserving the work incentive. The factual answers are interrelated.

Of course the report was prepared under pressure. But so was all the work of the Committee, its members, its tiny secretariat, and its widely ranging collaborators. That the Advisory Committee in two-and-a-half years produced a substantial final report, six sub-committee reports,[13] and nearly twenty contributory reports and memoranda was a tribute to the pace of wartime service that was evinced on other 'fronts' of the time in munitions, aircraft, tanks, and shipbuilding production, to say nothing of training programs and administrative undertakings of all kinds. But to suggest that it was hasty, in conception or in the materials assembled, was to forget that the writer had been lecturing on these subjects for more than ten years previously at McGill University; that he had been employed on a series of related research topics, all concerned at one point or another with employment, housing, education, and social welfare services in Canada; that he had multiple contacts with administrators and welfare specialists in Canada and the United States; and that from 1939, McGill University had been host to the International Labour Office (ILO) with its corps of social security experts, when they had to evacuate from Geneva at the onset of the war. It is true that there was a concentrated week of conference, with three Canadian experts and one of the ILO specialists, Mr Maurice Stack (with Dr Oswald Stein, then one of the most knowledgeable men on social security systems throughout the world); but their function was to comment *seriatim* on the several parts of the plan already in provisional draft. Finally, the writer knows from the experience of thirty years of editing that it is the skill, effort, and occasionally the inspiration of editing that turns research material into a usable and readable text. This requires unremitting concentration, and it is anything but hasty.

The recognition of the importance of employment policies in any reconstruction planning is abundantly evident. The context of the

Final Report of the Advisory Committee stresses every aspect of employment measures, from fiscal support and international trade to a variety of works projects, including reforestation and housing. The Social Security Report itself makes a basic distinction between 'employment risks' and 'universal risks,' which is carried through the total text; it emphasizes training programs and the strengthening of the Employment Service, and reinforces these with extensive appendix material. Indeed, nobody familiar with the experience and research of the 1930s would have done otherwise. The special emphasis of the American Social Security report has already been mentioned. The viewpoints of Beveridge are even more emphatic. The postulate of what full employment policies must be pursued is stated as a foundation at the onset of his report. Even more relevant, however, is Beveridge's pioneer work on the analysis of unemployment and the labour market, his contemporary analyses of the economics of recovery and reconstruction, and most of all his companion book, *Full Employment in a Free Society* (1944). Incidentally, a summary of the latter book contains the most lucid exposition of Keynesian theory of full employment known to this writer, and his emphasis on the *proper distribution of work opportunities* as well as of fiscal measures is still apposite today.[14]

It would take another book to recount what has happened to social security and full employment policies in the thirty years or more since the Marsh Report made the headlines. It is better to confine this account to the setting of the times, to aid the reader to make his own judgment of what has transpired in the succeeding three decades. But two components of welfare planning – medical care and children's allowances – merit further comment.

HEALTH INSURANCE

In Canada, health insurance was a special case, for many reasons. It had been in the Liberal party platform since 1919. In British Columbia a Health Insurance Act was actually passed in 1936, after many years of study had been given intermittently to the subject. Even though approved by a plebisite (1937), the medical profession resisted participation and the Act was never implemented. Similar legislation was enacted in Alberta (1935) and similarly shelved. In Saskatchewan, the 'municipal doctor' system had a long history, dating from the mid-1920s, and comprehensive medical care, with community health centres, was pioneered on a pilot basis in Swift Current. Studies preparatory to planning health insurance on a national scale had been made with the active co-operation of the Canadian Medical Association before the war, but in 1941 the subject received governmental recognition, starting with meetings of the Dominion Council of Health (provincial deputy ministers and others) and culminating in the establishment of the special Advisory Committee on Health Insurance (1942) under the chairmanship of Dr J.J. Heagerty (at that time director of public health service in the Department of Pensions and National Health). In 1942 and 1943, the Canadian Medical Association, the Canadian Public Health Association, and many labour, farm, and citizen associations passed resolutions in favour. In March 1943, the Heagerty Report was presented to the Parliamentary Committee simultaneously with the Marsh Report by the Honourable Ian Mackenzie, who undoubtedly foresaw a national Health Insurance Act as the signal contribution of his political career. The draft Bill, paying meticulous attention to the comprehensive survey of public health, medical care, financial costs, and contribution systems contained in the Report (on which medical representatives were a majority of the signatories) was received by the Committee in July 1944 and further prepared for consideration by the Dominion-Provincial Conference which had been scheduled for 1945.

The Social Security Report (p 267) recommended priority for health insurance with unemployment insurance – the two basics of 'universal' and 'employment' risks, respectively; and this recommendation seemed reasonable enough in the light of the events recalled above. Both the Heagerty Report and the Marsh Report recognized that provincially administered schemes would be essential, but both were striving for modes of national co-ordination that would be politically acceptable. The Heagerty Report instanced a model (provincial) act, complete contributory systems, and Dominion grants-in-aid. The Marsh Report invented 'degressive' contributions (p 150) to reconcile flat-rate personal contributions with graduated government subsidies. There is little doubt that had any such federal-provincial arrangement been consummated it would have paved the way for the additions and restructuring of the other components of a nation-wide social security system (p 196 et seq.). The breakdown of the Dominion-Provincial (Reconstruction)

Conference of the summer of 1945 left health insurance suspended, with only half of the four main grants (those for research and training, and for assistance in hospital construction) brought into action.[15]

In every civilized country, no social service is more basic than that of health care. Of course, this covers a wide area, from public health and disease control to well-baby clinics and family planning, to say nothing of such things as liaison arrangements with day-nurseries, schools, and social agencies. But access to doctors and other medical personnel (and meeting the financial costs) is the central issue, and it is sad that the record reveals every variety of compromise and resistance. Throughout the world, public health measures alone range from first-class to urban-rural inequalities, to despairingly overworked, to virtually non-existent. In health insurance the examples of truly comprehensive coverages, such as New Zealand, Britain, and Denmark, are so few as to make them the object of continuous study (rarely free from partisan objections, but invariably with acquiescence in their essentiality). In the United States, the compromise that alone gained Congressional approval was to limit coverage to the aged and a few related categories. A similar formula applied rigorously to low-rent housing helped to develop the public housing ghettos of the metropolitan areas, and in Canada to segregate housing for senior citizens from residential communities built for all groups (as people or families, not as categories). Escalating costs of medical care, as of housing, now show that extensive public provision over twenty years or more could have been a buttress against this 'income distribution component' of inflation. Canada, more dependent on provincial initiative than ever, has every variety of arrangement, with some fully comprehensive examples, notably in Saskatchewan.[16] The three most common compromises are insurance plans for hospital costs only (government co-ordinated), free or subsidized medical care for indigent persons only, and pre-payment (monthly contributions) schemes run by medical associations (private groups, usually controlled by medical personnel, with standard fee charges). Lack of Dominion-wide co-ordination has contributed to the lack of attention to many outstanding issues: the national extension of community health centres and other modes of group practice and co-ordinated practitioner care; the deployment of para-medical personnel, generically trained nurses, and travelling services; and the even more serious issue of high medical costs.

The growth of private and voluntary pre-payment schemes in almost all provinces, up to and beyond the time of the Hall Commission report (1964-5), was remarkable. By 1961, according to the data assembled by the commission, about 60 per cent of the population were members of one or another plan, though coverage varied considerably. By 1967, just before national medicare legislation was passed, the percentage was estimated at 70. While the experience of the private plans (some on a co-operative basis) was invaluable, they left a significant proportion of Canadians without provision; and there has been abundant evidence from surveys over many decades that these are typically the poor, and often the most in need. They are the so-called 'medically indigent'; and it is this group for whom the medical profession, who have always welcomed monthly pre-payment plans (which avoid both doctors' unpaid bills and the patient's financial catastrophe of a major illness or operation), have always advocated government aid. Without comprehensive health insurance, the indigent depend on hospitals, emergency wards, local agencies, and the medical care which comes with social assistance. In effect, this is 'state medicine' for the underprivileged. Completely comprehensive health insurance not only provides a national fund, contributed to by all citizens and supplemented by tax revenues which can also be collected by equitable means, but also provides through its statistics, its advisory committees, and a national supervisory department or Commission, a balanced picture of the country's health situations and a 'watch dog' on its financial costs. All this had to be reiterated in extensive studies by the Canadian Welfare Council in 1952-4 and in the massive report of the Hall Commission in 1964, before a modified national program was finally initiated federally in 1968.[17]

In Britain, the National Health Service with a substantial history (since 1948) illustrates the fully tripartite operation of general practitioners, hospitals, and local health services (including pre-natal clinics, home nursing care services, and community health centres). There are seven major advisory committees and over a hundred local executive councils for family practitioner services. The number of non-participating doctors in England is around two per cent of the total. What is of considerable relevance for Canadian examination is that extensive reorganization of the Health Service to fit into the new regional pattern of England is being undertaken, to come into force in 1974.[18] In the United States, the continuing problem of the unequal distribution of medical care is the ever-spiralling costs of doctors', specialists', and hospital bills, which the network of private insurance schemes only partially offsets. It is a safe prediction that extension of medicare beyond the aged must sooner or later be undertaken, with federal and state aid and administration.

CHILDREN'S ALLOWANCES

Children's allowances are a special case because they were a complete innovation, have been federal from the start, and point the way to the newest phase of social security planning, the guaranteed annual income concept. They have a long historical background: they were advocated by British pioneers in the 1880s when nearly all wages were low and a large family was almost universally a direct cause of poverty; the first applications, e.g., in Belgium and France, were accepted because minimum wage regulations, necessary though they were, would not have been enough to ensure adequate standards of living. The modern rationale, even in 1943, was very different. Provision for *all* children (whether the parent is unemployed or at work, whether there are two parents in the home or only one) is the key to consistency in a comprehensive scheme for both employment and universal risks. Without them, all administration and all rates and schedules are more complicated, and inequities may result because the family income may be greater, e.g., from unemployment benefits *plus* allowances than from wages *without* allowances. The key to consistency was not the over-riding argument as events turned out. Official and political opinion alike favoured the twin arguments of providing a new source of a 'purchasing-power floor' against the hazard of the post-war slump, and the vital constitutional fact that it was clearly permissible and administratively simple for federal disbursement. It was even possible, with little or no argument, to have the payments made to mothers. There was of course a flurry of frightened argument from those who did not understand the demoralization of poverty and those who translated the work ethic into 'population panic.' Within a few years, both Department of Welfare statistics and social agency surveys were reassuring as to the practical benefits of these small but reliable supplements to the family budget. One of the most revealing developments was the provision for continuing them to adolescents *provided they remained at school.* In the longer run, what is most significant is that both children's allowances and old-age pensions together are operative as components of 'guaranteed income' and so described. Today, the GAI concept has gained remarkable ascendancy in welfare discussions, and advocacy even by economists, all within the space of little more than a decade. There was indeed, in Britain, a phase when 'Beveridge principles' (i.e., reliance on a set of social insurance components) were condemned as out-of-date, but this phase was influenced at least in part by studies which showed that social security schemes by themselves do not guarantee the abolition of poverty. The most sophisticated welfare projections of the 1970s are directed as much against gross inequalities in income distribution and in access to services (and such basics as decent housing and adequate education), as against the risks which earlier Social Security studies sought to assemble for attack. And this concern has become more and more frankly and realistically international.[19]

Hindsight is very different from foresight, but one element stands out so much from any perusal of the Social Security Report that it cannot escape comment. In 1941, 33.4 per cent of male heads of families in urban areas had incomes of $1000 or less; in rural areas, 59.7 per cent. Relief schedules for families with small children in 1937 varied from $50-63 down to $22 per month (p 84). The adequate liberal (highest of four standards) budget for food, for a family with three children, was considered in 1939 to be around $53 a month (p 78). Rents in urban Canada in 1941 varied from less than $20 a month in smaller cities to less than $35 (average) in the larger cities. In Vancouver in 1941, one in five of all tenants were paying $15 or less. Rent and price controls during the War kept these rates, incredible as they may look now, relatively stable. No data could bear greater witness to the inflation which has characterized the last thirty years. There were, of course, ups and downs — prosperity booms and relative recessions. It is true also that the Canadian national income has risen prodigiously. There is greater productivity, more industry, dramatic additions to resources, notably oil and natural gas; there is also a much larger population. But prices, land values, wage levels, family budgets, consumer goods, household appliances, and national revenue itself, all establish an economy – and welfare dynamics – on a totally different scale in today's world. Whether it could or should have been foreseen is probably an unprofitable line of discussion. But one cannot escape the reflection that social security schemes would have been less costly to inaugurate and might well have offered more public knowledge and government action on controls had they been inaugurated in the first flush of post-war redirection. Had the first National Housing Act been operative in 1930 instead of 1937 (when houses could be built for $3500-$5000, though only 4900 were so built, under assisted home-ownership provisions – and no public low-rent housing built at all), who can doubt that today's housing situation would have been less of a recurring 'crisis' such as characterized in the 1960s? – to say nothing of its effects on employment, pre-war and post-war.[20]

A cartoon in a London newspaper toward the end of the war when acceptance of post-war reconstruction measures seemed to be lagging in Britain showed Beveridge saying to the Minister: 'May I introduce ...?' and profferring *half* of a working man (labelled 'the full employment part of the policy') to the other half, to whom the Minister is talking, labelled 'the unemployment insurance part.' This pinpoints the relationship between reports, governments, and public very deftly, and much more quickly than the long recital of social history necessitated here. Devotedly worked-out charts of the territory are essential before social goals can be staked out; history has proved devastatingly how each depends on the other.

NOTES

1 Employment Exchanges are worthy of mention, for these were set up (as Labour Exchanges in the first terminology) under the direction of a Board of Trade civil servant named W.H. Beveridge, well versed in the work of the Poor Law Commission of 1908, and through the advocacy of a Minister named Winston Churchill. Their purposes included not only registration of job vacancies, but the

beginning of adequate statistics and the application of 'tests of genuine unemployment by reference to the unsatisfied demand for particular kinds of labour' thus measured.

2 Detailed documentation of conditions, opinions, and political statements of the times has been assembled in a major compilation by Michiel Horn, ed. *The Dirty Thirties* (Copp Clark 1972). Barry Broadfoot has collected a series of recorded conversations under the significant title *Ten Lost Years: Memories of Canadians who Survived the Depression* (Doubleday 1973).

3 Examples were Harry Cassidy, *Unemployment and Relief in Ontario 1929-1932* (Dent 1932); F.R. Scott & H.M. Cassidy, *Labour Conditions in the Mens' Clothing Industry* (Nelson 1935); *Report of the Royal Commission on Price Spreads and Mass Buying* (King's Printer 1937); *Social Planning for Canada* (Nelson 1935); *Health and Unemployment* (Oxford Press & McGill University 1938) see note 4; L. Richter, ed., *Canada's Unemployment Problem* (Macmillan 1939).

4 For a comprehensive survey of all provinces for the period 1931-8, see Leonard C. Marsh, A.G. Fleming, C.F. Blackler, *Health and Unemployment* (Oxford Press & McGill University 1938).

5 This is far from a complete coverage of the complex political events which are the warp and woof of the 1930s fabric. The interested reader may review them expeditiously in chapters 16 and 17 of Kenneth McNaught, *The Pelican History of Canada* (Penguin 1969). Three sentences are tersely expressive: 'To implement the Rowell-Sirois plan would have required a combination of BNA Act amendments and policy agreements between Ottawa and at least a majority of the provinces. Such agreement was never reached. Throughout the Commission's period of research it was virtually boycotted by [the premiers of] Ontario, Quebec and Alberta.'

6 There were many other programs, e.g., the National Recovery Administration (NRA) and the Public Works Administration (PWA), the Agricultural Adjustment Administration, the Federal Surplus Relief Corporation, and the Farm Security Administration. Most of these 'alphabets' have passed into history, but they were virtually revolutionary in their day and none were launched without cries of concern. They made famous the names of Harry Hopkins, Corrington Gill, Harold Ickes, Arthur Altmeyer, and Arthur Burns. An excellent account is available in Corrington Gill, *Wasted Manpower* (Norton) which is particularly illuminating because it was written in 1939. (The United States did not enter the War till 1941.)

7 The difficulties of assembling comparable data and a general rationale for Canadian research and remedial measures can be gauged by reference to Leonard C. Marsh *Employment Research* (Oxford University Press 1935). The bibliography shows what types of studies were available at that time.

8 The Canadian Welfare Council was originally the Council on Child and Family welfare. Today it has been rechristened the Canadian Council on Social Development. 'Social development' is favoured in Third World countries, where it is related to community development programs, and also lends itself better to UN multilingual translations. 'Insurance' was not favoured in the US, partly because many of the component schemes are fiscal rather than actuarial, but also because insurance was claimed as a private preserve. Even these changes in terminology have significance.

9 In one of his books (see note 14), Beveridge records that briefs and memoranda were received from 127 different organizations other than government departments, and that the Committee met on 48 occasions. One of Beveridge's gifts was the capacity to sift such a great mass of data and varied suggestions into a coherent scheme.

10 Natural Resources Planning Board *Security, Work and Relief Policies* (US Government Printing Office 1942). The board issued a summary pamphlet (September 1942) entitled *After the War – Toward Security*.

11 It is an objective comment – not meant to be prejudicial – that the NRPB Report was as American as the Beveridge Report was British. Yet in broadcasts and articles at that time, Beveridge had to refute complaints that his plan was 'American' or 'Russian'! The Marsh proposals (they could not be a Plan in the Beveridge sense) were worked out quite independently, but the coupling of Beveridge and Marsh plans in the press led to some ill-informed allegations that the Marsh report was only a re-hash of Beveridge (and at least a few articles in Quebec that said it was 'English'!). The truth is that by 1941 there was a common stock of ideas and principles available to those who knew the literature.

12 Published separately under the title, *The Ganaraska Watershed: A Study in Land Use with Plans for the Rehabilitation of the Area in the Post-War Period* (Dominion & Ontario King's Printers 1944)

13 The Report on Housing and Community Planning was delayed till 1944, for good reason. It incorporated the most extensive surveys of every aspect of the subject ever made in Canada up to that time and

was three times the size of any of the other reports. Leonard
Marsh was the hard-pressed editor.

14 His earliest book was *Unemployment: A Problem of Industry 1909
and 1930* (Longmans, Green 1930). In 1931 he published *Causes
and Cures of Unemployment* (Longmans, Green) based on broadcasts delivered on the BBC. *The Pillars of Security* (Macmillan 1943)
reveals his views on wartime and peacetime perspectives and is en-
livened by a set of Low's cartoons. The summary of *Full Employment in a Free Society* (Allen & Unwin 1944) was published by the
New Statesman (London). Beveridge's capacity for lucid exposition
was his other outstanding gift (cf. note 9 above).

15 The basic 'Green Book,' *Proposals of the Government of Canada*
(Dominion-Provincial Conference on Reconstruction, Ottawa,
August 1945) is still well worth consulting, as an indication of how
employment, housing, agricultural, health, and other welfare
policies – even collective bargaining and 'productivity committees'
– might have developed. The health insurance proposals specifically
recognized the need for three-year adjustments to permit implementation by stages.

16 Hospital insurance was introduced in Saskatchewan 1947 and federal
hospital insurance legislation was enacted in 1958, but all provinces
were not participants till 1961. Comprehensive health insurance
('medicare') was introduced in Saskatchewan in 1962 (see note 17),
but the Swift Current comprehensive pilot plan dates
from 1946.

17 Basic references are *Royal Commission on Health Services* (Hall
Commission; Queen's Printer 1964); C. Howard Shillington, *The
Road to Medicare in Canada* (Toronto: Del Graphics 1972), a defen-
sive but fully documented survey of private and co-operative plans
throughout Canada. The hectic story of the opposition to the 1961
medicare legislation in Saskatchewan, medical as well as political, is
told in Robin F. Badgley & Samuel Wolfe's *Doctors' Strike* (Macmillan 1967). It includes an extensive bibliography on Canadian,
British, and American health-care surveys and legislation. Chapter 15
of *The Road to Medical Care* gives the details of the federal Medicare
legislation, introduced in 1965, discussed at several provincial conferences, subjected to opposition from both medical and political
sources, and only brought into operation in 1968 by federal government insistence.

18 A succinct and up-to-date reference is *Health Services in Britain*
    (Ottawa: British Information Service R515473, January 1973).
19 By far the most comprehensive analysis has been published by the
    Council for Social Development (the successor to the Canadian
    Welfare Council), thanks to a Nuffield Foundation grant which per-
    mitted an international colloquium to be held, with representatives
    from eleven countries: *Guaranteed Annual Income: An Integrated
    Approach* (Ottawa 1972). Another recent Canadian study, Norman
    Alcock's *The Emperor's New Clothes* (Canadian Peace Research
    Institute 1971), advocates the GAI as a new approach to overseas aid
    for the underdeveloped countries of the world.
20 A comprehensive account of the housing situation as it was in the
    1930s and of building progress under all available legislation after
    the war up to 1948 is given in Leonard C. Marsh, 'The Economics of
    Low-Rent Housing' *Canadian Journal of Economics and Political
    Science* (February 1949) 14-33. An examination of the sub-
    committee report of the Advisory Committee on Reconstruction,
    Housing and Community Planning (1944), will show how few of its
    recommendations were followed with any dispatch, in spite of its
    documentation on the urgency of the situation.

Report on social security for Canada

LEONARD MARSH

Letter of Transmittal

February 17th, 1943

Principal F. Cyril James
Chairman
Advisory Committee on Reconstruction
Ottawa

Dear Dr. James, – I have much pleasure in transmitting herewith a report, as requested by the Committee, on the principal matters involved in the consideration of comprehensive social security legislation for Canada. As the Committee is fully aware, the report is essentially a preliminary appraisal, not a final blueprint with all the details filled in; but it has seemed desirable to emphasize this in a prefatory note. In particular the report leaves open a number of alternatives, makes no decisions on rates of benefit and contributions, and incorporates no actuarial calculations.

Broadly, the subject-matter divides into four parts:

1 The nature of social insurance and of social minimum standards, examined from various angles, but particularly with reference to existing legislation in Canada and to post-war exigencies.
2 A special section is devoted to employment (primarily from the labour-market viewpoint, economic policy being referred to only incidentally). Some of this recapitulates topics which have already received considerable examination by the Committee and one of its Subcommittees. But it is desired to emphasize the important point that social security legislation in a post-war context has no firm foundation without special employment measures for the transition period.
3 Two detailed parts then examine *seriatim* all the branches of social insurance other than unemployment insurance. The review of existing legislation in this field in Canada, namely, workmen's compensation, old age pensions, and mothers' allowances, is included here in integral relation to possible insurance developments.

4 The concluding section brings together the most important
   matters calling for decision, particularly *(a)* the inter-relation-
   ship between units in a comprehensive scheme, *(b)* constitutional
   and administrative issues, and *(c)* the finances of social security
   legislation.

It is proposed to reserve for a supplementary study, to be prepared
later, an examination of provincial and local welfare services and
other constructive facilities most germane to a social security
system. The report as it now stands, however, is complete within its
own confines.

Faithfully yours
LEONARD C. MARSH,
Research Adviser

Prefatory Note

The purpose of this report, if it is to be put to best use, should be clearly understood. It is not a compendium of draft measures, ready to be implemented as soon as they are approved by Parliament or the people. It is an attempt to set out *(a)* the main features of existing statutory provisions for social security matters in Canada; *(b)* the methods by which these provisions can be improved and extended, particularly by transformation of the coverage and the technique to a social insurance basis; and *(c)* the principles which should be considered if the construction of a comprehensive social security system, suited to Canadian conditions, is to be undertaken in the most fruitful and effective manner. It is thus an effort in clarification as well as a survey. The field of social welfare legislation, even within the limits accepted in this report, is vast: it is, moreover, of concern to every citizen. Progress will therefore depend vitally on a wide understanding of the potentialities, and also the responsibilities and limitations, of social insurance methods. They demand debate before the blueprints are drawn up.

It is a pleasure to acknowledge the ready and helpful collaboration secured in the drawing up of this report, from: Dr. George F. Davidson, Executive Director of the Canadian Welfare Council; Dr. Stuart Jaffary, of the Department of Social Science, University of Toronto; and Miss B. Touzel, Executive Director of the Toronto Welfare Council. Dr. W.J. Couper and Dr. Allon Peebles of the Dominion Department of Labour acted as consultants on several points; and special thanks are due to Mr. Maurice Stack, of the International Labour Office staff, whose advice on social insurance practice in other countries was a particularly valuable ingredient in the discussions.

L.C.M.

PART I

THE BASIS OF THE TASK

1. CANADIAN PERSPECTIVE

The war, or rather the unprecedented production effort that the war has called forth in Canada, has changed the face of the Dominion so far as social needs and social security problems are concerned. It is not only that mass unemployment has been eliminated, with such unemployment as still remains limited to special problems of transferring between jobs, production hold-ups in industrial plants, and other types of interruption of working time which do not leave workers completely without prospect of further employment. In spite of the heavy demands of the Treasury for revenue to finance the war, consumer incomes have increased in several sections of the population. Earnings in many families have been brought above their previous levels through better-paid or more regular work on the part of the main breadwinner, the employment of additional members of the family, or even in some cases through the allowances now payable from state funds for the members of that family who are serving the country in uniform. There are still broken families—in some respects more than ever before—and not only because of the absence of fathers or sons overseas, but because members of the families have found work away from their home towns, and again because many housewives are now full-time or part-time workers on one of the home fronts of the war effort. There are still problems of distress, for war bereavements have been added, and on a growing scale, to those of normal times. But full employment, whatever may be its special wartime pressures, has removed the chief characteristic of the Canadian social welfare picture as it was in the thirties. It has erased from the lives, if not the memories, of many thousands of families, the hopelessness and tragedy of seeing no means of making a livelihood in sight, and no means of maintenance other than doles from municipal or provincial governments, unskilled and dispiriting relief work, or assistance from the voluntary charitable agencies in the cities of Canada where these existed.

It is certain that this background of social and economic insecurity has not been entirely forgotten by many who are employed or contributing to family earnings now; and it is equally certain it must not be forgotten in projecting our minds forward to the post-war period, in planning in advance what measures should be taken to deal with the re-employment problems of that period, and on a wider plane seeking to give reality to the aspirations and hopes which the peoples of the world are more and more clearly voicing: that organized provision will be made in the post-war world for the risks and contingencies of family life that are beyond the capacity of most of them to finance adequately from their own resources.

These risks and contingencies are not solely those of unemployment. But it is understandable, against the background of the depression thirties, why unemployment should dominate most other considerations. If earning power stops all else is threatened. For the moment it is not necessary to pause to distinguish the differences in the risks of unemployment, sickness, accident, more normal but none the less serious events from the point of view of the working budget such as the increase in the number of children; and other factors. There are certain basic lessons to be learned from the experience of the thirties in which all the hazards of life—at least as they appear to the low and middle income groups—seemed to be swallowed up in the great vortex of unemployment.

The first is that provision for unemployment, both economically and socially, is the first and greatest need in a security programme designed for the modern industrial economy. A second is that in the absence of organized provision for particular categories or types of need and contingency, unemployment relief—itself the extension of provision intended only for destitution of multiple forms—draws into itself all other kinds of need: sickness, disability, widowhood, desertion, loss of residence requirements and so forth. Provision for simple destitution without any particular analysis as to cause may be barely justifiable when the scale of such assistance is small, as it was in the small parish or village of long ago when only a few persons in each community found themselves at any particular time without any means of subsistence and beyond the support of any relatives. It is completely indefensible, and of a nature to defeat efficient and constructive administration, once it attains national dimensions.

Canada has experienced all the problems of undifferentiated relief provision, and the consequence of having little or no measures designed for specific causes of distress and need. These deficiencies, in point of fact, are not solely in what is usually known as social security legislation, Some of them are due to the inability of municipal governments, whether in terms of finance or of administrative facilities, to handle many of the problems which constitutionally may still be interpreted as their responsibility. The basic framework of government itself has still not been adapted in any radical fashion—except recently for the vast effort of the war—from that which at the time of Confederation seemed proper for a country of the New World that did not know the modern problems of unemployment or public health or lack of economic opportunity, and was still in very large measure a constellation of small communities.

It would be a mistake to assume that a social security programme is entirely a matter of specific pieces of legislation, each covering a field marked off for itself alone. Social insurance involves an administrative organization, which is important for Canada not solely because it is a federal community but because of its problems of sheer distance. The proper methods for decentralization and regional administration demand the most careful consideration. None the less this much is clear. The only rational way to cope with the large and complicated problem of the insecurities of working and family life is by recognizing and legislating for particular categories or areas of risk or need. One of the contributions made by the social insurances, almost without the change being observed, is the advent of classified maintenance or treatment, or what in some countries has been called categorical provision. As will be indicated later, there is still need for development or rationalization of some of these categories. But this much may be said in advance. The establishment of organized provision for even one defensible area of need, as, for example, through the institution of unemployment insurance or health insurance, makes immensely easier the handling and the sorting out of the other types of need which still remain.

The Method of Social Insurance

An explanation of these areas of social contingencies will be made in a succeeding Section. First, it will be well to state simply what social insurance means, and why the approach through social insurance methods is appropriate. There are three basic reasons:

(a) In modern economic life there are certain hazards and contingencies, which have to be met, some of them completely unpredictable, some of them uncertain as to time but in other ways reasonably to be anticipated. They may be met in hit-and-miss fashion by individual families or they may be met by forms of collective provision. Some of the risks may never strike any individuals or families; but we know from experience that, *collectively speaking,* these problems or needs are always present at some place in the community or among the population.

(b) For a large proportion of the population, incomes are not sufficient to take care of these contingencies through their own resources. It is no answer to this point to say that this would not be true if wage rates and earnings were higher than at present. As one of the Rowell-Sirois reports has summed up the matter, "It is impossible to establish a wage which will allow every worker and his family to meet the heavy disabilities of serious illness, prolonged unemployment, accident and premature death. These are budget-shattering contingencies that strike most unevenly." The inadequacy of even moderate incomes to provide for such things as major illnesses has now been measured by more than one authoritative investigation.

(c) The third principle, which really links together the first two, is that of the collective pooling of risks. Social insurance is the application on a much larger scale of the principle of pooling which has long been the basis of insurance in the more restricted sense (commercial insurance against fire, etc.). A great number of people may be liable to a certain risk, but only a few of them at any one time. At the time the hazard strikes, they may draw on the resources gathered through the contributions of many, including their own.

The understanding of social insurance, however, is still confused because too much emphasis is placed on the second word and too little on the first word

of the phrase. Social insurance brings in the
resources of the state, i.e., the resources of the community as a whole, or in a particular case that part
of the resources which may be garnered together
through taxes or contributions. It does not mean,
more particularly for phenomena subject to such
variability as unemployment, that there must be a
precise actuarial adjustment of premiums to risk in
each individual case. The contributors who do not
draw on the fund help to aid the unlucky ones who
suffer unemployment or some social casualty. Some
social insurance provision may have to be frankly
viewed as no more than the gathering together of a
fund for a contingency whose total dimensions are
uncertain, but whose appearance in some form or
magnitude is certain. In any circumstances it is
better than having no collective reserves at all, or
leaving the burdens to be met by individuals in
whatever way they can. Of course, the more refine-
ment that can be made, in the light of experience,
between revenues required and current disbursements, the more systematic and economical for its
particular task the social insurance fund becomes.
The most important and serviceable of these devices
is the provision, now written into all modern legislation, for careful annual review of the finances of
the scheme, and their relation to current contribution
and benefit rates. This is the real "actuarial"
continuity in social insurance arrangements. The
basic soundness of social insurance is that it is
underwritten by the community as a whole. In
the broadest sense, the question is one of determining
what, in relation to the national income, can or
should be made available to deal with certain
contingencies and liabilities; and, having decided
the scale and quality of the provision by reference
to what we can afford and to what are justifiable
standards for a civilian community, of raising the
money and administering it for the purpose
concerned.

As experience with social insurance has grown, there has been increasing recognition of the advantages of this pooling of individual risks by collective means along with state control and participation. It is very emphatically commented upon in the Beveridge Report in terms such as the following:

"When State insurance began in Britain, it was felt that compulsory insurance should be like voluntary insurance in adjusting premiums to risks. This was secured in health insurance by the system of Approved Societies. It was intended to be secured in unemployment insurance by variation of contribution rates between industries as soon as accurate valuation became possible, by encouragement of special schemes of insurance by industry, and by return of contributions to individuals who made no claims. In the still earlier institution of workmen's compensation, adjustment of premiums to industrial risks was a necessary consequence of the form in which provision for industrial accidents was made, by placing liability on employers individually and leaving them to insure voluntarily against their liability. In the thirty years since 1912, there has been *an unmistakable movement of public opinion* away from these original ideas, that is to say, *away from the principle of adjusting premiums to risks* in compulsory insurance *and in favour of pooling risks.*"

The Beveridge recommendations go so far in this direction as to envisage not merely complete inclusion of all persons involved in a particular category of social need, but the collective administration of the funds for all the major categories of need in a comprehensive scheme.

It may be questioned why, if these extensions of the pooling idea are valid, social insurance should not be financed solely by taxation, rather than the contributory method. The answer depends a good deal on practical considerations. If a widely com-

prehensive and unified scheme is not possible immediately, contributions serve to demarcate the section
of the population for which it is intended to cater.
Secondly, they have certain distinct administrative
advantages, through applications, records and other
ways, relating the individual directly to the service
rendered or benefit received, and serving to facilitate
the enforcement of conditions attached to benefit.
For some groups, though not all, it is an advantage
to be able to make small periodic payments, which
would be less feasible under a tax scheme (although
developments of income tax payment methods are
lessening the distinction between taxes and contributions in this respect). But whatever the method
of assessing the contributions, since it is in the
interest of the insured person to maintain them
regularly, his relation to the administration is more
likely to be a responsible one. Generally speaking,
the wider the area over which it is sought to make
benefits available, the more important this becomes.
And the proprietary interest which citizens as
contributors come to feel in the satisfactory working
of the scheme is not without psychological as well
as administrative virtues.

None of these considerations should obscure the
possibility of combining both contributory and tax-
revenue methods. In effect, it is this combination
which the Beveridge recommendations propose to
develop extensively, and the combination has been
effectively in operation in the comprehensive New
Zealand system for several years. It is important
to note, indeed, that state contributions or outright
grants (e.g. in the form of marriage or maternity
grants) administered in conjunction with an insurance system are much more likely to be payable
without introducing the flavour of charity or the
equal disability of irresponsible gratuity.

This is really the logical outcome of planning a
better distribution of existing or anticipated income.

both in point of time and as between the whole
population or certain classes of it. Much of it is
not necessarily additional expenditure, but the
replacing of inefficient expenditures by more efficient
methods. This is best recognized to-day in the case
of health insurance. Large expenditures are already
made both by governments and by citizens for
medical care, much of it ill-advised, much of it
in the later stages of an illness or disease when it is
least able to be effective. Taxes in modern communities are similarly a major method of redistrib-
uting incomes, and of securing through individual
contributions certain objects of collective expenditure. Social insurance administration, of course,
brings to the disbursement of payments and services
certain appropriate conditions. But the ability to
put these conditions into effect on a fair and uniform
basis is one of its major advantages. The genius
of social insurance is that it enlists the direct support
of the classes most likely to benefit, and enlists
equally the participation and controlling influence
of the state, at the same time as it avoids the evil
of pauperization, and the undemocratic influence of
excessive state philanthropy.

Relation to the Post-War World

The purpose of this report is to look forward, not
backward. It would not serve this purpose if it
were not geared closely to consideration of the vast
economic and social changes which are going on
now, and which must continue only with the difference of changes in purpose and direction, once the
war is over. There have been certain compelling
arguments for the community types of social
provision ever since the growth of large industrial
communities. But there are additional reasons, and
some reasons which change the force of the old ones,
for planning the overhaul and extension of our social
legislation at this time.

The first is that social security has become accepted as one of the things for which the peoples of the world are fighting. It is one of the concrete expressions of "a better world" which is particularly real to those who knew unemployment, destitution, inadequate medical care and the like in the depression periods before the war. To others the idea of better social security measures may be less of a reaction from previous hard experience; but it is an intelligible recognition that it is one way of realizing nationally a higher standard of living, and of securing more freedom and opportunity through the use of such income as is available once social insurance has taken care of the minimum.

Whatever assessment may be placed on the first and rather broad interest in social security, a second one is completely realistic and timely. The end of the war means demobilization of much of the civilian as well as the uniformed population and, no matter how short may be the period of transition, there are risks and difficulties attached to the process of re-employment against which all appropriate facilities must be mobilized. It should not be forgotten, in this connection, that the re-employment problems of the post-war period include the reassembling of many thousands of families.

A third and equally realistic consideration is that the transition period will show in more ·marked contrast than any other, differences in respect of social provision for Canadian citizens when they are in the army or in some other branch of the services, and when in ordinary civilian life. The provisions which the state extends to its armed forces and their dependents in time of war, and to ex-service men's families after war, go far along all the avenues of what is usually comprised in "social security"— provision for children's maintenance, widowhood, medical care, disability, unemployment, retraining, and other contingencies.

The standards and allowances and the attention given to many varieties of need will, rightly or wrongly, be measured against standards of livelihood and welfare in the civilian world. Some of these differences may be entirely justifiable. But nothing short of an objective appraisal of existing legislation, the requirements of transition, and the adjustment of such civilian deficiencies as may have been rendered more prominent by improved attention to groups affected by the pressure of war, will meet the situation.

The final point in gauging the need and validity of a social security programme in post-war Canada is only indirectly a welfare matter at all, but it is a strategic factor in economic policy generally whose importance cannot be over-emphasized. One of the necessities for economic stability is the maintenance of the flow of purchasing-power at the time when munitions and other factories are closing down and war activity in many other spheres is being liquidated. Sound social insurance, which is a form of investment in physical health, morale, educational opportunities for children, and family stability, is a desirable and a comparatively easy vehicle of expenditure. It is not only an eminently appropriate peacetime alternative for expenditures now being devoted to destruction: it is also a form of using some of the deferred backlog of consumer expenditure to which reference is so often made only in terms of radios, frigidaires and other tangible consumers' goods. In this perspective, a wide and properly integrated scheme of social insurance and welfare provision of $100,000,000 or $500,000,000 is not to be regarded with the alarm which, with inadequate understanding, it might otherwise occasion.

Some extracts from a recent statement made by the Chairman of the Social Security Board in the United States (A. J. Altmeyer) are extremely relevant on these points:

"Because of the manner in which benefit and eligibility rights are accumulated in advance of the receipt of benefits under social insurance, the contributory nature of its financing, and the automatic processes inherent in its operation, it is inevitably destined for an important role in the post-war period. The only basic question is whether a comprehensive system should be set up now, so that benefits will be immediately available at the end of the war to assist in alleviating the hardships of that period, or whether changes should be delayed until these hardships are actually occurring for millions of families.

Provided expansion is undertaken now, social insurance can play a dual role in the economic readjustment and reconstruction that will be necessary when the war ends. On the one hand, it can provide protection to individuals and families against the loss of income which they may suffer for one reason or another after the war, when a decline from the high levels of wartime production would increase greatly the incidence of risks leading to such losses. On the other hand, from the standpoint of the economic system as a whole, social insurance can aid in maintaining consumer purchasing power if national income exhibits a tendency to shrink and thus can assist in maintaining employment at higher levels...

The general sense of security which would result from the continuity of income provided by these various types of protection would provide a better life for the great mass of people. Knowledge that these programmes are in operation would give a sense of security to all who are protected, a sense of security which is the most potent antidote to fears and worry over the uncertainty of the times. Viewed from the present, therefore, the post-war period would not be anticipated with fear and apprehension because of the readjustments that will be inevitable but as a period when the economic

sacrifices made during the war will seem to have
been worth while. . .

If employment declines sharply after the war,
the need for a strong social insurance system will be
critically urgent. Even if our economy stays
geared for the long run to high levels of employment,
many millions of workers and soldiers may be
temporarily unemployed while we are changing over
from a war to a peacetime economy. It is precisely
in such circumstances that disbursements under an
expanded programme will be most likely to exceed
receipts and will be most useful in sustaining
general purchasing power."[1]

Subjects Not Within the Scope of the Report

This report addresses itself particularly to those
forms of individual and family need which arise
when earnings are impaired or interrupted by
unemployment, illness or accident; to the economic
problems which are directly incurred by failing
capacity through age, or loss of support through
disability or death; and to the family contingencies
requiring exceptional expenditure, particularly those
connected with birth, death and marriage. There
are, of course, a number of fields of social welfare
provision which might be considered in any exhaust-
ive survey of social facilities. Nutrition has become
so important a matter in itself that it is now a separate chapter in any social welfare book. The
proper provision of housing, and the elimination of
bad housing, is so universally recognized as a fundamental attack on many social ills that it also is a
separate topic in itself. There are certain inven-
tories—of hospitals, sanatoria, etc. or of institutions
for orphans, crippled children, etc.—which raise
questions of the adequacy of our capital equipment

---

[1] A. J. Altmeyer, "The Desirability of Expanding the Social Insurance
Programme Now", *Social Security Bulletin*, November 1942, pp. 6-7.

no matter what legislative provision there may be for care. The advent of health insurance will raise some of these questions more prominently. Education is of course a fundamental not only in social welfare but for many other aspects of civilian life. Better provision for passing the young worker from school to employment, and codes governing juvenile labour, would not be fully rounded out without attention to the treatment of juvenile delinquency. These and other problems will not be forgotten by anyone who has in mind for the future the fullest utilization of our human resources. They are excluded from consideration here because this report is concerned with one special and strategic method of covering, *through family income maintenance* in particular, some of the most widespread contingencies. The necessity for welfare administration improvements is referred to, wherever it is most directly relevant to the extensions of social insurance here reviewed. But this is another topic, demanding its own special report.

2. CATEGORIES OF SOCIAL NEED

In the history of social security legislation, the advent of health insurance and unemployment insurance at first sight seemed to clear the picture of provision for all contingencies considerably. It was obvious that they covered a large area of all problems of need and interrupted earning-power. But in fact they still leave territory in which a good deal of rationalization is called for. This is all the more true because there has been a considerable tendency to regard the British situation as a model and to follow the forms of legislation adopted there, without paying much attention to the devices accepted as compromise expedients or the anomalies which may have become incorporated in British practice. Clearly, these need not be adopted by those who follow after, particularly when it is possible to start from a clean slate.

In point of fact, both unemployment insurance and health insurance are neither so clear-cut nor so provident of full solution as they may seem. Unemployment insurance is properly adapted, by itself, only to certain of the shorter-run forms of unemployment; it does not deal with unemployability and certain forms of occupational rehabilitation needs; it becomes seriously ill-adapted if a large number of formerly insured classes are given unconditional allowances; and so on. Health insurance may or may not deal with public health and preventive medicine; hospital facilities as distinct from general practitioners' service; the interruption of income as distinct from the need of medical care. Even when some insurance is already in existence, therefore, it may be helpful to subject the total field to review.

A simple classification of the main contingencies is as follows. Its purpose for the moment is not to indicate how each kind of problem may be attacked;

but to emphasize that each is one of the hazards that every family of low or moderate income fears, for typically the amount of protection they can finance through savings, budget allotments for doctors' bills, life insurance, or retirement annuities, is too small.   The rates of incidence are of course very different; the risk of sickness is greatest, the risk of permanent disability or widowhood much smaller. But throughout the community at large, the risks are constantly making their appearance as realities.

I. *Unemployment.*—It is hardly necessary to stress the effect of this on family income, and the problems of need which may arise from it.   It is perhaps necessary to distinguish between unemployment in the sense of lack of work which is not due to the fault of the wage-earner, but to industrial causes; and unemployment or inability to work due to physical or mental defects.   But that the whole phenomenon is a major risk which has to be met in any modern society by collective as distinct from individual provision, is beyond question.

II. *Sickness and Medical Care.*—Sickness as a risk in the life of the individual as breadwinner or as a member of the family may be simply a problem of securing proper medical care.   But it is a problem which has to be made by collective provision because individual incomes are not sufficient to provide for the contingencies, or to pay for the desirable amount and quality of services.   Particularly when it strikes the breadwinner, however, it is also a problem of interruption of earning-power.   A serious and prolonged illness means not only medical or hospital bills but destitution if there are no sources to fill the gap created by the cessation of wages.

III. *Disability.*—At some points the line between sickness and disability may be hard to draw.   But clearly there are certain categories of disability where the cause or results or both are such that special provision is called for.   As a category of

social need, the burden on the family may be the
need for support of disabled member; or it may be
interruption or impairment of earning-power on the
part of one of the breadwinners.

IV. *Old Age and Retirement.*—The inability of
persons whose earnings during working life have been
low, to save enough to provide for the period when
they are no longer able to work with the same vigour
or regularity, has been earlier recognized as calling
for state assistance than most other contingencies.
As time has gone on, however, it has been recognized
that a pension may be appropriate at ages earlier
than those usually described as "old". The most
generalized form of the category would be the
appropriateness of retirement under any particular
set of circumstances in which it was not reasonable
or desirable for the individual concerned to attempt
to earn a living. A more common approach concerns itself with all cases of need in which the chief
wage-earner is no longer able to work at a reasonable
living wage.

V. *Premature Death.*—The death of the breadwinner (usually the husband) if he has had no means
or opportunity for building any savings or insurance,
may be a catastrophe for the family for economic
reasons apart altogether from others. The problems
of widowhood and orphanhood do not need explanation; but they have by no means been dealt with
consistently in most countries. The special problem
of funeral expense, a very real one for most low-
income budgets, has even more rarely received
comprehensive attention from the national point of
view.

VI. *Family Needs.*—Over and above all of these
contingencies is a factor which reduces the income
of many a family to levels inadequate for the proper
health and maintenance of its members—the size
of the family itself. Family needs, in this sense,
do not constitute a risk of the same type as those

listed above. But the inflexibility of wages or earnings (no matter what the level of skill) as compared with the needs of varying-sized and particularly of large families, is important enough in itself to constitute a sixth category or area in which social insecurity may arise. It is the chief reason for the recognition, already implemented in several countries, of *childrens' allowances* (also termed "family allowances" and "family endowment") as the logical complement to the more familiar social insurances. Certain contingencies which are normal, rather than risks, particularly the extra expenses due to marriages, births and deaths, may or may not be recognized as subjects for provision or assistance through the social insurance framework.

All of these contingencies together may be summarized in threefold fashion. (1) The first group comprises *interruptions of earning capacity*. These may be intermittent as in the case of unemployment or sickness; or prolonged as in the case of disablement. Every gainfully occupied man faces at some period in his later life the special interruption due to old age. Not all gainfully occupied persons face unemployment in the urban or industrial sense. (2) The second group is that of *occasions requiring special expenditure* which may place a strain on the family budget. Some of these are normal, as in the case of births, or deaths if the latter come in later life. Others such as accidents or major illnesses are less predictable. Finally, there is the possibility of (3) *greater continuous budgetary needs than the family income* can accommodate. If the basic wage of the husband is too low, or in the case of a farmer, if his holding is too small and unproductive, the latter condition may be chronic even if he has no children at all: other methods than social insurance are needed to remedy these situations. If the family's income is in other respects moderate or adequate apart from the circumstances of a large number of

children, the situation can be met through family
allowances.

Sir William Beveridge, referring to the substantial
series of studies of living conditions which have
been made in Britain within the last decade,
summarizes them as indicating that from three-
quarters to five-sixths of all want (according to the
particular measurement of poverty chosen) was due
to interruption or loss of earning power, and practically all of the rest due to "failure to relate income
during earning to the size of the family". It would
be a safe guess to take twenty per cent as the
minimum proportion of poverty due to large
families in Canada.

Modes of Attack

The differences between attempting to meet these
problems through social insurance and other methods
are discussed in detail in Section 4. In the absence
of social insurance legislation, poverty and unemployment have been met, in Canada as in other
countries, only through public assistance or poor
relief. Because there is a difference between social
assistance as it has been, and what it might become,
a preliminary reference is helpful.

Social insurance may be defined as the special
technique of organizing provision collectively by
securing contributions from various groups for a
need which cannot be left safely to individuals' or
families' own resources. It is concerned fundamentally with raising and broadening a national
minimum (the nature of which is discussed in later
sections). This concept can be applied to wide
areas of the population, measured geographically or
by income; and the modern tendency is to extend it
to cover the whole citizen body. *Social assistance*,
in the form of public assistance in which it has had
the longest history, is directed to meeting the same
social needs, but more or less by definition is

restricted to the sub-marginal groups of the population, whose needs are met on a compassionate or
charitable basis. It is not always clear, unfortunately, that it is concerned to raise standards
beyond subsistence. It is not inevitable, however,
that public assistance be as restricted as it so
commonly is. If social insurances exist to provide
a basic minimum for the majority of the population,
there is room for social assistance or public welfare
measures which are supplementary or even preventive in form, as for example some of the best
public health measures are to-day. Social assistance
may be at any stage between two extremes: one, an
anachronistic and unsatisfactory form of general
relief for all kinds of destitution, dependent mainly
on the proof of complete lack of means; the other, a
modernized and specialized series of constructive
welfare services. It is no accident that the latter
when found in this form is usually developed in
relationship to the practices and institutions set up
by insurance methods.

One important distinction, which runs throughout
all public welfare matters, is that between *(a) income
maintenance* and *(b) services*. Income maintenance
involves the provision of cash payments, whether
for temporary periods for unemployment, etc., long
periods as in the form of pensions, or grants for
special emergencies such as funeral expenses. *Services* are usually directed to the same contingencies,
but not in monetary form. Medical care is the
outstanding representative, but there is room
within the social insurance system for a variety of
preventive and restorative services: convalescence
for the sick, vocational rehabilitation for the disabled, training facilities for the unemployed, are
good examples. The two types of provision are not
always required for every case, nor need this be
administered by the same agency. Each should be
considered for its appropriateness to the particular
situation it is sought to remedy, and to the par-

ticular section of the population concerned.[1]

The distinction is relevant in the consideration of a final classification which should be noted, referring to the coverage (in terms of persons) for which each unit in the social security scheme is appropriate. Three groupings are particularly important.

(a) Some contingencies affect the *whole population,* whether occupied or not, and whether juvenile or adult. Chief if not unique among these is the need for medical care, though funeral expenses might be regarded as a special case. Children's allowances since they must be universal to be effective, are another special case.

(b) Some contingencies may be insured on the basis of risks affecting the whole *gainfully occupied population,* i.e., farmers and rural workers, the self-employed, as well as urban wage earners and other employees. Besides the need for medical care, these groups require protection for long-term disability and old age, and (in the case of married women) widows' pensions.

(c) Finally, some contingencies are confined wholly or mainly to *employed persons;* or by some definitions, the wage-earner or urban-worker population. The most obvious of these is unemployment; however, sickness is a counterpart to the extent that absence from work in the case of the employee is a direct cause of loss of income: a sickness cash benefit scheme is therefore appropriate for the urban wage earner. Income maintenance in the event of industrial accident and

---

[1] Both insurance and assistance are, of course, additional to the basic resource for most people, namely, wages and earnings, on which standards of living and individual security depend in the first instance. Also both social assistance and social insurance approach in their more highly developed forms to complete state provision, or some part of it (as, for example, when children's allowances financed solely from tax revenue, are established to complete a social insurance system).

certain disabling diseases is also recognized (through workmen's compensation) as a special system need confined to employees: potentially these could include all rural employees, but this coverage so far is exceptional.

Other examples could be given, but these are enough to illustrate the main point, that a total social security plan may properly be built in different dimensions for different sections of the population. What are usually known as the universal risks—the need for medical care, pensions in the event of disablement, old age retirement pensions, and widow's pensions—should be considered for the whole gainfully occupied population. Sickness cash benefits, unemployment benefits, and certain others, if they are not definitely inappropriate to non-wage-earner categories, would certainly be difficult to administer. It would be equally inappropriate, however, to confine provisions for e.g., old age or widowhood on an insurance basis to urban workers, on the ground that their contributions are more easily collectible. These considerations are all examined in the ensuing sections.

The Need for Integration

Though the categories have here been set out broadly to emphasize their nature, this has not been done without awareness of the fact that they become more refined in administrative practice, or restricted initially at certain points so as to be made susceptible to legal or actuarial handling. These restrictions, however, should be distinguished from some which are the product of inadequate legislation and are inherently much less justifiable. Even when national provision is advanced to the point of setting up social insurance systems, there may be a tendency for these schemes to solidify and mark off arbitrary or illogical boundaries. Industrial disability and accident, for example, are recognized as a matter requiring organized attention, while other accidents and disabilities, which may be equally onerous for the ordinary family, go almost unrecognized. Or old age and the need for retirement comes to be thought of as something which happens only at the age of seventy.

When legislation is mostly of the assistance type, especially if it springs from a past of undifferentiated relief for the destitute, a logical approach to specific classes of risk or need is even less likely. For fully effective social security planning, it is necessary to do more than visualize the categories which have here been outlined. It is necessary to be aware of associated and comparable contingencies: to appreciate, for example, the similarities and transitions between disability and old age; or between unemployment and certain forms of sickness so far as they involve absence from work. When all this has been done, it is finally necessary to recognize the essential unities of social security—to fit together, in other words, all the branches of social insurance and social provision in such a way that they support each other, and work together as a coherent administration. There is abundant experience to prove that this requirement will continually present itself; most of all in regions or districts where welfare services have been most greatly lacking or unorganized in the past. There is abundant evidence also to show the obstacles which will be left on the path of progress if a piecemeal approach is adopted. In a federal state the warning is all the more necessary. The demand for comprehensiveness is not mere academic straining after perfection: it is one of the practical realities of economic and efficient operation.

3. MINIMUM STANDARDS AND EXISTING SOCIAL LEGISLATION

For three reasons it is important to review at this point the most relevant measurements which have so far been made of defensible standards of living for Canadians. A yardstick is needed, first, because the starting-point of all social security discussion is the level of family income or, particularly in urban centres, of wages. It should be stated at the outset that this report is equally concerned with both rural and urban needs as the subject of social security legislation. It is relevant to note, however, that Canada is now definitely past the stage of being primarily an agricultural or rural country. Its population passed the predominantly rural mark at the time of the last war: it is hardly necessary to emphasize the acceleration which has been given to its industrialization by the present war. Wage levels, accordingly, while they do not tell the whole story of Canadian standards, have become more significant with time. Average levels of farm income remain much harder to determine, but certain broad estimates are possible.[1] For both these and for wage levels, there is no objective means of visualizing the total situation and the need for a social security structure unless we know what the main representative incomes are, and what these levels mean for family budgeting and family needs, as nearly as possible in quantitative terms.

---

[1] For a review of available measurements (for 1930–1939), see Marsh: *Canadians In and Out of Work,* pp. 173-177. "In general, there is a strong presumption that farm income follows a flattened pyramidal distribution: a minority group on established, debt-free, well-equipped farms; a large middle group with fluctuating fortunes not unlike the skilled worker, potentially able to make a minimum living but heavily liable to founder in depression; and a fringe below the subsistence level which, if urban unemployment figures offer any parallel, is considerably larger than the total actually on relief." Even for the middle group referred to, the range of income might typically be from $700 to $2,000.

The second reason is the need for some gauge to apply to existing legislation and social assistance practices. In part of this field, even information as to actual monetary rates cannot be properly interpreted without knowledge of the procedures of administration and the way these are apt to work in practice for the dependent groups and individuals concerned. The assessment cannot be merely statistical; but statistics help to present some picture of a complex situation.

The third and most important reason is that social security systems are primarily designed to lay the foundation of a social minimum. What this minimum should be is a matter for definition. Certainly, however, it means the direct elimination of poverty. It raises the level of those families whose incomes are inadequate at present levels or whose family needs too great, to permit proper provision for health care or savings against the risks of disability or unemployment. It prevents penurious old age and the necessity of parents becoming dependent on their married children in later life, and straining the resources of these younger families.

The Basis of Computed Standards

To obtain a standard which can easily be used and compared, it is necessary to state it in dollar terms. It may be admitted at once that such criteria cannot be used as if they were completely precise tools, the micrometers of social engineering. None the less, substantial progress must be recognized in the assessment of more and more of the quantitative factors making up a living standard. It is not so very long ago that food needs would have been regarded as almost unmeasureable; but there is to-day enough authoritative understanding as well as actual experience of food requirements to enable them to be discussed with a reasonable degree of confidence. It is worth noting that the physical requirements in respect of such matters as housing, fuel, and clothing do not require the same degree of scientific knowledge; it is entirely valid to appeal to the experience of those who know the actual types of these things available, and the extent to which they are or can be fitted into the household budget in particular environments.

The need for judgment will perhaps always remain greatest in assessing rural standards. Partly because of this, but also because of the paucity of studies adequate to the point, only computations secured from urban centres are referred to in this section. In Appendix VI, such material as can be procured is assembled, to examine how far a regional variation of a standard minimum might be feasible on the basis of rent differentials; the difficulties of such regional variation as already obtain in existing social assistance in Canada are discussed at the end of this section. At this juncture, an important circumstance, so far as standards applicable to social insurance are concerned, should be noted. The units paying cash benefits (unemployment insurance and sickness benefit schemes) to which wage-level comparisons are most relevant, are payable only to industrial or urban wage-earners. Disability pensions, old age pensions, and survivors' pensions, it is argued elsewhere (Section 14), may validly be placed on a national flat-rate basis, even though this may involve some differences in the purchasing-power of the benefits, in different areas, or as between town and country. The special case of children's allowances is considered in Section 15.

The most authoritative work on living standards has been done with special reference to food. The League of Nations, through its international Nutritional Committee, has set the basis from which all other specialists have proceeded, in the assessment of the dietetic content and amount of food whose consumption is necessary to maintain health and vigour. With a few modifications appropriate for the North American continent the most systematic translation of these into actual food budgets has been made by the Bureau of Home Economics of the United States Department of Agriculture (referred to below). For the special purpose of administering relief to the unemployed and destitute, computations relating to food have been made by various agencies in Canada including the organized social agencies in Montreal and Toronto, and by the relief departments of the Prairie Provinces; probably the most detailed enquiry, however, has been conducted under the auspices of the Ontario Medical Association, which set up a special committee on relief diets in 1933. These latter scales have had the advantage of more than one reassessment since that date, and have been measured against the experience of social agencies in the provinces. The caloric standards adopted are somewhat lower than those recommended by the League of Nations committee and than some of the American standards; but the budget amounts for relief purposes which have been set by reference to them are now above the average of Canadian provinces generally.[1]

Before passing to the full budget, of all household items additional to food, it is important to set out the chief differentials in possible budget calculations, and the qualifications which should apply to them. The necessity for resolving the idea of a standard into at least four different concepts is most succinctly presented by reference to the levels defined and

[1] For comprehensive review of minimum budget food standards, including the League of Nations recommendations, the Bureau of Home Economics (or Stiebeling-Ward) and Ontario Medical Association computations, see Marsh, Fleming and Blackler: *Health and Unemployment*, Chapter 20; and Grauer: *Public Assistance and Social Insurance*, Appendix 6 of the Rowell-Sirois Report studies, pp. 23-26. In supplementing these, advantage has been taken of two recent Canadian studies, *The Cost of Living*, special compilations made by the Toronto Welfare Council in 1939, and Tisdall, Willard, and Bell: *Study of Relief, Food Allowances and Costs*, report made to the City Council of Toronto, 1941.

computed by the Bureau of Home Economics of the U.S. Department of Agriculture (Table 1).

The desirable minimum to which the whole of the social security fabric may be geared by contributory techniques depends on the share of the national income which it is decided should be devoted to the purpose. It must be decided also by reference to the minimum quantities of the essentials of life sufficient to maintain the nutrition, health, and decency of the family as a unit. It is reasonable to compare the standard with some of the lowest of existing wage rates, but it is not an inherent necessity of social insurance principles to do so. Social insurance and its related measures themselves set a standard once they are instituted. A series of considerations must determine what that standard is to be, but the higher it can be set, the better for the country concerned.

It will be helpful to present these standards first in their most familiar form, i.e. for a more or less representative family, of five persons. The "moderate" standard represents something like the level of living in a city, of occupational groups with incomes of about $1,800 to $2,400. The "liberal" diet, much more generous than this one, would involve little or no attention to economy, and includes a variable range of luxuries. For the lower-income groups, including typical wage-earner families as well as families without the full requisites of self-support, the Bureau examined two standards. The first is a basic minimum which can be called adequate if it is understood that only the essential commodities are taken into account. It contains no luxuries, but does cover the "requirements for maintenance and growth over an indefinite period, furnishing a small margin of safety for nutritive essentials" and a promise "of limited choice as to quality". The other is a restricted minimum intended for emergencies or short periods only.

Priced in Canadian terms, the actual food articles in these budgets, which may be characterized as liberal, moderate, desirable minimum, and subsistence respectively, would have cost the following monetary amounts if they had been bought in 1936; and the comparable prices for 1939 (computed by reference to the cost of living index) are added.

During most of the depression years in Canada the relief rations which were made available to unemployed families bore a relation only to the lowest of these levels, the subsistence or emergency budgets. Apart altogether from a wide variation in the rates in force in the various centres throughout the country, deficiencies of 5 per cent were common,

TABLE 1.—MONTHLY AMOUNTS NEEDED TO MEET FOOD BUDGETS AT FOUR LEVELS

(Stiebeling-Ward Standards, U.S. Bureau of Home Economics)
(Five-person family: average)

Standard (Food only)	Index	Monthly Amounts	
		1936	1939
		$	$
I. Liberal................	145·2	51.07	52.86
II. Adequate, moderate......	115·1	40.48	41.90
III. Adequate, minimum......	100	35.17	36.40
IV. Restricted, emergency....	70·5	25.90	26.80

Source: Reproduced from *Health and Unemployment*, p. 166. 1939 estimates added.

and others of 15 to 20 per cent by no means exceptional.

These facts must be taken into account in seeking any standard on which to build social insurance

benefit rates. To avoid any possible misunderstanding of the limited character of the subsistence
or relief budget, it is desirable to assemble all the
qualifications which apply to it.

1. The scale of living presupposed for the emergency budget, is essentially a short-period one.
"Followed over a long period, the practice called for
in the emergency budget may prove harmful to
both health and morale".

2. It is unsuitable to long-term unemployment
benefit because of the risk that employability may
be impaired. Under any constructive policy an
unemployed man must be regarded as eventually
returning to employment: he will not be able to
take advantage of this if his physical capacity is
liable to be easily overtaxed.

3. It presupposes the most rigid economy, and
skill in both purchasing and food preparation. A
monetary allowance gives no assurance that it will
be spent in the same way as the original minimum
calculation; but it is made by selecting, often down
to small fractions, the most economical means of
securing nutritive elements many of which may not
be known or available to the ordinary purchaser.
Even if the purchaser has some dietary knowledge,
the small quantities which hand-to-mouth budgeting
forces upon the poorest housewives may easily
prove more expensive than the retail purchases of
the middle-income groups who can afford larger
units.

4. In close calculation of minima, it is unlikely
that sufficient attention can be paid to the differences
of nutritional need dependent on the age and sex
of members of the family. This is particularly true,
for example, of the needs of children during the ages
of 13 to 18.

5. The absence of a margin in the calculations for
non-essential expenditures does not prevent, and

can hardly be expected to prevent, the use of the food money for other purposes. Many relief budgets do not include allowance for such things as soap, matches, cleansers, etc.; apart altogether from such innocuous luxuries as tobacco and newspapers. Most of all, of course, there is no margin whatsoever for emergencies such as sickness or accident.[1]

A Canadian standard for the wider matter of a full family budget, covering all the items necessary to ensure health, reasonable living conditions and general self-respect, has been provided by a special study undertaken by the Welfare Council of Toronto in 1939. While the computations made relate only to the Greater Toronto districts, and the budget therefore constitutes a gauge for metropolitan conditions only, it was guided by reference to the studies of the Bureau of Home Economics and the Ontario Medical Association already referred to; it reflects also the knowledge of social workers, of the purchasing habits and requirements of low-income families, and the limits to the adjustments they can reasonably be expected to make.[2]

Desirable   Living   Versus   Assistance   Minimum   Standards

The purpose of this budget was to set the line at which there would be certainty over a long period

---

[1] It is true that these needs would be covered once comprehensive social insurance were in effect. But if this standard is used as a gauge of wage levels, it must be remembered that some allowance should be made for social insurance contributions.

[2] The budget is intended to show a minimum which would exclude any unreasonable expenditure, and assumes continuous and efficient management on the part of the housewife. Only the most economical foods were included. The operational items were selected on the advice of the trained workers of the Visiting Homemakers' Association. They include small charges for gas, coal, electric light, water, ice and cleaning materials; car-fare to the extent of 75 cents a week; and less than 50 cents a week for the replacement of household equipment. Rentals ($25 a month for 5-roomed house with three bedrooms as minimum for family of five) were judged from a sample study of actual houses meeting reasonable requirements of accommodation and repair. Since the budget is intended as a wage standard, it includes items for life insurance, group medical care, and a small amount of savings for contingencies, including dental care. The sum available for these, ($3.57 a week), includes no provision for maintenance in old age. Allowances for advancement and recreation ($1.39 a week), include newspapers, church and club contributions, nominal pocket money for children, but do not include alcoholic beverages, tobacco or provision for vacations.

for better than subsistence standards for a family of
five. Provided there was good management in the
home and the principal wage-earner suffered no
losses or reductions from unemployment or sickness,
there would be reasonable promise of a minimum
level of health and decency. Valued for 1939,
which is an appropriate basis, this would require
$28.35 a week, or $122.85 a month. The income
required for the food items only would be $34.66 a
month in this "living-wage" budget, and this
provides a means of comparison with other standards.
Of the Stiebeling-Ward dietaries, it is comparable
with the "minimum adequate" level, which at 1939
(all-Canadian) prices would require about $36.40 a
month. The most systematic examination of minimum food requirements so far made in Canada,
the Tisdall-Willard-Bell report, yields a figure of
$43.20 a month, averaged for 3-children families of
differing age and sex groups, at 1941 prices. Since
1939 prices were about 10 per cent lower, the
equivalent figures for 1939 would be about $38.90.
By both these tests, therefore, the standard employed here is not an excessive variation of the
"minimum adequate" level.

To further the evaluation for social insurance
purposes, it is useful next to divide this budget into
two parts, (a) the amount attributable to the
requirements of the parents (or a husband and wife
without children living together)—the "two-person
unit" as it may be conveniently referred to in other
sections; and (b) the average amount attributable
to the maintenance of a child in a family household. This computation produces a figure of
$16.00 weekly as the desirable or living-wage
minimum for the two adults, and an average for
each child (which must be approximate because
the needs of children of different ages vary) of
$4.10 weekly, or about $17.00 a month.

These are standards which ought to rule, at least

under urban conditions, if either wages or benefit payments are not to raise any deficiency problems in the course of a long period. If concessions are made, however, to the possibilities of restricted provision in emergency periods, to the areas of sub-marginal incomes already existent, or to the exigency of keeping down the gross contributions for a comprehensive national scheme, points can be found at which items can be excluded or pared down. A careful assessment of the Toronto Welfare Council budget has been made, and the reductions possible on a subsistence basis result in figures of $10.30 weekly for two adults and $3.40 as an average for each child. These would be monthly amounts of $44.50, and say $14.50, respectively. The restrictions thus embodied include more crowded housing accommodation and the absence of any allowance for advancement expenditures or savings at all, on the grounds that there is least room for safe economy on food. The lower standard must be regarded as conceded rather than recommended: a level which it is desirable to raise. In social insurance terms, if it is used to set benefit rates, the assumption or the hope would really be that supplementary sources of income might be available. The benefit rate would be a nucleus, perhaps an encouragement, for personal or industrial provision, through annuities, superannuation, and the like. It follows, of course, that application of means tests would be quite inappropriate.

It will repay the attention given to examine the two standards presented here in relation to a number of other familiar concepts of income, as well as other details previously noted which help to give meaning to the standards.

The ruling rates which have been set in Canada for minimum wages vary somewhat as between provinces, and are presumably subject at present to some adjustment for cost of living increases. One

TABLE 2.—DESIRABLE LIVING MINIMUM BUDGET, AND RESTRICTED ASSISTANCE MINIMUM

(Toronto Welfare Council and Adapted Standards)

(a) FAMILY OF 5 (3 CHILDREN)

	1939		1940–41	
Standard (All Items)	Week	Month	Month	Year
	$	$	$	$
Desirable Living Minimum	28.35	122.85	131.45	1,577.40
Assistance Minimum	20.39	88.36	94.54	1,134.48

(b) FAMILY UNITS (1939)

	Man and Wife		1 Child (Average)	
Standard (All Items)	Week	Month	Week	Month
	$	$	$	$
Desirable Living Minimum	16.00	69.29	4.12	17.85
Assistance Minimum	10.26	44.46	3.38	14.63

Based on *The Cost of Living*, Welfare Council, Toronto, 1939; and adaptations explained in the text.

of the highest figures, in British Columbia, is
$15.00 weekly; or in certain trades in which the rate
of 40 cents an hour is set, $16.00 a week if a 40-hour
week is assumed.   Even in Ontario, however, rates
outside the metropolitan area may be as low as
$10.00 or $12.50 a week according to locality.
It is relevant to add that minimum wage rates for
men, which are a fairly recent institution, are
admittedly set in relation to rates which were
originally intended to secure a minimum living level
for single women workers.[1]

A good indication of representative wage levels in
Canadian factories is provided by the statistics
of weekly earnings, averaged for all manufacturing
industry in the summary bulletins of the Census of
Industry division of the Bureau of Statistics.
For male wage-earners only, these national averages
have moved up in the last five or six pre-war years
from $20.30 to $22.23 a week, the latter being the
figure for 1939.   Corresponding figures for female
wage-earners in 1939 were $12.77, i.e., just above the
usual minimum wage.

The best perspective of all would be complete
figures on the distribution of incomes of families
throughout the Dominion.   Thanks to new material
provided by a sample count, undertaken by the
Dominion Bureau of Statistics, of the earnings data
of the Census, an illuminating table can be compiled
giving a part of this picture, for a year (1940-1941)
in which the full results of increased war production
had not yet taken effect.   The table is particularly
valuable because, besides giving contemporary
figures (comprehensive data having been available
only for 1931 until recently), it is possible to distinguish clearly between heads of families and other
individuals, and also between persons located in
urban and rural areas.

---

[1] A convenient source of reference for details of the computation which
seems to have been used generally as a Canadian standard is Grauer,
Labour Legislation, appendix study to the Rowell-Sirois Report; p. 251.
The figure as computed in 1933 is $12.50 a week.

It must be noted that the tables do not measure family income as such. This qualification becomes important, however, only for the family in which there are several extra earners of adult or near-adult wage level. A good guide for this correction is available from the result of the detailed enquiry undertaken by the Dominion Bureau of Statistics in 1937-1938 of typical family incomes and expenditures, for the purpose of improving the basis of its cost of living index.[2] This showed earnings of the father as accounting for by far the major share of the total family income, averaging 92.4 per cent for the whole income range, and between 93 and 95 per cent for families with incomes of $1,000-$1,500.

The Assistance Minimum budget indicated above would require an annual income of $1,134 a year. For the year 1940-1941, if $1,000 earned by the head of the family is assumed to be equivalent to this amount (i.e., taking some account of other earners), 33.4 per cent of urban families were below the Assistance Minimum. In rural districts, at a conservative estimate, the figure is more nearly 50 per cent. This estimate is conservative because it is based on the assumption that money income, earned by the father, of only $850 is equivalent to the urban family figure. The 50 per cent represents a much smaller absolute number than the number of urban families, but the proportion is none the less striking. In practice, some of the families in this sub-standard third or half would be above and some below the Assistance Minimum, according to the number of children in the family, because an average family of three children is assumed. This is an important qualification, but the implication is more significant than the merely statistical

---

[2] *Family Income and Expenditure in Canada, 1937-1938.* Dominion Bureau of Statistics, 1941. Further examination of the relation between individual and family incomes, and also details of the differences between occupational classes (Marsh: *Canadians In and Out of Work,* Chapter 8) suggests that wage-earner families in which more than ten per cent of the family income is contributed by members other than the husband are exceptional.

TABLE 3.—EARNINGS OF MALE AND FEMALE EMPLOYEES
IN CANADA, 1941

Distinguishing Male Heads of Families and Other Workers,
and Urban and Rural Residents.

(a) TOTALS

Earnings (Year)	Male Heads of Fami.	
	Urban	Rura
Under $500	114,900	103,1
500— 750(a)	85,900	48,5
750—1000	123,200	40,0
1000—1250	191,200	49,5
1250—1500	114,900	25,0
1500—2000	180,400	35,8
2000—2500	75,000	12,9
2500—3000	27,200	3,7
Over 3000	44,800	6,0
Total	975,700	324,5

(a) i.e. $500—$749, and similarly for other categories.

(b) PERCENTAGES

Earnings (Year)	Male Heads of Famil	
	Urban	Rura
Under $500	11·8	32·2
500— 750	8·9	15·1
750—1000	12·7	12·4
1000—1250	20·0	15·2
1250—1500	12·1	7·6
1500—2000	19·1	10·8
2000—2500	8·0	3·9
2500—3000	2·9	1·1
Over 3000	4·7	1·8
Total	100·0	100·0

Source: Special sample count (10 per cent of all census schedules, with
for adequate representation of all main localities.) Figures provision have
been rounded to nearest hundred.

Other Male Workers		Female Wage-Earners	
Urban	Rural	Urban	Rural
219,900	203,900	279,800	107,200
113,400	44,000	132,600	24,300
90,300	22,700	73,300	10,600
76,100	17,600	36,200	3,600
30,800	6,200	12,100	1,000
32,800	7,700	11,200	800
9,000	1,900	2,800	200
2,500	400	700	—
2,800	500	500	—
577,600	304,900	552,200	147,700

Other Male Workers		Female Wage-Earners	
Urban	Rural	Urban	Rural
37·6	67·3	50·0	73·4
19·6	14·4	24·1	16·1
15·7	7·4	14·1	6·9
13·3	5·6	6·7	2·3
5·5	2·0	2·3	0·6
5·8	2·4	2·1	0·5
1·6	0·6	0·5	0·1
0·4	0·1	0·1	—
0·5	0·1	0·1	—
100·0	100·0	100·0	100·0

Employees include all wage-earners and salaried personnel from age of 14 upwards. Earnings include all income from salaries, commissions, etc., but not pensions, income from investments, or relief payments.

correction, i.e., the large family may be the cause
of poverty.

Taking the Desirable Living Minimum as a gauge
and making similar assumptions, another 32 per cent
of urban families, and another 23 per cent of rural
families, are between the lower and the higher
minimum standards. This is another way of saying
that particularly large families, heavy sickness rates,
or long spells of unemployment, would drive them
definitely below desirable living standards; while,
on the contrary, health insurance, childrens' allowances and other insurance provisions would serve
to maintain them comfortably at or above minimum.
For the lower income strata previously referred to,
the need for insurance techniques to ensure even a
maintenance minimum is even more clearly indicated.

Evaluation of Past and Present Provision

1. *Unemployment relief.*—Care of the unemployed
through municipal relief is now happily almost
entirely past history, but it is necessary to recall
some at least of the main features of the situation
so far as assistance standards were concerned.
Relief schedules were not only very frequently
inadequate in amount but widely variable in range.
The differences may be graphically illustrated by
the following table relating to 20 medium-sized cities
and towns whose relief allowances (autumn and
winter) were ascertained by the Canadian Welfare
Council in 1937.

Even allowing some downward adjustment of the
Assistance Minimum because of its metropolitan
origin, the highest provision among the cities here
listed is 15 to 20 per cent short. One municipality
provided a maximum allowance for a family of 5 of
$16.65 per month, or less than 20 per cent of the
standard. It is true that shopping costs were lower
in this municipality, but the advantage is unexplain-
able in any such terms. Many smaller municipalities knew even poorer standards.

TABLE 4.—RELIEF SCHEDULES IN FORCE IN CANADIAN
MUNICIPALITIES, 1937

Population	Amount for 5 persons	Maximum, any sized family.
65,000	$ 51.00	$ 76.20
63,108	48.45	86.41
60,240	16.65	24.27
60,000	21.66	36·83
53,209	63.70	98.35
40,185	39.48	74.61
39,082	34.55	56.50
32,862	50.00	70.00
32,000	52.00	80.00
30,900	30.07	45.77
30,000	35.00	60.00
26,500	45.33	72.65
26,000	50.00	75.00
25,000	48.40	79.32
24,372	14.54	60.91
24,158	52.00	80.00
23,439	60.35	85.78

Source: Special compilations made by Canadian Welfare Council.

A basic reason, as reviewed in one of the Rowell-
Sirois Report studies, was the difference in municipal regulations "regarding eligibility for relief.
Great hardship is caused by a tendency in some
places to cut groups of unemployed persons off relief
on technical grounds without making any other
provision for them. Many smaller municipalities
either give no relief whatever or very inadequate
relief. Municipalities generally show wide variations in the amount of food, clothing, fuel, shelter
and medical care allowed. In some places no
provision at all is made for clothing and medical
care. Careful studies by the Canadian Welfare
Council on the actual schedules of relief and assistance given in municipalities throughout Canada
give ample statistical proof of this variation in
standards. It is to be expected, of course, that
there will be regional differences in the cash value of
relief, but the variations referred to are between
cities and communities in the same region, or in
comparable regions".

Because of the importance of the housing situation in future policy, it is worth while to quote another passage. "With rent, too, cheapness is the criterion. As a result, there have been frequent evictions in the cities, which aside from their demoralizing influence, involve not inconsiderable costs for cartage and temporary shelter. 'Rent allowances vary greatly as between provinces and municipalities, and in some cases receive scant attention. In Nova Scotia, for instance, rent is granted upon notice of eviction when the applicant appeals to the relief office. He is then instructed to find new quarters at the lowest possible rental, and is allowed a maximum of $10 to pay the first month's rent, after which rental payments become the responsibility of the individual unless he is again evicted.' Relief rental policy also has an effect upon the housing problem because utterly inadequate rents offer no inducement to the owner to do necessary repairs and result in undesirable housing conditions."[1]

2. *Unemployment insurance.*—In contrast to unemployment relief, the unemployment insurance system provides uniform benefits (subject to wage categories) for all duly qualified claimants. This is so important in relation to future developments that unemployment insurance is separately considered in Section 7.

3. *Disability.*—Under Workmen's Compensation, if the male wage-earner suffers partial or temporary impairment as the result of industrial accident, the weekly compensation amounts made available for the family are assessed as a direct percentage of previous wages. On this basis, whether or not Workmen's Compensation payments are adequate or inadequate depends, in the same fashion as for unemployment insurance, on the extent to which

---

[1] Quotations from Grauer: *Public Assistance and Social Insurance*, Appendix 6 of Rowell-Sirois reports, p. 24. Quotation in Grauer's text is from Canadian Welfare Council survey referred to in the preceding table.

earnings themselves meet a desirable living standard. Disability pensions paid to ex-servicemen appear almost invariably to be adequate. The standard rate for 100 per cent disablement for a family including three children, for example, is $137 a month; and for parents and four children, $147 a month.

In a few provinces mothers' allowance legislation takes account of the family situation if the father is totally incapacitated; but since no benefit is assigned for the specific maintenance of the man the total allowance in terms of family needs is a relatively reduced one.

— 4. *Widowhood.*—There are major differences between the situation of a widow whose husband was a member of the services, the widow whose husband died as a result of industrial accident which was covered by Workmen's Compensation, and widows in need of assistance who are not eligible under these categories but apply for Mothers' Allowance in one or other of the provinces which have this legislation. The Department of Pensions provides $107 per month for the widow of a soldier with four child dependents. Under Workmen's Compensation, payments in the event of fatal accident are made at standard rates. The variations here depend on the province of residence, and may range between $30 and $40 per month for the widow and between $7.50 and $12 for children, which are relatively adequate. Full orphans are provided for under Workmen's Compensation by payments of $15 a month, a reasonable figure judged by the minimum assistance computation considered above.

Mothers' Allowances, however, range approximately from $4 to $7.50 monthly per child. Though the allowances to the mother herself of about $30 to $35 may meet some of the first child's needs, these are inadequate sums for a number of dependents. **The deficiencies in the basic budgets for Mothers'**

Allowance claims are rendered relatively greater
because of the long period over which the families
must subsist on this allowance, i.e. until the youngest
child is 16 years of age.   Older children are allowed
to contribute, but very commonly in this case
means tests reduce the allowance proportionately.

5. *Old age pensions.*—Even if the maximum grant
set down in the Dominion statutes ($20 a month)
were secured by all applicants for old age pensions,
they would not guarantee to two elderly persons
living together a tolerable minimum.   The assumption which is often made that the income needs of
aged persons are much lower than others is
questioned by those with experience in assisting
these groups.   It would not be valid, therefore, to
argue therefrom that $40 a month is adequate at
this advanced age.   In fact, however, almost
universally the pensions paid are lower than the
statutory sum as the result of means-test deductions
(referred to elsewhere in Section 12), and the
average pension at present is about $18.   It may
be further added that if one of the marriage partners
has personal means sufficient to bring his total
income to the minimum allowable amount of $365 a
year, the total income for husband and wife would
still be markedly below the desirable minimum level.

6. *Allowances for soldiers' dependents.*—The separation allowances made for wives and dependents
of men in uniform are a special case, and perhaps
not to be regarded as strictly belonging to a social
security system.   But it is of interest to note that
they operate on a scale which is readily defensible,
and in harmony with desirable Canadian standards.
The family incomes which result call for careful
interpretation since an important proportion of them
is made up by assigned pay.   Typical figures,
however, for men in the low ranks, e.g. from lance-
sergeants to privates, in the army, are as follows:
$35 allowance to wife, and allowances for the first,

second or third child of $12, $12, and $10 respect-
ively.   Added to $20 assigned pay, with the possible
addition of five days' pay, or $9.50, it would be
possible for a wife and three children to receive
$98.50· a month.   Allowances for children, more-
over, which are paid for boys up to 16 years and for
girls to 17 years, are available for either up to the
age of 19 if satisfactory progress is made at school;
and the period may be indefinite for the child who is
physically or mentally infirm.

It is significant that dependents' allowances have
recently been extended to include statutory amounts
for fourth, fifth and sixth children ($8 a month).
Other special contingencies likely to affect families
of enlisted men are now met in substantially flexible
form through a special fund administered by the
Dependents' Board of Trustees. The primary
contingencies were understood as being death,
sickness, special accidents such as fire, etc., but there
is little doubt that unusually large families were
also the occasion for assignments by the Board.
As noted above, statutory rates have been added to
cover families of up to six children; the Dependents'
Board of Trustees has authority on proof of need to
give additional allowances for children in excess of
this.

The closeness with which dependents' allowance
arrangements measure up to the standards indicated
in this report are illustrated by a special example.
The Welfare Council of Toronto has made a special
study of the needs of a family composed of a mother
with four young children, assuming (as in the
standard budget cited above) a level higher than
subsistence but economical as to budgeting.   The
prices of the necessary articles and services (at
Toronto rates) call for $109.93 a month.   The in-
come provided for such a family under dependents'
allowance provisions as indicated above (including
the new statutory allowance for a fourth child)

would be $106.50.

Anomalies in Provisions for Children

The widely varying rates and conditions which apply to children when they are the subject of assistance are important in themselves, but also a particularly relevant contrast to the straightforward adjustment of status which a national system of children's allowances would provide.

While most relief schedules applied by municipalities for unemployment cases set varying scales according to the number of dependents, it is doubtful if it can be said that children were considered systematically. Standards which have been determined on the basis of nutritional and relief needs consider the variations due to age and sex; but it is questionable if there is any really valid basis for the assumption that children's needs diminish as the number of children increase. This, in effect, was the principle of many relief schedules. The motives were understandable; large families were a specially heavy charge on the relief rolls; and municipal relief appropriations had to be husbanded through every type of economy, particularly when revenues were shrinking and demand for assistance due to growing unemployment increasing. But some schedules were tapered off to such an extent that extra children in the family were provided for by sums of only a few cents a week.

Under other social legislation in Canada children are provided for only as dependents in special circumstances. The child of a man covered by Workmen's Compensation who is killed while at work may receive, if his mother is alive, income varying from $7.50 to $12 a month, depending on the province of residence. If his father was not killed but completely disabled by the accident, the child may share in a family budget of varying amounts depending on his father's past wage level and paid in most provinces at 66 per cent of that level. If the father of the child was not covered by Workmen's Compensation, i.e., if the accident occurred outside the workplace, or if his father died from some non-industrial cause, his mother might secure assistance on his account to the extent of amounts varying from only $4 to $7.50 a month, according to which of seven provinces constituted his home. In one of these provinces he would have no claim to assistance if he were the only child of his widowed mother. In the other two provinces his mother would be dependent on the ordinary poor relief facilities of the district, subject to such modifications as might be provided through services from charitable sources. In two provinces his mother would be able to secure payment on his account if his father were completely disabled (from non-industrial causes), though, in effect, the allowance made presumably on his behalf would be reduced because the father would share the family income. Orphans, and children who for other reasons do not enjoy a normal family life, constitute yet other, and important, special cases.

The contrast in the provisions for the children of soldiers, sailors and airmen on active service, which recognize specifically the claims of children in the family budget, are significant. The amounts payable are fixed, and uniform for all classes and throughout the Dominion (the only variation depending on rank). In the event of disablement or of death, rates of pension, up to the fourth child, are equally determinate and uniform without regional variations. But amounts in terms of family budgets, as indicated elsewhere, are reasonably adequate.

In all provinces except Prince Edward Island, where the legislation exists but has not been implemented, neglected or dependent children are covered by Children's Protection Acts, and may become wards of the Children's Aid Societies, the practice usually being to guarantee support at varying rates which are chargeable to the municipalities. Typical rates are 70 cents a day or $20 a month, but there are sizeable variations from this. Provisions made for illegitimate children are, more frequently than not, insufficient to allow the mother to keep the child if she so desires. Some provinces have legislation enforcing collection of support from the father, but because of the difficulties involved collections are usually small and the mother frequently has to face the necessity of parting with her child, or supporting it on very small income if she is working. In such cases adoption or placement in foster homes is often the only means of guaranteeing adequate care.

Variations in Assistance Rates: Regional Aspects

For a variety of reasons some of the most obvious anomalies in existing social assistance show up in the form of regional variations. Not all of these reasons are differences in basic costs: others are insufficiency of information on scientific standards, varying periods and histories of developments in welfare programmes, and undoubtedly the lack of strong or centralized leadership, whether expressed in social insurance measures or in other ways. These variations came to light most strikingly in unemployment relief schedules in the thirties, because unemployment had to be handled through municipal and other agencies of public provision which, at least theoretically, were available for all categories of destitution. They reflected differences of community backgrounds and resources and even the varying views of administrators. Standardization was effected in some areas through provincial policy, but this was by no means common. The divergence in unemployment relief rates has already been referred to, but divergences in regulations and scope of provision were almost as common. One of the most important, made particularly noticeable after Ontario set up a medical relief scheme for the whole province, was the difference in recognition of unemployment and of sickness as a direct cause of family need. In some areas where public relief programmes were non-existent or discontinued, families who could prove temporary or chronic illness might be granted assistance under the local poor law, but would not be regarded as eligible if the head of the family was unable to provide for his family by reason of being unemployed.

As will be indicated in other sections, the lack of uniform or adequate standards still continues in provision for problems other than unemployment (Sections 12, 17). Even in so comparatively simple a matter as old age pensions, the range of variation is high. That there are differences in *costs* of living as well as standards of living in various parts of Canada is undeniable. It is easy also to draw misleading inferences from any one series of figures by itself. It is of considerable relevance, for instance, that the rural, farm, and village population is 62 per cent of the total in the Maritimes and 68 per cent in the Prairies as compared with only 36 per cent in Ontario.[1] Rents in particular are apt to be low in the small towns. In farm areas, also, it is reasonable to assume that contributions in kind to the monetary income may be available. On the other hand, some low standards are the expression of backward development. Referring to the differences not only in old age pension rates, but in percentages of persons over 70 in receipt of them, one of the Rowell-Sirois Report studies suggests, "This is another indication of the fact that there are poverty-stricken areas in Canada which inevitably increase the costs of any social service. Northern New Brunswick is such an area. The social services

---

[1] Figures from a special compilation in Marsh, *Canadians In and Out of Work:* p. 114.

can have no remedial effect on these conditions;
what is needed is some sort of national re-settlement
or regional economic planning. The taxpayer, of
course, has to bear the hidden costs of such backward and economically hopeless communities."

Again, there may be considerable justification for
variation in wage levels above what has been called
the desirable living minimum where different regions
include different combinations of the higher occupational scales. (Some of the figures in the tables
of Appendix VI, which reflect the uneven location of
manufacturing industry in Canada, are an illustration). There is less if any justification for
variations in the food subsistence minimum, which
by close calculation is confined to the bare essentials
of living and leaves no margin for economic fluctuations, shopping contingencies or personal taste.
Even rent differentials, while they undoubtedly
exist, might become considerably less important if
standardization is effected, so far as the lowest
units of accommodation are concerned, through a
national housing programme and appropriate modifications of present rent control. In general, minimum standards ought to be buttressed as minima;
if prevailing conditions of life are inferior, there is a
case either for assistance from a national source, or
at least fiscal devices (such as the Rowell-Sirois
Commission sought to formulate) which would
support local incentive to raise the levels to and above
this minimum.

The undesirability of the situation is, of course,
not simply the extent of anomaly in itself. The
fact is that low standards do not avoid the need for
effecting, sooner or later, an improvement in the
situation, nor the need for a systematic categorical
approach to particular types of care. Two para-
graphs from one of the Rowell-Sirois Report studies
express this well. "The deficiencies and lack of
standards in the administration of unemployment
aid become more serious for the individual family

on relief as the duration of the depression lengthens.
The needs of the individual family increase for a
variety of reasons,—the wearing out of clothing
and household equipment of all sorts, the exhaustion
of available financial help from friends and relatives,
the piling up of dental and medical requirements,
etc. But the latter part of a depression is the very
time when the unemployed family is likely to be
faced with arbitrary reductions of relief grants and
a rising price level. Undermining of physique and
destruction of morale are then inevitable. The
state must later pay the permanent costs of unemployability, illness, crime and immorality. It does
so under such headings as poor relief, mothers'
allowances, hospitalization, costs of tuberculosis and
mental illness, penal costs and so forth." And
again: "The lack of standards in relief administration has injured the taxpayer and continues to do so.
It makes possible wasteful and inefficient day-to-day
administration. Over the long run, it will increase
costs to the taxpayer in the ways just indicated."

The wisdom of building an adequate assistance
minimum is relevant not only to social security
measures, but to all forms of public assistance.
As the point has been put by a social worker of long
experience whose views were consulted in the preparation of this report, "There is no security to the
beneficiary in a programme which under-provides
for basic needs or whose administration or means
test procedures and principles do not enlist the
confidence and co-operation of those in need of
state aid. Inadequate provision increases health
costs, reduces ability to benefit from training or
re-employment, and encourages fraud. In fact it
ensures it. Whether in insurance or assistance
programmes, these conclusions enforce the need for
an adoption of basic minimum standards."

4. SECURANCE OF THE SOCIAL MINIMUM:
SOCIAL INSURANCE PRINCIPLES

Social insurance is one way, and an important way, of raising standards of living, and attacking poverty. Other ways have been tried in the past, not all of them effectively; and a multiple attack on the problem will need to be continued in the future. The role of social insurance methods will be clearer if they are considered comparatively.

An attempt to set forth the primary causes of poverty, i.e., of the existence of incomes at or below subsistence levels of living, would take the discussion too far afield, into the nature of the economic system, or social disorganization, and of international breakdown. But the secondary causes of poverty, and the methods of attacking them, can be more easily defined. Obviously low wages are a cause of poverty, and accordingly, minimum wage laws have grown up to insist that payments for work performed must have some relation to living needs and standards. Public assistance, or poor relief, in its least developed form, simply operates by supplementing or replacing earned income, but does so under conditions which, for most people, are unpleasant and deterrent. Unemployment, which removes earning-power altogether by sweeping away jobs, has dominated all other phenomena of modern industrialism, but the social hazards of sickness, accident, incapacity and death may also destroy income in their own way. One direct cause of poverty, namely, too large a family in relation to the income available, if often not ranked as clearly with other immediate causes as it should be. A brief examination of the relations and differences between wages, assistance, and insurance is necessary not only to clear up certain confusions which are common, but to point the way to more

constructive developments in the future. Against
this background it will be easier to appreciate the
significance of social security of wide coverage
contemplated or in action, in countries comparable
to our own.

1. *Wages and Minimum Needs*

Wages are primarily a payment for services or for
productivity; their relation to family needs, if it
exists at all, is indirect. It is true that the wages
of adult men are supposed in some rough kind of
a way to be related to the budget required for the
maintenance of a wife and possibly one or two
children. Minimum wage calculations for men are
constantly beset by the argument as to whether
they should cover family needs or not, or only the
support of a wife; and the computation of minimum
wages for women usually follow more or less im-
plicitly similar suppositions, by being related only
to the expenditure requirements for the maintenance
of the woman as an individual. Fundamentally,
insistence on relating a wage rate to family needs is
illogical. There is no reason why a man who has
a large family should get a larger wage or salary
than someone performing the same work, who
happens to be unmarried or to have no children at
all. At the lowest level it is equally indefensible—
in industrial as distinct from social terms—to raise
the meagre wages of the unskilled labourer because
they will not take care of a family. The proper
approach to intolerably low wages, and easily the
most desirable in the long run, is to raise the efficiency of the worker himself; either by improving
his training, education or skill or—a remedy whose
importance is frequently forgotten—by placing him
in an environment in which his efficiency will be
improved. This environment may· necessitate reform in his home conditions, or of the organization
and equipment of his place of work. The latter is
the real argument for the minimum wage forced

upon industries which exploit cheap labour; they must become more efficient so that they can pay better wages, if they are to stay in business at all. Supplementation of poverty-line incomes, without any reference to constructive attacks on the problems, are merely palliatives if indeed they do not delay reform.

The implication for social insurance planning is that the issue should not be confused by any assumption that a minimum standard of family income, and the basic or unskilled wage level, are the same. Assuming that the "minimum" in the sense of the desirable level per person has been settled, the next point to decide about the minimum standard is the number of persons to whom the minimum is intended to apply. It may validly for certain purposes be a typical or representative family with two or three children. It is more consistent and effective for a social insurance scheme, however, to plan in terms of an individual who could be regarded as the typical "contributor unit."

This representative individual for social insurance planning is the single man who, in all probability, in course of time will become a married man. It is on this basis that in those countries in which there is a background of experience in social insurance planning, the practice has become accepted of building up the unit calculations. If a man's contributions are regarded as providing for himself and for his wife, actual or potential, it is reasonable to argue that in the earlier stages of his participation in the scheme he is in a sense providing for a future situation; if on the other hand he does not marry, it is still reasonable to expect him to continue a somewhat larger contribution than it might otherwise have been, in his capacity as a citizen of the country making some contribution to the married members whose responsibilities are greater.[1]

The important question which still remains, is

the proper method for providing for children as
dependents in all the circumstances of family
hazards and emergencies. It is easier, not harder,
to answer this question, and to administer the
scheme, if we begin from the basis outlined above,
which is a genuine social insurance postulate, than
from a concept already confused taken over from
wage rate considerations which are not appropriate.

2. Social Assistance

Public assistance measures, particularly in the
form of income allowances, are concerned with
meeting the needs of the family as a unit. Because
of reasons of economy, and also because the groups
aided are typically in the lower income strata in
any event, the tendency has been to take strict
account of the claims of all the units of the family
on whatever allowance was available. In other
words, when the amount available, whether of food
or of income, is limited, distribution according to
need is an almost inevitable principle.

The practical difficulties have shown themselves
in two ways. It is only by rigid economies and
often by questionable restrictions that it is possible
to make the minimum allowance "go round." On
the other hand, particularly if the minimum is more
liberally interpreted, it is possible for the allowance,
drawn up for the whole family, to be larger than the
wage which the principal earner could get if he were
employed. This is the more likely if his work is
usually unskilled and irregular so that his earnings
are substandard at the best of times; it is the more
likely if his family is large so that the minimum
itself is stretched to include them. Whatever may
be the answer to the anomalies in this situation,

---

[1] This incidentally is consistent with the principle which it will be
relevant to remember at other points in this report; that social insurance
is concerned with the equitable administration of contributions made to a
common pool, not with the claims of each individual to receive back in
benefits exactly the payments he has made in the past.

it is necessary to ask, when a social insurance system is being devised, what must be done to avoid them under this improved method of general provision.

Insurance is not superior to assistance simply because it makes a more logical approach to the relation of income to needs. The first and compelling reason for the growth of insurance systems is that they avoid the undesirable features of almost all assistance situations. Assistance, to begin with, is almost inevitably based on the lowest subsistence rates. It has dealt with only those who demonstrably have not been able to help themselves. Indigence or destitution, the complete lack of any means, is the first test for the receipt of aid. Its standards accordingly, however much they may be redeemed by skilled administration and sympathetic service, must be lower in goods or income than those regarded as available for the self-supporting.

Possibly it may be denied that this "less eligibility" standard is accepted or applied in Canadian assistance services. A second defect is more clearly evident. This is the lack of certainty, in the sense both of objective determination in advance and of continuance over time, which characterizes relief provision in the eyes of the recipient. There are a number of reasons, many of them hingeing on the test of continuous destitution, which may remove the "right" to the week's allowance. Social assistance in this sense does not give security, but barely tolerable subsistence; it might almost be said to sustain insecurity.

Assistance measures, if they are the only means of providing for certain forms of distress and not constructive measures, supplementary to the social insurance framework, inevitably involve application of a means test. The means test, or ascertainment of all the sources of support available to the individual or family, may be for two different purposes, although in practice they are easily confused. The investigation may be needed in order to prove that the claimant has no means whatsoever or that his means are so few as to render him for all practical purposes completely destitute. It may be required, on the other hand, for the purpose of supplementing an inadequate income, to bring it up to a reasonable living standard. Unfortunately it is all too easy for the emphasis to be on the first rather than on the second aspect of the task. Everything depends upon the standard of administration and upon the training of the personnel. In a situation already made harsh by the conditions of poverty, inquiries as to means may be regarded as an inquisition and bitterly resented. The possibility of supplementation being a constructive function is always there, and in the hands of a trained social worker it may be achieved. But all too commonly supplementation is distasteful because along with the assessment of existing means goes the power to decide the amount of supplement. If there are no standards predetermined or set by law, it is easy for public assistance in unemployment and other matters of social need to be arbitrary, or vacillating with changes in regulations and the differing views of administrators.

This does not mean that there is no possibility of workable income-exemption limits set in statutory terms, or made declarable by a simplified procedure. There are a few examples of such tests which are acceptable and in operation without friction, e.g., the income declarations required in setting maintenance grants under the British scholarship systems; and a number of features of the new consolidated social insurances in New Zealand. But it is significant to note that these standards or limits are set for matters which are concerned with something above basic subsistence. In much the same way deductions for income possessed would be much less objectionable for old age or retirement pensions if the limits below which income was allowable were much higher.

3. *Social Insurance*

Social insurance is a direct and complete remedy for the most painful feature of assistance at low income levels because it obviates altogether the need for a means test in every specific case. The benefit under a social insurance scheme is available according to certain objective tests of eligibility which are clearly set down and known to all parties. The amount to be obtained is relatively certain, and subject to certain reasonable conditions; so is its duration. The insured person knows "what he is entitled to"; his benefit comes as of right, and not from charity. Further than this, there is a proper machinery for adjudication in the event of doubt or dispute.

These are advantages of social insurance which meet the psychology of the dependency situation. In addition, however, there is a weighty material consideration. The community resources which are brought into operation are extended far beyond the responsibility area usually considered in assistance or relief cases, i.e., the family and other relatives; they comprise, in effect, all the population with any liability to comparable situations. This is a great virtue of the social insurance network, strengthened as it is by its compulsory features, which voluntary schemes can never hope to equal. It is particularly designed to cover the groups who are most likely to need it, whereas many voluntary schemes must be restricted to persons who must be above the lowest levels in order to afford the premiums. And it is perhaps particularly worthy of note that social insurance technique almost alone brings in effectively the "lower middle" income classes who are not able to provide health services, savings, etc., enough to guarantee their own risks, who are seldom buyers of expensive individual insurance, but who also avoid, often with great effort, descending to the ranks of the destitute and thus getting services on a free or charitable basis.[1] In general, the wider the pooling principles are extended, the greater is the mobilization of purchasing-power—which would not otherwise go there—towards certain risks and emergencies which can be foreseen, collectively speaking, but are not capable of precise prediction in the individual case. Finally, the almost universal experience is that by virtue of administrative economies and for other reasons, and certainly in terms of the material advantages of security, health conservation and family stability, the advantages are bought relatively cheaply.

4. Children's Allowances: The Key to Consistency

How should this distribution be extended for the recipients, as distinct from the contributors? At this point some confusions still remain in some countries as to whether the purpose of the insurance should be (a) to sustain the needs of the family, whatever its size, or (b) to maintain (possibly at a reduced level), the chief wage-earner's income as such. The difference of idea may even appear in the same piece of legislation, for example in workmen's compensation, which for disablement cases provides two-thirds of the wage of the disabled men, but in the case of fatal accident provides allowances for children below certain ages. This may not raise any particular difficulty so long as it is applied in a few pieces of legislation which do not combine in an attempt to cover the whole field of social risks. Once a comprehensive scheme is in sight, however, and even in the more basic elements of social insurance (for health and unemployment) serious anomalies arise if the attempt is made to stretch the monetary benefit in dependency circumstances to cover all the members of the family, while retaining

---

[1] Cf. Marsh, Fleming, and Blackler, *Health and Unemployment*, for an appraisal of medical relief, in which it is pointed out that "this development has placed an important group, that of low-income families which are more or less self-supporting but unable to provide for proper medical expenditures in their budgets, at an unfair disadvantage." (p. 177).

links to the wage or income scale at the input end of
the insurance system. The first is the possibility
of benefit receipts being larger than the wages
usually obtained by the wage earner. The other
is the danger of over-insurance, or taking on more
risks or claims than the fund can support.

Unemployment insurance as it is at present scaled
in Canada is not yet fully adequate to become a solid
basis for all further social insurances. A larger
differential between the benefits payable to single
and married men than is embodied in the present
total scale would be preferable (Section 7). But its
principles are entirely adaptable. In spite of
representations to this effect, extra benefits graduated according to the number of children in the
unemployed contributor's family have not been
added to the basic rate. Assuming, of course, that a
comprehensive social security scheme is going to be
constructed in the future, this is a definite gain so
far; and by it the scheme has avoided the dilemmas
which follow relentlessly once children's allowances
are added to the ordinary or standard rates of benefit.

Everything depends on the recognition of the
special place of children's allowances. If the needs
of children as claims on the family income are
recognized only in the insurances, certain questions
inevitably arise. Why are children's needs recognized in times of need and not in the normal situation
through wages? Why should children get more
specific attention when the family is under some
handicap or in distress, rather than the reverse?
Another question accompanies these because the
children's allowances added to benefits are almost
invariably restricted (by a limit to the numbers
recognized, or a tapering rate). If assistance is
extended to one or two children, why not to all?
If the point of view is that of broad social need,
why should not the large families have an equal
claim with the smaller ones?

The first part of the answer to these questions is the distinction which has already been emphasized, between income maintenance and health or other services. There is no difficulty in extending services, particularly those of medical care, to the utmost; and it is reasonable also to construct a social insurance system, rather than a strict actuarial structure, comprising a simple contribution but a highly flexible benefit.

The extension of medical benefits to the children of the insured family should be unrestricted; or to put the point more positively, health insurance should specifically be designed so as to make it possible for this to be the case. The advantages in terms of national health are too obvious to require emphasis; and it is also true that there are hardly any examples of health insurance schemes in which children's rights to medical benefit have not been included. It is worth while pointing out, however, that this is not a comparable situation to the receipt of unemployment benefit, or for that matter sickness cash-benefit. The counterpart to the medical care branch of health insurance coverage is rather the placement (and perhaps training) functions performable by the Employment Offices; and it is entirely desirable that the employment office should provide training facilities for the children of an unemployed man if these are appropriate in their case. The analogy should not be pressed too far, but it may help to clarify the main point. Part of the answer to the situation is to move towards generosity in whatever *services* may be appropriate for children, particularly if they help to take off some of the strain of the dependency condition.

Conclusion

The maintenance of income, however, is something which can only be taken as far as the wage system will allow. It is therefore suggested here, as a

principle which will go far to clarify public understanding both of minimum wage problems and of
social insurance problems in the future, that the
normal coverage of an adult worker, if it is to be
extended at all beyond the individual, should not
go further than his marital partner.

It is probably desirable to reiterate immediately
that this does not mean that agitation for improvement of low and substandard wages should
cease. This battle must be taken up on its own
grounds. It will be no advantage to the cause of
social insurance, however, if it is used as an illogical
weapon in the battle, either to attack existing wage
scales, or as a lever with which to attempt to prise
them up. If the Canadian social insurance system
is built in full realization of its limits, it will have
everything to gain from improvement in wage
standards generally. The unemployment benefit
scale, it may be noted, need not hinder this. If
wages rise generally, the lowest benefit scales will
simply become obsolescent, so far as adults are
concerned.

The picture becomes complete only when the
approach to child maintenance is made systematic,
and the obligation for proper attention to children's
needs put where it belongs. Of course, if nothing
further were to be done about the situation of
children in dependent families, in times of unemployment, sickness, widowhood or disability, our
system of social insurance would be evidently
incomplete. We should have improved provision
substantially beyond the situation left entirely to
assistance methods; but the improvement would be
partial, and there would still be vital territory to
cover. Facing the situation, it would be hardly
defensible to say that provision for children's social
security must wait until the general level of Canadian incomes had risen to the point where even the
minimum income would be so high that children's

need could invariably be accommodated. The practical answer to the situation is that children's needs should be met as a special claim on the nation, not merely in periods of unemployment or on occasions of distress, but at all times. This is the basic case for children's allowances. It is an important incidental, but still only incidental, that it is the one technique which, until we reach entirely new levels of income, removes the anomalies both of the wage system and of a social insurance system if that system is optimistically but unwisely designed.

It has been argued, in full recognition of the unpopularity of the argument, that minimum wage questions should not be confused with those of inadequate rates of social insurance. It must be equally made clear that it is unwise to attempt to bring children's allowances into being through the back door. This is what has happened in some countries. They are recognized for dependency situations only. When these are provided for on a relief basis, acceptance of their validity is still restricted on the score that too liberal an allowance for too many children would bring the income of the family above ·wage levels. Applied to the monetary benefits of a particular social insurance scheme, the restrictions are even more prominent. Children's allowances, actually, have a basic claim in any really clearsighted system of social security, for both normal and dependency situations. There is no reason why that valid claim should not stand on its own merits. If this claim is understood and accepted, our future social insurance structure will be better built at the outset, and easier to maintain and improve in the future.

Examples of Existing and Proposed Comprehensive Schemes

The potentialities of comprehensive social insurance may be illustrated at this point by a brief analytical review of the systems either in existence or recently proposed for the countries most comparable to Canada. In particular, Great Britain and New Zealand have moved farthest on the road to complete coverage in social security measures. The present schemes in Great Britain, while they merit all the esteem of the pioneer, are nevertheless a patchwork, to which many modifications and improvements have been added from time to time. They already cover in different degrees most of the area of social need. But Britain, as everybody knows, now has its Beveridge plan, which proposes to reform and unify every unit in the present fabric, and bring many new elements into a consistent system. New Zealand has made the most rapid advances in recent times. Its reforms made since 1938 give it the most comprehensive scheme, perhaps the only fully consistent scheme, at the moment, in the world. The United States has extended contributory insurance over the widest area, already covering 50,000,000 employees. Big gaps and deficiencies were left in spite of the innovatory character of the Social Security Act of 1935; but proposals such as were embodied in the Elliott Bill presage a radical extension, particularly to bring into insurance agricultural and other non-wage-earner groups. It is true that the Elliott Bill introduced in the previous session of Congress has lapsed, and that the present policy of the Administration has still to be restated in detail; but the Bill corresponds to the views of the Social Security Board, and to the recommendations made by the President to Congress in October, 1942.

The essential features of the extended New Zealand, British and American schemes can be presented most easily by means of the schedules at the end of this Section. The differences as well as the similarities are of interest. The outstanding omissions in the United States plan are the absence of complete health insurance, and of children's allowances. Before examining these, it is of special interest to refer to the Australian situation, which does not yet conform to this degree of coverage but promises to do so.

The Commonwealth already possesses federal non-contributory schemes of invalid and old-age pensions (1908); children's allowances for all children except the first (1941) and maternity allowances, which are small lump-sum grants towards the expenses of confinement; widows' and orphans' pensions (1942); and workmen's compensation laws in every state. There is a well-developed friendly society organization (including trade union bodies) which provides sickness benefit, funeral benefit, and general practitioner treatment for a substantial minority of the working population.

In 1938 a federal National Insurance Act was enacted, but it has never been enforced. It provided for the compulsory insurance of wage-earners against sickness, disablement, old age and death, according to the pattern of British legislation. The situation has since been changed by the introduction of *(a)* widows' and orphans' pensions and *(b)* children's allowances, while *(c)* a growing conviction that the health needs of the population cannot be adequately met by a medical service relying on individual medical practitioners is leading to consideration of a comprehensive national health service.[1]

It is reasonable to expect therefore that an Australian plan will soon emerge, which will propose the introduction of insurance for sickness, cash benefit and unemployment benefit, the conversion of finances to a contributory basis, and the estab-

---

[1] The most recent proposal (February 1943) is to lay the foundation for a comprehensive scheme, to be developed progressively, through a National Welfare Fund, commencing July 1943 with an annual assignment of £30,000,000 or one-quarter of all personal income-tax revenue. The Fund is to be devoted to "health services, unemployment or sickness benefits, family allowances, or other welfare or social services."

New Zealand (Social Security Act, 1939)	Great Britain (Beveridge Plan)	United States (Elliott Bill)
1. Scope of Compulsory Insurance—		
National (unitary). All ordinary residents.	National (unitary). All residents, in three contributory groups: (i) employed, (ii) other gainfully occupied, (iii) unoccupied.	Federal. All gainfully occupied, in two contributory groups: (i) employed, (ii) other gainfully occupied.
2. Needs and Risks Covered—		
Unemployment. (Training services separate).	Unemployment. Training benefit. Rehabilitation services.	Unemployment (pre-existent) for wage-earners; state schemes. Vocational rehabilitation services
Complete medical care for all residents. Sickness cash benefit.	Complete medical care for insured persons and their families. Sickness cash benefit. Maternity cash benefit.	Limited hospital care for insured persons and their families. Sickness cash benefit. Maternity cash benefit.
Workmen's compensation (pre-existent) remains unaffected.	Workmen's compensation replaced by supplementary arrangements for permanent industrial disability. Permanent disability pensions.	Workmen's compensation (pre-existent: states) remains unaffected.
Permanent disability pensions.		
Old age benefits. Widows' and orphans' benefits. Children's allowances.	Old age benefits. Widows' and orphans' benefits. Children's allowances. Funeral grants.	Old age, widows' and orphans' benefits, supplemented by Federal-State assistance for the aged and for dependent children. (Social Security Act, and proposed amendments.)
Discretionary emergency benefits for exceptional cases of distress.	Supplementation in cases of need, by national assistance.	

lishing of a national health service. But it is significant that the State governments have recently agreed to ask their Parliament to consent to the delegation of wide powers to the Commonwealth, especially in the social security field, in order to ensure these results.

3. Rates and Conditions of Benefit

(a) New Zealand

Grant of benefit is not strictly dependent on previous regular payment of contributions, though there is power to refuse benefit if contribution obligations have not been complied with. All cash benefits (except superannuation) are subject to a means test which allows of high exemptions.

Apart from the operation of the means test, the rate of each kind of benefit varies only with the number of dependents: an invalid, for example, receives 30/- a week for himself, 10/- for his wife and 10/ for each child, plus a cost-of-living bonus. Children's allowances (6/- a week for every child) are payable only when the breadwinner is *not* receiving benefit.

Sickness (cash) and unemployment benefits are indefinite in duration, but there is power to impose stricter conditions for the continued grant of unemployment aid at a certain stage.

The superannuation benefit is a special form of old-age pension which is payable without means test and which, beginning at £10 a year, increases by £2.10s. at yearly intervals up to a maximum of £78.

(b) Great Britain

Grant of benefit is strictly dependent on previous regular payment of contributions, except for periods of sickness and unemployment. There is no means test.

The rate for adults varies only according as the

beneficiary is a single person or married couple, being 24/- or 40/- respectively. Children's allowances, at an average rate of 8/- a week, are payable whether the breadwinner is earning or on benefit, and are continued after the death of the father or both parents.

The old-age pension, like the New Zealand superannuation benefit, rises gradually from 14/- a week in 1945 to 25/- in 1965: it is granted subject to retirement from gainful activity.

The *self-employed* are not insured for sickness cash or unemployment benefits, or supplementary benefit for permanent industrial disability. The *unoccupied* are not insured for these or for permanent disability benefit.

(c) United States

Grant of benefit is subject to payment of contributions, and in case of permanent disability, old age and survivors' benefits, they must have been paid for at least half the period lapsing between entry into insurance and the occurrence of the contingency insured against. There is no means test.

Benefits consist of a basic rate for the single person, varying on the number and rate of the contributions paid, plus a percentage of that basic rate for the wife and each child. The basic rate of disability, old-age and survivors' benefits is heavily weighted in favour of low wage earners.

The old-age benefit is granted subject to retirement from gainful activity.

The *self-employed* are not insured for sickness cash or unemployment benefits.

4. *Contributions and Finance*

(a) New Zealand

Financed, as to about two-thirds of the cost, by the "social security charge", which is a tax of 5 per cent on all incomes, and by a registration fee of

£1 a year; the remainder of the cost is borne by general revenue. Employers collect the social security charge on wages and salaries. The charge on other income and the registration fee are paid by the individual directly. Payment is enforced by penalties for late payment by prosecution; no employer may engage a person who has not paid his registration fee up to date. Exemption from payment of charge and tax is granted temporarily in cases of hardship.

(b) Great Britain

Financed by joint contributions of employers and employees and by personal contributions of other insured persons. State pays whole cost of children's allowances, most of medical care, one-third cost of unemployment benefits, one-sixth cost of other cash benefits and initial deficit of pension insurance: about half entire cost of plan.

Contribution rates depend on status (employed, others gainfully occupied, unoccupied) and sex, being higher for men, whose insurance provides for their wives. Contributions are collected by stamps and cards; in the case of employees, through the employer.

Persons with less than certain minimum income, e.g. £75 a year, are exempt from contributions and are not insured: these are cared for by assistance.

(c) United States

Financed entirely by *(a)* joint contributions of employer and employee, and *(b)* personal contributions of others gainfully occupied. The joint contribution is 12 per cent of earnings, and the personal contribution (for disability, old-age, survivors' benefit and hospital care) is 6 per cent of earnings. The joint contribution is paid in the form of quarterly cheques, drawn by the employer and based on the payroll.

PART II

EMPLOYMENT

5. A NATIONAL EMPLOYMENT PROGRAMME

The greatest change in statutory provision for social and economic risks in Canada since the depression period of the thirties is the establishment of unemployment insurance. So great is the change indeed that it may seem to some to be a principal answer to unemployment hazards in the near future. Only a little knowledge of the complexity of the unemployment problem, and of the economic policy necessary to deal with it, however, is enough to show that unemployment insurance is only one weapon in varied armoury of attack; and even this weapon, as will be indicated later, has only a very restricted range.

The only basic answer to unemployment is employment—not any kind of task work it is true, but employment carrying a reasonable level of remuneration and reasonably satisfactory working conditions. The first positive measure in providing social security, therefore, is a programme which will make work available, or, in other words, which will offer wages rather than subsistence maintenance to the farthest extent to which it is possible.

This is not merely the depression argument that something ought to be received by the state in return for what is paid to unemployed men in relief or doles. In a post-war context, employment provision through public organization in the transition period has an altogether special place. In terms of employment and expenditure, the end of the war means a huge curtailment in the labour market for wartime forms of production. The extent to which peacetime forms of production will fill up this gap depends on the recovery of world trade and the reconversion of domestic industry on a scale which has never had to be contemplated before; and until this adjustment is completed the gap will be filled only if the governments of the world, Canada

included, sponsor programmes of peacetime investment and development almost commensurable in
size to present wartime levels. How long this
highly critical transition period will last could be
the subject of a wide variety of calculations. It
might optimistically be put at as little as six months;
it might be nearer three years. The war has given
us ample experience of the delays and difficulties of
"tooling-up" for a completely new pattern of production in Canada (and if it is permissible, the
phrase can be extended to agriculture and the primary industries as much as to manufacturing); the
economy will be so completely on a war basis before
victory is achieved that the necessary scale of
reconversion will be immensely greater than at the
end of the last war.

There has been a remarkable acceleration of recognition in recent times that there are plenty of useful
public projects and forms of developmental expenditure which need to be undertaken, not merely as
stop-gap expedients, but as desirable social and
economic improvements. There is a great range of
enterprises, which will almost certainly only be
undertaken through public initiative, which will
directly remove wastes, eyesores, social costs: projects like the redevelopment of congested terminal
facilities or of blighted areas in cities, the replacement of slum dwellings, the extension of rural
electrification, the rehabilitation of eroded and cut-
over areas in the country; which yield productive
assets as well as give employment, and help to
open up opportunities for private investment as
well as channelling public expenditure in desirable
directions. The mobilization of these projects is
an economic security task for the future which
must be considered now.

There is, of course, nothing new in the idea of a
works programme. There is something new—or at
least as yet untried—in the idea of national em-

ployment programmes operating *on the basis of inter-national collaboration* as a specific anti-depression measure in the period of post-war dislocation. From the domestic point of view, the new factor for Canada is the scale of the programme and the challenge of bold conception and operation which it presents. The volume of wartime expenditure which is now producing full employment in Canada is in the realm of two or three billion dollars a year. Whether substitute or anti-depression expenditures have to be made on this scale in straight expenditure *in public works form* depends on a number of calculations which still demand analysis—the extent and time of utilization of purchasing-power reserves in the hands of consumers; the proportion of public expenditures which may be anticipated in other forms (in particular, social security disbursements); the proportion of projects (on the model of Part I of the National Housing Act) in which a relatively small amount of government expenditure may stimulate a large volume of private expenditure; the effects of the "multiplier" principle in general; and so on. But it seems reasonable to assert that the employment reserve for Canada will not be safe unless it is part of at least a billion-dollar programme in the first post-war year. Before more ambitious figures are proposed, it is to be noted that even half of this amount would vastly exceed any volume of work projects ever before assembled (except during wartime) in the Dominion.

One point should be made plain beyond fear of misunderstanding. There is no parallel, and nothing in common, between a public investment programme designed to be part of the grand economic strategy of the post-war years, and the relief works which characterized the depression thirties. With some honourable exceptions, the work projects drawn into the unemployment programmes of those years were patently inadequate and poorly timed. They were far too small in volume. Because of the unfortunate view which prevailed that they should use the maximum amount of labour instead of being ruled by efficiency standards, they provided employment, for the most part, only for unskilled and manual labour; and the rotation system of giving short spells of work to successive bodies of men served further to lower the respect accorded to them. The unemployment experience of the thirties in these fields is such that the very term "public works" gives rise to hostile associations, which confuse any discussion of an employment programme unless the conception and intent of these programmes is clearly defined. There is no need to deny such contribution as the relief work programmes did actually make. They produced some physical assets to set against the expenditures for involuntary idleness and the backlog of demoralization which was the legacy of the period. But a few figures will show that, above all, they did not measure up to the dimensions that the emergency demanded.

The total municipal, provincial and federal public projects designed or accelerated for unemployment relief purposes (excluding housing) employed as many as 75,000 men for only one short period, viz.: three months in 1934. The average number of men employed per month was in no year greater than 56,000, and the most typical figure was 20,000-22,000. The fluctuations in the works and the total of employment, moreover, had no organized relation to the course of the trade cycle or to other anti-depression policies.

It is true that a more substantial case can be made for the assisted housing programmes. Figures have recently been analysed for the main period of operations of the Dominion Housing Act and the

National Housing Act, commencing in 1935. If the
record is to be clear, it must be admitted to begin
with that this was too late a start. The best
feature of the two Acts is the extent to which they
served to encourage additional investment as the
result of expenditure from government sources.
Taking the period 1935-1940, government loans for
housing amounted to $15,500,000; the total loan
value of the houses built was $77,000,000. Even
so, the total number of houses built under Part I
of the National Housing Act, in the course of seven
years was only 23,500. Against this must be set
the fact that house building had almost completely
stopped in the worst years of the depression. Calculating from the total loan value figures, in the
period 1937-1939, 43 per cent of all houses erected,
as far as the records are available, were built as the
result of government assistance. No one knows
just how many individual workmen took some part
in this building programme and gained some income
thereby. But careful assessment of the investment
and employment brought into being through all the
on-site and off-site work (a total expenditure of
about $92,000,000) indicates that the seven-year
programme gave employment which would be
equivalent to the full-time work of 63,000 men for
one year. The calculation takes a realistic view
of the limits of the construction worker's year,
since it assumes an "equivalent" year to be one of
forty 48-hour weeks. This is an average of only
about 9,000 men per year.

If Part II of the National Housing Act had been
utilized as was hoped, the story might have been
considerably different, and this is an important
qualification which must be applied in considering
the relativity of any such figures to the future.
None the less it must be clearly evident from these

incomplete figures that even the housing programmes
which were well conceived, did not supplement such
other public construction as was initiated to any
effective scale, measured against the fact that the
total volume of unemployment during 1930-1939
so far as it can be estimated, varied from 250,000 to
700,000 persons of wage-earner status. A conservative estimate of the average for the decade of the
thirties would be 300,000 unemployed.[1]

TABLE 5.—NUMBER OF PERSONS EMPLOYED ON
FEDERAL, PROVINCIAL AND MUNICIPAL RELIEF
WORKS: MONTHLY AVERAGES—1932-39

Year	Monthly Average	Year	Monthly Average
1932	20,156	1936	20,212
1933	22,175	1937	15,170
1934	56,108	1938	9,603
1935	25,047	1939	21,141

From monthly figures, reports of the Dominion Commissioner of
Unemployment, e.g., *Report on the Unemployment and Agricultural Assistance Act, 1939* (Department of Labour, 1940), pp. 37-39.

What must be envisaged for post-war purposes,
therefore, is a much vaster programme of public
investment and development; a programme which is
planned and put into effect as an integral part of
economic stabilization. Public investment programmes in this form have been advocated as part of
the attack on peacetime depression; but as a special
post-war phenomenon, programmes must also be
directly concerned with physical reconstruction and
conversion from the war economy. Both of these
requirements can be further underlined. The programme must be actuated not by mere reference to
the number of unemployed men but by the role of
public expenditure and total fiscal policy in the
national, and indeed in the international, economy.
It is investment expenditure, not employment,

[1] *Canadians In and Out of Work*, pp. 364 et al.

which is the motive force. Full employment is the objective, it is true; but full employment arises from successful mobilization of all the productive resources of the nation. The economizing of human effort through all the devices of organization and technology is a proper part of this mobilization. It would be as absurd to concentrate on the labour-absorption capacity of projects in the post-war period as it would be absurd to-day if the criterion of munitions production were to be their ability to use up labour, rather than to turn out the maximum output per unit of total resources. If the investment is productive in itself, it will contribute its stimulus to employment in other and more enduring ways.

The second and related requirement is that the particular units which make up the total programme must be justified by their economic merits and their social benefits. It should be a special quest in their planning to seek out how they will contribute to productivity, how stimulate further investment, including investment by peacetime industry, how contribute to social welfare where no immediate or industrial objective is in view. More systematic and more responsible protection and utilization of Canadian national resources, in forests, mines, water and soil must obviously be in the forefront of these programmes. On the purely economic side, reconversion and adaptation of our manufacturing industries will be of more urgent necessity than ever before in Canada; not only for the stability of the domestic economy, and not only because the pace of technology has been so greatly accelerated, but also in order that the Dominion may contribute its share in the restoration of productive power in other parts of the world, on which alone the long-run hope for international reconstruction depends. Because of this, as well as the strategy of anti-depression policy itself, the Canadian investment programme must be implemented in co-operation with the United States and the other members of the United Nations.

So far as welfare criteria are concerned, it is particularly relevant in this document to enter the reminder that the creation of a social security system brings about directly a stronger demand for what might be called collective consumer goods or social utilities—housing, hospitals, schools, libraries, urban and rural recreation facilities, and so forth. Housing in its best and widest sense, including rural and urban environmental planning, is obviously of special and particularly far-reaching importance. It is apposite to add also, in projecting our objectives into their post-war perspective, that full employment under the insatiable pressure of war can be too full. There should be room for leisure and culture, for projects therefore which promote the fruitful use of leisure, and the wider cultivation of all that makes up education and welfare, in the projects we plan for a better peacetime way of life. These considerations should affect the character of many of the things we decide to build; they should include community centres, youth hostels, demonstration nurseries, kitchens, houses and farms, research stations of all kinds, as well as roads and power plants.

It will be of considerable importance to make room for small as well as large enterprises. One compelling reason will be the need for projects which can be started easily, which will be flexible in using varied kinds of skill and adaptable to varied communities. There is a place for maintenance and repair undertakings as well as major construction jobs, for arts and crafts, domestic as well as industrial, for projects which are partly instructional (perhaps linked with the Dominion-provincial training programmes), as well as employment for wages. Projects of these types, even organized on a nation-wide basis, cannot be effective unless there are large enterprises to carry the major weight of the transition; but promoted with sufficient energy, they can render it flexible, provide room for experiment and community effort, and (as suggested in Section 8) produce many a better alternative to unemployment assistance in individual cases.

The programme of major works will not be realized without imagination and intensive organization. It demands, first, a co-ordinated effort of mobilization in which provinces, municipalities, utilities and private industry must be invited to join. It involves, secondly, the organization of all appropriate technical aids in the engineering and physical features of the programme. It involves, thirdly, much closer attention to long-term budgeting on capital account, on the part of all governmental authorities, than has yet been achieved in Canada. It is not enough to be satisfied that a project can promise certain economic results, or even that it has been the subject of an engineer's report and worked out to the blue-print stage. It is necessary also to project into the future the actual costs of the projects, their relation to the normal revenue available annually, and the conditions under which the five, six, ten year plan, or whatever it may be, can be accomplished or accelerated.[1]

Finally, it involves the formulation of a low-interest-rate policy and its injection into all the sections of the national programme in which it has any justifiable place. There are some precedents in Canada for these weapons of stimulation and expansion. The Housing Act embodied federal aid in this form as well as other inducements; the limited extent to which advantage was taken of it in practice, however, necessitates that it be further examined—

---

[1] The Subcommittee on Post-War Construction Projects has reported in detail on the administrative features of a national programme, and is currently studying financial aspects.

not only by the federal government which initiated
it, but by the other governments and parties whose
collaboration it was intended to enlist. The Municipal Improvements Assistance Act (1938) accepted
even more directly the principle of easing the
financial charges for worthwhile projects by author-
izing loans from the Dominion government to
municipal bodies at two per cent. Undertakings
were limited to a special definition of "self-liqui-
dating projects", and provincial approval was
necessary. Out of a total of $30,000,000 available,
only $7,740,000 was utilized. These results are
disappointing against the perspective of the needs
of the depression years, and the policy has now to be
projected against a much bigger demobilization
problem in the post-war years. Again there would
appear to be a direct implication that all parties
concerned should examine why a measure whose
principles are sound should not have been put to
more dramatic use.

In so large a task a clear understanding of its
magnitude is the first and most important step
towards hastening its achievement. The emphasis
which has been indulged in here is necessary, because
a great visualization and planning effort is even more
imperative for a construction programme than in the
building of a social insurances programme. Without
an investment mobilization against the first shocks
of economic demobilization, without an employment
programme to sustain the country while industry
and agriculture are moving towards a new peacetime
equilibrium, the social insurances structure will
have no solid foundation. In the widest sense we
must have a policy for economic security as well as
for welfare security, which is what "social security"
usually implies, for the two security programmes can
be built to buttress each other. But in each of them,
be it noted, the word "security" is paradoxical.
Social security merely anchors the basic minimum,

the absence of poverty. It will completely accomplish this limited result only on the condition of bold acts of income mobilization. An employment programme likewise, amidst the welter of post-war tasks, is a guarantee of successful transition, not of boundless prosperity. The engineering of each, far from implying a capitulation to timidity or insulation, requires efforts of courage and initiative which alone will succeed.

6. OCCUPATIONAL READJUSTMENT: PLACEMENT,
GUIDANCE, AND TRAINING FACILITIES

The second positive measure which is needed in a
full-employment programme is a system of facilities
which will help to equip people to find work, or to
give them access to new skills if there are no openings
for those they already possess.

It is impossible to overemphasize the significance
of the Dominion Employment Service as the agency
for the development and coordination of these
functions. The reorganization of the Service on a
national basis was a big step forward, made possible
by the amendment to the British North America
Act in 1940. It implemented, incidentally, one of
the most emphatic recommendations of the National
Employment Commission of 1936-7. Under heavy
war pressures in the administration of National
Selective Service and manpower mobilization orders,
valuable experience has been gained, and the Employment Offices should be much better equipped
than ever before to play their basic part in the redirection of workers who have to find new jobs in
the peacetime economy. It is still necessary, however, not to lose sight of the fact that labour market
organization in the post-war period will demand
personnel of the highest calibre, nationally and
regionally.

The manner in which the functions of the Employment Service grow ever more important with extensions in the social insurance structure, also their
special role in the future of unemployment assistance
organization, no matter what strengthening of the
unemployment insurance system may be undertaken,
will be made clear by other sections of this report.
Furthermore, a positive and constructive approach
to social security legislation will require the development of rehabilitation measures as well as placement

facilities, and various elaborations of the concept of vocational guidance as applied on a mass scale. These will call for co-operative effort between government and industry, ingenuity in the development of training and educational techniques, the harnessing of administrative science to mundane and "practical" situations, of which there are now many wartime examples, but which will have to be worked out anew for the problems of peace.

To elaborate on this modernized concept of placement work as it may be performed through the Employment Service would take this text too far from the immediate purpose of the report. A special word is necessary, however, on the role of training schemes, both in relation to the post-war period, and as part of a comprehensive social insurance scheme.

Recognition of the need for a variety of training facilities, adapted to the realities of the labour market and to the wide range of educational inequalities, has been slow in Canada, though accelerated markedly by the distress and pressures of the pre-war depression years. Most of the reasons for the need are not the product of depression conditions, but of long-run deficiencies. The large proportion of unskilled workers on the unemployment relief rolls gave emphasis to the need, however; so also did the growing problems of youths who were unable to find employment after leaving school. Other reasons which still remain are the inefficient articulation of technical school facilities with the elementary educational system, and with industrial demands, in almost all the provinces of Canada; continuous changes in the technology of industry itself; the need of agriculture for an increasing leaven of science and technical training in its personnel, if it is to retain its reserves of youthful labour and improve its efficiency.

Apart altogether from the intensification of these needs in the post-war period, training facilities have a special and constructive relationship to unemployment insurance. For many categories of workers the proper requisite in the event of unemployment is not maintenance in idleness, or even employment on works projects, but training. British experience has developed several types, all of them supplementary to the regular educational system—schemes concentrating on physical rehabilitation, courses giving a general acquaintance with tools and factory techniques; more elaborate training in specific crafts; projects in "continued" (or dovetailed) education. In the United States, special prominence has been accorded the technique of the Civilian Conservation Corps, which combines physical fitness and open-air programmes, supplementary education, and training in conservation methods and in appreciation of the value of natural resources. In Canada this particularly useful supplement to labour market organization was emulated (in the form of the National Forestry Project) on only a small scale; but the youth training programmes, starting with only a few hundreds in 1937, have been greatly expanded in size and experience since the youth training schemes became the War Emergency Training Programme covering pre-employment training of all kinds, for adults as well as youths.

Attendance at courses of instruction is already written into the Canadian unemployment insurance Act as one of the statutory conditions for the receipt of benefit; it would obviously be even more relevant for workers who have exhausted their benefit rights, or who for other reasons apply for unemployment assistance (Sections 7, 8). In any case, training should be brought into operation for all unskilled workers, particularly if they are still young, as soon as they show lengthy unemployment records (if they do not apply for training voluntarily); for an im-

provement in what they have to offer an employer is
their only hope, in normal times, of getting better
paid or more regular work. "Training benefit," in
the form of a maintenance rate payable only on the
condition that appropriate training courses are
taken, has been suggested as an apposite provision
for the normally self-employed and other non-wage-
earners who would not be eligible for ordinary unemployment benefits. It has been proposed also as
a requisite for the receipt of a widow's pension if the
woman has no children or is below a certain maximum age (say 50) and has reasonable prospects of
becoming self-supporting. Special vocational instruction and placement arrangements are already
being organized for war casualties. There is no
reason why similar provisions for physically handicapped civilian workers should not be extended on a
national basis; and this will in fact be specifically
desirable in the advent of a disability pensions
scheme. The training or retraining of middle-aged
and older workers which amounts to rehabilitation
is perhaps the most difficult; indeed, it is impossible
without specialized attention and "case work," and
the cooperative goodwill of employers. It would
obviously not be profitable in a depression situation,
in which jobs were hard to find even for the skilled
and physically fit. But this is equally true of any
training programme, whether for youth, for returned
soldiers, or for war workers adapting themselves to
peacetime enterprises. Training programmes are
critically dependent on success in the economic
branches of "full employment" policy. But the
dependence in reciprocal: the best policies of monetary and fiscal adjustment, national works programmes, and industrial and agricultural reorganization, cannot be fully implemented unless the machinery for a flexible redirection of labour is also
set in motion. A half-hearted approach to either
would be equally detrimental to both. The obvious
requirement is that placement and training pro-

grammes and plans for economic expansion should
be built side by side.

It is not necessary to emphasize further the crucial
importance of turning the fullest resources of training and re-training to the problem of occupational
transference immediately the need for war production is ended.   Fortunately, Canada starts off with
certain assets in this field.   The enhanced range of
pre-employment classes, accelerated teaching for
skilled men in the armed services, supervisory training schemes, spare-time vocational education courses,
can be examined for adaptation to post-war use.
The rehabilitation machinery (under P.C. 7633)
provides a strong framework for men who wish to
extend their training or education after demobilization. Above all, the Vocational Training Co-
ordination Act, passed in 1942, provides a basis and
an opportunity for a co-operative programme of
courses and projects on a national scale, if its facilities
get the response they deserve.

In immediate preparation, however, there is still
much to be done. It is not at all certain, for example,
that the capacity and equipment of our existing
technical schools is sufficient to meet the heavy
demands which will be made upon them in the first
post-war years.   Again one of the specific problems
of administration which has to be carefully envisaged
and worked out—as far as possible, before the end
of the war—is the proper relation between training
projects under the Vocational Training Act, present
apprenticeship conditions, regular technical school
facilities, and the contributions which management
and workers in wartime plants can make by looking
ahead themselves. All this involves responsibilities
for the Employment Service and requires a strengthening of its resources if it is to act, through its
national machinery and its local committees, as a co-
ordinator. The Committee on Reconstruction has
received reports on several of these topics from one of

its subcommittees. Because placement and training facilities have become so generally recognized to-day as an integral part of constructive social security measures in the employment field, some of the most relevant recommendations of the subcommittee referred to are reproduced in Appendix IV. It is of interest, also, to precede these with the official statement of the policy of the Employment Service, as set out in the first report of the Unemployment Insurance Commission.

7. UNEMPLOYMENT INSURANCE

It is an immense advantage to have, in the Unemployment Insurance system, the basis for systematic attention to a large part of the unemployment problem. Its operation during the war period means that experience in administration is being accumulated as well as contributions to the unemployment insurance fund. Not least of the advantages is the strengthening of the Employment Service as an administrative agency; and also the growing improvement in statistical resources. Both the analysis of unemployment insurance records, and the inventory of current labour movements now being developed through the Employment Service, have obvious relevance for advance forecast and actual administration on the post-war period. As the biggest piece of social insurance in Canada so far, its coverage, rates of benefit, and general principles of construction are of special importance. No extensions of the social security structure can afford to ignore its existence and the necessity of coordination with it wherever this is reasonable; equally it is necessary to examine how far the unemployment insurance machinery is a satisfactory base from which other social security units might be built.

It is to be noted first that unemployment insurance is confined only to employees—mostly to urban wage-earners. The restriction, as in the case of Workmen's Compensation, is appropriate to the nature of the risk protected; though, equally, there is no inherent reason why coverage should not be extended to rural wage-earners and to others who are subject to the risk in their capacity as employees, but are administratively difficult to include. Unemployment insurance, however, as a unit in a social security system is decidedly superior to Workmen's Compensation in one respect, namely, its national and unified structure. This does not mean, be it noted, that unemployment insurance is not decentralized regionally: on the contrary, the system is organized on a fivefold regional basis, while a network of some two hundred offices and branches ensure servicing of all the principal areas of the Dominion.

Coverage, measured in terms of insured persons, has increased from its original numbers to a figure of 2,500,000 or 2,600,000 (as at the end of 1942).[1] Much of this increase has been due, not to extension of the scope of the act, but to expansion of the working force itself. The most notable increase, as might be expected, has been in the manufacturing field; the present estimate is that at least 1,250,000, or about half of all the insured workers, are in manufacturing industries. It is not possible to say exactly how many of these latter are engaged solely in wartime production, but an estimate puts them at about 825,000. The latter figure would indicate very substantial coverage of war workers, but possibly a small portion of the total as not yet eligible. Manufacturing, however, is probably one of the best covered fields. There is still a sizeable list of excluded employments. These involve particularly (a) agriculture, forestry, and fishing; (b) private domestic service, and (c) stevedoring and shipping workers, as well as (d) governmental employees, police forces, etc., (e) nurses and teachers, (f) most classes of workers earning $2,000 a year or more;[2] i.e., both "good risks" and "bad risks", some of which would help to set off the others in an expanded scheme. It should be noted that, looking towards a comprehensive social security system, the desirability of in-

---

[1] The exact total of persons is not yet available as existing records, which are based on books issued, are not free from duplications. It is probably safer to take the lower rather than the higher of the two figures mentioned.

---

[2] Workers engaged in air transport are excluded along with workers in water transport, though it is doubtful if the irregularities of the two types of employment should be regarded as parallel. Another dubious exclusion is of employees of hospitals not operated for gain, as on a par with employees of charitable institutions. Certain other exclusions, e.g., family workers, are obviously necessary ones.

clusion depends on more than the liability to unemployment alone. If sickness cash benefits, disability, widows' and old age benefits are involved,
it is of much greater necessity to have an inclusive
basis so far as the employee section of the population
is concerned; and the willingness of most persons to
be drawn in as contributors will also be enhanced.

Estimates of the total employed population, under
war conditions, are both difficult to make and
subject to change. The figures of a special sample
count of the census data just released give 2,808,000,
as the total of wage and salary workers for mid-1941
(of whom 720,000 are females), exclusive of men on
active service. Allowing for the comparatively
rapid intake of women workers, which is still going on,
it would be reasonable to expect the employee population to be well above 3,000,000 by the end of 1943,
and it was probably at 2,900,000 by the end of 1942.

Various amendments to the Unemployment Insurance Act are under consideration; for loggers,
seasonal sawmill workers and stevedores, on the one
hand, and employees of governments and public
utilities on the other. It has also been proposed
that the present wage limit should be raised to at
least $2,500. If all of these were implemented
probably half of the present uncovered population
would be drawn in. It is reasonable to assume that
many of those who are most specifically war workers
(in munitions plants, etc.) may not wish to continue
in gainful employment at the end of the war. This
would be particularly true of young women, and it is
estimated that about 135,000 of the 825,000 previously
referred to are females. A sizeable proportion of
this number, even though they have only slender
benefit rights by the end of the war, might perhaps
be regarded as requiring no special protection from
the social insurance point of view. Even if these
allowances are made, however, there are substantial
gaps which will have to be considered as the subject

for unemployment insurance legislation, or other facilities in the event of unemployment, or both, before the war is over.

Members of the armed forces are of course a special group. A total of the order of 500,000 or 600,000 may obtain benefit rights on discharge, which will put them on a par with civilian workers who have been building up contributions for varying periods over the last two years. An ex-service man, providing he is able to complete a minimum of 15 weeks in insured employment within a year after discharge, secures a credit of contributions equal to his period of military service since July 1941 (the date at which unemployment insurance came into operation), the equivalent employers' and employee's contributions being paid by the Treasury. Since ex-service claimants, once established as insured persons, come under the operation of the "one-in-five" rule in the same way as civilian workers, and since special direction is given to the Unemployment Insurance Advisory Committee to exercise surveillance over this source of withdrawals from the Fund, these arrangements cannot be regarded as weakening its present financial status; this augmentation of the number of potential benefit claimants must be remembered, however, in envisaging the post-war situation.

The unemployment insurance fund at the present moment has a reserve of $100,000,000 and to this it is adding under wartime conditions approximately $60,000,000 a year. This is a substantial sum, but it could easily be made the basis of exaggerated optimism. It must be placed against the large number of workers now covered who will have claims upon it in the event of unemployment at the end of the war. It is conceivable that, at least for short periods, well over half of the insured total, and it is certainly possible that 1,000,000, may draw benefits at least for short periods.

A second consideration is the limited duration of most of the benefits which will be available. Payments into the fund were started in July, 1941; since benefits under the Canadian scheme are limited to the period of contribution (roughly in the proportion of one week's benefit for every five weeks' contribution), it would take five years for an insured worker to build up a claim which would assure him the maximum allowable protection for one year. On the assumption that the war terminated at the end of 1943, those workers who have been in the scheme from the beginning, if they had had no periods of unemployment previously, would have rights to benefit which would maintain them for about 24 weeks. This would be true probably of the majority of the present insured population, but the newest workers, particularly those whose first employment has been in the war plants, would have claims of much shorter duration. The significance of this fact depends, of course, very much on the calculation of how long will be the period of greatest stress during the transition. If it is only to be six months, the unemployment insurance situation may be viewed with some equanimity. If re-establishment of peacetime industrial employment at a high level can hardly be expected until two years after the end of the war, however, the situation demands serious attention. It is obviously desirable to consider now not merely the broad question of extension to other categories and occupational groups, but what provision should be made for those who exhaust their benefits, whether at the end of six months or more rapidly; what provisions should be made for persons not covered by unemployment insurance at all (and these latter will range from groups who could anticipate steady employment down to casuals and partially employed individuals who are unable to qualify); and other related questions. These are examined further in the succeeding Section.

Adjustment of Benefit Scales

An important matter which has to be considered before the view can be taken that the present structure of unemployment insurance could meet all that will be required of it, is the level of benefit rates, both absolutely and in relation to scales of benefits under other pieces of legislation. Details of the wage categories and benefit rates are listed in Table 5. In the assessment of these, it is an important fact that the great majority of the workers covered are entitled to receive benefit at one of the upper three levels. It must be added, however, that the probable incidence of unemployment is greater among individuals in the lowest categories, many of whom are unskilled or irregular.

TABLE 6.—WEEKLY RATES OF UNEMPLOYMENT BENEFIT
PAYABLE TO CATEGORIES OF WAGE-EARNERS, AND
APPROXIMATE NUMBER OF WAGE-EARNERS, END OF
1942

Category	Weekly Earnings	Approximate Number Insured	P.C. Distribution	Benefit Rate (a)	Benefit Rate (b)
				$	$
0	Less than $5.40 (or under 16 years of age)......	49,400	1·9	....	....
1	$ 5.40– 7.50	23,400	0·9	4.08	4.80
2	7.50– 9.60	52,000	2·0	5.10	6.00
3	9.60–12.00	119,600	4·6	6.12	7.20
4	12.00–15.00	231,400	8·9	7.14	8.40
5	15.00–20.00	444,600	17·1	8.16	9.60
6	20.00–26.00	522,600	20·1	10.20	12.00
7	26.00–38.00	1,157,000	44·5	12.24	14.40

Material supplied by the courtesy of the Unemployment Insurance Commission.

(b) The second or "dependent" schedule is payable to (i) a man whose wife is wholly or mainly dependent on him, (ii) a married woman with a dependent husband, or (iii) a widow or widower with dependent children under 16.

The present scales provide rates which are approximately half the wage-rates of the categories concerned, and there is only a very restricted recognition
of the extra dependency obligations of married men,
the second schedule of rates being about 15 per cent
higher than the first. Evaluating these by reference
to the standards cited in Section 3, it will be seen
that only categories 6 and 7 ($12-$14 a week) reach
or exceed the assistance minimum, with category 5
possibly marginal if the recipient happens to live
in a low-cost community. None of the categories
(based also on the two-person unit) reaches the
"desirable" minimum or "living wage" standard.
In particular, it is evident that the extensions
applied in the second schedule do not provide
adequately for a second adult, for contributors
earning less than $20 a week (all categories below 5).

Since the greater proportion of insured workers
are in the higher categories it could be argued that
the unemployment insurance system, taken by itself
and for limited objectives, is relatively adequate.
(This adequacy is of course more readily assertable
by comparison with past unemployment relief rates,
but these cannot be accepted as a valid standard).
There is much more to the matter than this, however. The graduated scales of present unemployment insurance, as it is recommended elsewhere,
are appropriate to other basic insurances set up
under Canadian conditions; and there are considerable advantages to be gained from assimilating at
least the contributory scales of the new schemes
to them as far as is possible. The two-person unit
is even more fundamental, for a structure built up
logically with a children's allowance system. Looking forward to future social security planning,
therefore, adjustment at this point appears as the
most urgent preliminary action which should desirably be taken now. In the present scales, the
"dependent rate" is larger than the "single rate"

by only about fifteen per cent, and it is recommended that this differential should be increased. It will be desirable, as far as possible, to graduate the increases so that the percentage improvement is greatest for the lowest scales.   In category 7, perhaps the most important, a differential of about 33 per cent would be sufficient to bring the dependent benefit rate to the "desirable minimum" standard. In the middle and lower categories, while increases of even the single-unit benefit rates may seem desirable, it would be better to raise the double-unit benefit only.   Considerations of preserving or improving the mobility of labour are important at this part of the wage scale, particularly for young and single workers (probably a majority) in the lower categories.   If these workers have an adult dependent, however, (assuming child dependents will be covered by children's allowances), it is reasonable to assume they will be anxious to get into better-paid occupations, even if the augmented (two-unit) benefit brought the rate much nearer the average wage in their preceding employment.

There are several methods by which this increase in the claims placed upon the fund might be handled; by direct government contribution for the amount of the improvement, by some adjustment of contributions, or a combination of both.   The matter is of more than sufficient importance to justify changes in the rate structure, and also the revision of the actuarial calculations that have been made so far. If part or whole of the adjustment is financed through increase in the contribution rates, it would be possible to do this without destroying the very desirable features already embodied in the scales; (1) the differentiated graduation so that employers pay higher proportional contributions for the lower-paid workers, and (2) sums of such amounts as to permit multiples of six (for the purpose of calculations in terms of daily units).   It is desirable, however, to make the changes in such a way as not to require larger contributions from the lowest categories, certainly those below category 4.

Besides the prime advantage of setting a systematic standard to which all other contributory insurance could be linked, this adjustment would take an immediate step towards reducing the anomalies which will otherwise appear when wartime allowances are curtailed. There would be a distinct psychological advantage in announcing these preparations for the transition now. And if increased contributions are required they could be inaugurated now, at a time when earnings are relatively high.

It is impossible to ignore the fact that rates set up under special war measures and for the armed services are particularly likely to be regarded as setting standards. If nothing is done now, anomalies in post-war circumstances may appear even for the same individual. As statutory dependents' allowances, the wife and two children of an enlisted man today receive $84.60 per month, and this amount is for three persons, the father not being in the home. This is equivalent to a wage income of about $20 per week. On demobilization the ex-service man will be entitled to unemployment insurance benefits under the rehabilitation scheme; but these benefits will be only $12 a week and the father will now be in the home. In the case of this ex-service man a demand for increase or supplementation, for example, would probably run in terms of continuing the dependents' allowance scale until he is re-employed. The proper course, however, is not to supplement the insurance rate because other types of provision do; but to set the total structure of social security to a feasible scale, and preserve its logic as far as possible. Piecemeal adjustments are a danger which threaten every social insurance system if its requisites are not examined carefully in advance. Proper adjustment now will be relatively easy: under post-war stresses it will be hard;

and inconsistency in rates once started may become more and more of a handicap to efficient administration.

Compared to this matter, other improvements are of minor weight, but it may be noted that the unemployment benefit scale for the very lowest categories 1 and 2 are so small as to have no justification as amounts sufficient to support a dependent. In practice, a considerable number of the insured persons in these categories are youths, female workers, or partial workers, whose incomes at best are not much more than small contributions to a family budget. It would not be possible to increase the benefit rates very much without reaching the primary wage level itself. The fact is, however, that little can be done through the unemployment insurance system as such, for employees working at these rates. The workers concerned should receive special attention at the hands of Employment Service officers, to ascertain if their wage rates are justified, or if their skills or working conditions can be improved. But the first necessity so far as scales are concerned is to ensure adequacy at the three levels which account for 70 to 80 per cent of the total insured working force; and this is the more important because by far the greater proportion of married wage-earners are in these categories.

Other Attributes of the Unemployment Insurance System

Before leaving unemployment insurance, two features of the present system are worthy of note for the suggestions they offer in the construction of other social insurance units. The first of these is the principle which was adopted that all administrative costs (provided for, in the Canadian scheme, solely by Dominion government grant) are a separate charge, and in no way payable from the Insurance Fund which is composed solely of contributions (including government contributions made as such).

This procedure may seem obvious enough; but its advantages, in keeping clear the relation of administrative costs to the total scheme, and making easier the surveillance of contributor-revenues in relation to the amounts paid out as benefits, are worth underlining. The device of meeting administration costs by outright Dominion grant has itself much to recommend it. This need not wholly preclude consideration of examples in which provincial participation in administrative expenses might be appropriate; but there are merits in an arrangement in which the Dominion government has specific interest in the efficiency (and also the adequacy) of administration.

The second feature, well known to students of the subject, but probably not yet widely appreciated, is the extensive machinery which now exists for the adjudication of disputes. "Hard cases" and doubtful cases under an insurance system have an opportunity for fair hearing, before panels composed of employers' and employees' representatives, with neutral chairmen. Such panels have been established in over thirty centres. If the decisions of the Courts of Referees thus contributed are appealed, an Umpire (a Judge of the Superior Court) takes the case under consideration and gives a final verdict.[1]

Requests for references have so far been very few, but the machinery will unquestionably be called into greater operation in the post-war period. The suggestion of most relevance here is that careful consideration should be given to developing this

---

[1] An exception to this procedure was planned for the simpler but more extensive matter of decisions on occupations and employments intended to be covered by the Act, particularly at the initial stages. "Doubtful cases were referred to Regional or Head Office Coverage Committees for administrative rulings. The five Regional Committees working in close co-operation with the Head Office Committee provided uniform application across Canada in matters of coverage under the Act......If an inquirer is not satisfied with the rulings given by these Committees, he is entitled to ask for a formal decision by the Commission which is given after further inquiry into the details of the case. The decisions of the Commission are subject to appeal to the Umpire." (First Report of the Unemployment Insurance Commission, pp. 10, 17.)

nucleus of the machinery for the settlement of all
social insurance and related questions arising directly
out of administration. It would be unfortunate
indeed if a piecemeal approach to social security
legislation were to produce a series of different
arbitration procedures, not merely doing similar
work but continually raising the possibility of
conflicting decisions. It would on the other hand
be a great boon for the future to build up a unified
body of administrative law, and (through the citizen
committees) better acquaintance, both regionally
and nationally, with the interrelations and the
objectives of the various branches of social provision.
Even familiarity with unemployment insurance in
Canada is not yet very extensive; it should not be
too much to suppose that an appropriate extension
of the present combination of lay and technical
personnel could be brought together to equip themselves for the interpretation and development of a
comprehensive system.

8. UNEMPLOYMENT ASSISTANCE

There are a number of compelling reasons why unemployment assistance measures additional to unemployment insurance must be considered before the end of the war. Some of these have already been indicated. The first is the limitation in the coverage of the Unemployment Insurance Act itself. Unless much more substantial extension is undertaken than is at present contemplated—which involves the overcoming of several administrative difficulties—there will remain some hundreds of thousands of workers not covered by the scheme. The second is the limitation in the duration of benefit, the importance of which could become very great if the period of transition is difficult and prolonged. Thirdly, whatever may be done in extension of the Act, smaller groups of various types will not qualify, or may be eligible for benefit for such short periods as to be indistinguishable in practice from the non-insured. Among these will be casual and irregular workers, many of whom move frequently from one occupation to another. If one of these is a non-insurable occupation, or a non-wage-earning activity such as farming, unemployment insurance would not be very helpful.

It will be necessary to lay plans for some assistance in any case: it is only the dimensions that are indeterminate. They can be small or large. Even in the best circumstances, of favourable economic conditions and of much wider coverage of social insurance measures, loopholes in some categories undoubtedly remain. The Beveridge Report, outlining the most comprehensive system hitherto considered in Britain, still assumes that for a limited number of cases "national assistance subject to a uniform means test" will be needed. So far as Canada is concerned, there are wide areas uncovered. Failing any other legislation in Canada,

the only recourse for the non-insured unemployed
would be municipal relief. It can hardly be denied
that one of the strong reasons for considering unemployment assistance anew is the inadequate and
repellent character of the relief measures of the past.
However much or little administration beyond the
insurance-machinery level has to be relied on, it
must be reformed and made more efficient than
municipal doles to the destitute.

This is the negative aspect of the matter. There
is a positive one which has already been indicated,
but which should be restated in the present context.
Everything possible must be done to support and
promote mobility of labour in the immediate post-
war period, because great occupational change-over
in these years is inescapable. In European countries
unemployment insurance has often been blamed for
the immobilization of labour under depression conditions; though with knowledge of the tangle of
municipal residence restrictions in the thirties as a
background, it will be easier for Canadians to
appreciate that the principal immobilizer is prolonged unemployment itself. A practical aspect of
the post-war situation, however, is that even if all
the wage-earners in the country were now within
the insurance scheme, the question would eventually
arise, if they relied only on benefits to tide them over
the transition period: can they anticipate continuing
in exactly the same industry or occupation in which
they first became insured? Unemployment assistance measures in Canada, therefore—as in other
countries in a post-war context—must be designed
as constructively as possible, in relation to public
employment projects, to training and transference
programmes, and to the co-operation of industry in
utilizing the services of the Employment Offices.

Almost any plans will raise the question of
division of responsibility between Dominion and
pro vincial authorities; or, in the terms which were

recommended by the Rowell-Sirois Commission, between responsibility and provision for employables and unemployables. At the Dominion-Provincial Conference in January, 1941, it is to be assumed from the Prime Minister's statement at that time that the government accepted the Commission's recommendations that the Dominion government should assume full responsibility, in respect both of finances and administration, for the employable unemployed. The passage of the Unemployment Insurance Act was a part fulfilment of the recommendation. It still remains true, however, that the administrative arrangements necessary to incorporate these principles are by no means settled. The problem is one not only of tax resources, but of existing welfare machinery, both provincial and municipal. It would of course not be enough to argue that burdens not already assumed by the Dominion government must be regarded as provincial—or, if constitutional obligations are still to be interpreted rigidly, municipal. Action to meet the whole situation is advisable which will take account of wartime developments since the Rowell-Sirois Report was written, and also the proportions of the problem as it is likely to appear under post-war conditions. But it is important to remember that there has been no change in present law, other than that for unemployment insurance, which *authorizes* the Dominion to undertake plans.

Assuming that constitutional issues, if any, are resolved, there are two direct methods of providing supplementary assistance: a special extension of the Unemployment Insurance Act, or of its benefit conditions; or the setting up of appropriate facilities for non-insured workers of status otherwise comparable to the insured.

The first would, of course, have many advantages, if it could be done simply by bringing in new classes as contributors. It would drastically lessen the

need for a substantial federal assistance scheme; and
it would have the incidental advantage of beginning
the collection of contributions now, when they might
most helpfully be drawn from consumption channels.
Administrative difficulties would be admittedly great
for some categories, however, and many marginal
groups would still remain. A compromise arrangement would be to bring a number of categories into
insurance by means of a government grant, making
up the equivalent of past contributions sufficiently
to give the new groups a sizeable amount of potential
benefit claims (similar to the procedure already
adopted for members of the armed forces under some
of the provisions of P.C. 7633). It is a distinctly
better method than that of the unconditional "out-
of-work donations" or bonuses which were attached
to the Unemployment Insurance Fund in Britain
after the last war, and which were the beginning of
the "dole" because of their loss of contact with any
actuarial principles. The method should perhaps
not be considered entirely out of court for non-
military workers; but its application would call for
very careful consideration if justice were to be done
to workers who have paid contributions for some time
in regular fashion. If considered at all, it should
perhaps be applied only to specific occupations
whose inclusion so far has been prevented, not by
their being particularly bad "risks," but by administrative difficulties now overcome.

The other method is to set up an Unemployment
Assistance or Unemployment Aid administration
under Dominion government auspices. This procedure recommends itself because the workers uncovered by insurance are not the only ones in question. Besides those who are employable (and,
therefore, presumably Dominion government responsibilities) but have for one reason or another been
unable to qualify, there will be the workers who have
satisfied the necessary conditions for receiving

benefit for a period, but whose unemployment or inability to get satisfactorily relocated has exhausted their benefit rights. Unless there is no doubt at all about their unemployability, these workers, and also insured persons disqualified for technical reasons other than misconduct under Section 45 of the Act, should of all groups be the most automatically eligible for claim to Unemployment Aid.

Administration of Unemployment Aid

The logical location for the service dealing with Unemployment Aid is the Dominion Employment Service, or some appropriate branch of it. Desirably this should have some similarity to the Unemployment Insurance Administration section in the local office, but also certain differences. Unemployment Aid and Unemployment Insurance administrations may require day-to-day access to each others' records, but the experience of Britain is a warning, if warning is needed, that insurance benefits and Unemployment Assistance must be kept separate so far as recipients are concerned. This requirement does not, of course, apply to the Employment Office, which must be available on completely equal terms for all unemployed persons. By the same token, the placement section of the office must be freed from assistance or insurance duties (unless the office is, for example, a small one in a rural district) so that it can give its full time to finding jobs. Not only are the needs of assistance claimants identical with those of insured persons, in respect to placement, transport facilities, training and other requirements for re-employment. The whole administration which comes under the authority of the Unemployment Insurance Commission is equipped to deal with these claims—with employment records or the means of obtaining them, a network of offices covering all parts of the country, and staffs familiar with employment mat-

ters. The services that the local offices would have
to perform would be: (1) to register those applying
for unemployment assistance and to keep the registration up-to-date; (2) to decide in terms of the conditions set forth for the receipt of unemployment
assistance, whether a person should receive such
assistance, in what amounts, and for how long a
period; and (3) to issue the cheques or vouchers to
those entitled to receive them. The chief administrative problems would arise in connection with the
second of these functions. The first, however,
would be no more than an extension of what the
offices already do.

Every endeavour should be made to standardize
the basic rates payable under Dominion unemployment assistance, with flexibilities allowed under
reasonable conditions. The principle that unemployment aid, being non-contributory, should be at a
rate lower than a contributory insurance benefit, is
generally accepted. Assuming that the "dependent
class" benefit scales are augmented to bring them
nearer to two-person standards than at present, a
flat rate of reduction, preferably of not more than
about 10 per cent, might be applied for Unemployment Aid administration.

The personal aspects of Unemployment Aid
administration are of particular importance. As a
unit in the staff of every sizeable office there should
be available a competent interviewer with experience
in family welfare work. Prolonged unemployment
engenders family difficulties of various sorts, evidence
of which is often presented in the employment
interview. Such a consultant service, available to
all applicants wishing to use it, would add a valuable
complement to monetary assistance, in the form of
maintenance of morale and perhaps of employability. It is highly desirable that a simplified
process for the determination of need should be
worked out. Payments would be made subject to

office verification and it should be quite feasible with experience to assess needs on the basis of an office interview and a simple declaration by the applicant of his resources.

The Definition of Employability

It is obvious that the determination of whether a person is to be adjudged employable or not will be of great practical significance. This is not only because it will presumably determine Dominion responsibility for aid. It is in line with the argument already set forward, that the effort to find new or more suitable employment must be intensified rather than weakened, for applicants at the assistance stage. It is important also if disability pensions are to be available for those persons really incapacitated or unsuited to continuing in the labour market, (Section 11).

There has been much rather abstract discussion of "employability", but it is important to realize that the vagueness of the concept is whittled away (1) by the proper functioning of the Employment Service, which can offer the ultimate test of a job, (2) by unemployment insurance administration experience, in testing availability for employment, and (3) by the development of training schemes, especially if they are adapted to cases of minor physical handicap. It would be still further clarified if health insurance and disability pensions were in effect, providing tests of incapacity from a medical point of view.

In practice, the local offices would play the largest part, in making sure that the applicants for unemployment assistance were capable of and available for work. For this purpose the mechanism is already operating because the same tests must be applied to those who apply for benefits under the Unemployment Insurance Act. It is true that differences would be encountered between periods of

high and low employment. When the labour
market is active as at present, the testing of capacity
to work offers little difficulty. If an applicant for
benefit is offered a job and does not take it because
of incapacity he is not entitled to benefits. Since
there are relatively few claimants for benefit, and
since most claimants are offered jobs within a short
period, determining whether or not the applicant is
capable of work has not been a serious problem.
Moreover, as the applicant for benefit must appear
in person at a local office, he must presumably be in
physical condition to do so (though as argued in
Section 11 this situation is not fully covered without
sickness cash benefits). All of this means, however,
that the whole situation is clearer and easier if there
are appropriate types of employment available—
even if they are substitute employments, or training
projects. If a period of widespread unemployment
lasting for some years had to be faced, the problem
would become more serious, assuming that the
provinces were administering relief schemes for the
unemployable. It would, however, be to the
interest of the provinces to reduce the numbers listed
as unemployable and the most effective method of
doing so would be to improve their rehabilitation
services.

So far as establishing the status of the unemployable—rather than the maintenance of employability—
is concerned, health insurance would measurably assist
the whole administration. Unemployability (which
is a form of incapacity) may be classified in three
ways: *(a)* Permanent and complete unemployability arising because of old age, complete disability
such as cases of paralysis, etc., *(b)* Temporary
unemployability arising because of illness or accident, *(c)* Partial or limited unemployability arising
out of loss of limbs, the sight of one or both eyes,
etc. If a cash benefit scheme were in operation as
well as health insurance, most of the second group

could be provided for. The test itself would probably require a doctor's opinion; taken in conjunction with that of the employment office, it would settle most cases.

The case of the partially unemployable is the most complicated because it is a function of the condition of the man and of the labour market. In a time of great labour scarcity a man might be employable, who in a time of widespread unemployment would be unemployable. Again, a man who for example loses his eyesight may be unemployable until he is trained for a new occupation, and even after training his employability will be more restricted than a man with full eyesight. In this connection the creation of special training schools for the handicapped would be important. The responsibility of operating such schools would not of course devolve upon the local offices. Indeed these might very appropriately be provincial government functions. It would, however, be the office's responsibility to refer handicapped persons in need of training to the appropriate school and to endeavour to obtain positions for them after their training was over. Once again the existence of disability pensions would simplify many cases. As recommended elsewhere, the most desirable procedure would be to give the individual the benefit of the doubt until inability to take a job or to benefit from rehabilitation courses had been proved.

These problems of administration have been pursued in some detail in order to show that the social insurances and their supporting services offer the best aid in establishing a satisfactory method of Dominion unemployment assistance, and of working out the division of federal-provincial jurisdiction in marginal cases. The greater the extent of social security measures, dealing with specific contingences and types of dependency, the greater the extent to which the Employment Office will be spared the burden of dealing with miscellaneous and undifferentiated relief tasks. Much will depend on the welfare services of the provinces, (the discussion of which is not undertaken in this report). But the reformed and developed Employment Service holds a key position, provided it is properly staffed for the task. Another part of the machinery should also be referred to again. The provisions for adjudication and appeal in insurance cases, already described, could undoubtedly be utilized for assistance cases, provided that standard assistance regulations are set up, with a considerable contribution to fair administration. There would already, with comparatively little augmentation, be facilities for regional operation. There seems to be no good reason, equally, why the Courts and the Umpire should not be adaptable, given due provision for provincial representation, to the tasks of arbitration of Dominion-provincial disputes on unemployment cases, such as the Rowell-Sirois Commission proposed to assign to a separate Appeal Board.

The Role of Special Assistance Projects

It has been implicit in the consideration of employment in this part that a fourfold approach is to be made—that a national development programme, occupational transference facilities, unemployment insurance, and unemployment assistance, are to be planned and operated in close relation to one another. One possible unit in an integrated programme remains to be clarified before this section is completed. It has been suggested[1] that some employment projects, distinct from those forming part of the national post-war development programme—which would employ workers in the

---

[1] E.g., by H. M. Cassidy in his recent book, *Social Security and Reconstruction*, (Ryerson Press, Toronto), Chapter VII. (By courtesy of Dr. Cassidy the manuscript of this book, which deals solely with Canada, was made available in advance of publication.)

normal way at prevailing rates of wages—should be
organized deliberately for groups coming within the
scope of unemployment assistance. They would in
effect be supplementary and partially subsidized projects for special categories not absorbable in ordinary
industrial employment. These groups make a wide
and very varied range—white-collar workers, artists
and related professional groups, young persons still
in need of training or education, members of farm
households whom it is not desirable to move from
their districts, older persons unfitted for heavy
work, and so forth. In the United States, the
W.P.A. "white-collar" projects, the National Youth
Administration and Civilian Conservation Corps,
and some branches of the Farm Security Administration programmes (including the Food Stamp
Plan) have demonstrated the wide scope for
ingenuity which offers itself. Community projects
of various kinds which were developed for the
unemployed in Great Britain (particularly in the
"depressed areas", through the National Council of
Social Service) are probably less well known, but
also relevant. Not all of these projects are "depressed areas" enterprises, but they recognize an
element of low employability for one reason or
another. So far as the projects are rehabilitative
(particularly for young persons), they may help to
make this a transitory stage. In Canada, some of
these schemes might be geared to the machinery of
the Vocational Training Act, some might possibly
be developed as extensions of the P.F.R.A. system.
Their claim should not be ignored, whether for
rounding out a large-scale capital works plan, or—
probably more appropriately—as a deliberately
designed set of alternatives to unemployment
assistance.

What is important is that such a programme, if
adopted, should be frankly recognized as a supplementary and subsidized system. It should pay
only maintenance wages or assistance rates, some

possibly in the form of training benefits. The
proper relation of federal and provincial (or other
local) participation is of much consequence. It is
doubtful if the programme would be advanced
beyond an experimental and fragmentary stage
without federal initation and assistance in financing.
It would be necessary also for the unemployed to be
referred to the projects through the Employment
Service, and to be at least partly within national
control so as not to impede desirable transferences
of labour. At the same time provincial and local
sponsorship of particular schemes would be highly
desirable. So far as they related to depressed areas,
or districts with especially heavy unemployment or
agricultural distress, it is particularly important
that they should not be relied on as the sole means of
assistance, i.e., without reference to educational,
health, and other social welfare services, which may
be seriously lacking in this area. American experience has demonstrated again and again that, in their
absence, an assistance project which is to be successful will be forced to take on various welfare functions
as auxiliaries, to the benefit of the residents, it is
true, but to the detriment of the project as a mode of
employment. This leads once again to the general
counsel that the whole of the national machinery
for dealing with employment will function more
efficiently, unclogged with other problems of individual and social deficiency, if it functions within a
framework providing a national minimum of coverage against major causes of poverty and insecurity.

PART III

THE UNIVERSAL RISKS: SICKNESS, INVALIDITY, OLD AGE

9. HEALTH INSURANCE (MEDICAL CARE)

Health insurance is one of the most widespread forms of all the social insurances. Details of systems in force have been set out in many documents (including one of the most convenient Canadian references, the appendix studies of the Rowell-Sirois Report) and it is not necessary to reproduce them here. It may be noted, however, that prior to the war some thirty or more countries provided for this need through social insurance methods, and the great majority of them through compulsory schemes.

It is not necessary to do more than restate the essentials of the case for health insurance, since this has now been put forward from many quarters in Canada. The case is really a twofold one; the importance of adequate medical care as a basic need in itself, required by all members of the population; and the economic necessities which support the contributory approach towards attaining it. The key fact is that most family incomes, excepting only those at the highest levels, are insufficient to meet the costs of continuous or serious illness; while a great many family men put off consultation with a doctor or a hospital for fear of the bills; and this has been verified by successive studies since it was first brought sharply to light by the Committee on the Costs of Medical Care in the United States. The most important complementary fact to this conclusion is the one emphasized recently by the intensive investigations made through the National Health Survey of the U.S. Public Health Service, the burden of which is that both frequency and severity rates of illness are in general higher among the lower-income groups.

The general case for health coverage is well summarized in the report on the subject in the Rowell-Sirois documentation. First, "it is increasingly felt that the physical fitness of the population is a matter of basic public interest like education." Secondly, "preventive medicine is being used to only a slight degree of its potentialities", particularly because "many low-income receivers are unable to obtain regular examination and diagnosis. Meeting this need would not only save life and health but would probably reduce state expenditures on hospitalization and institutionalization, mothers' allowances and other social services". Thirdly, "the loss occasioned by sickness is a very important one for industry, and to the extent it could be reduced, industry would benefit." Finally, better health care would render incalculable benefits in terms of higher survival rates and preventable ill-health, disability and disease. The special case is equally well verified, in the statement that "every commission appointed to investigate health insurance in Canada"—by which reference is made to the Royal Commission on State Health Insurance and Maternity Benefits in British Columbia, 1932; governmental commissions on health and medical services in Alberta in 1929, 1933 and 1934; one of the reports of the Quebec Social Insurance Commission, and others—"has found the average wage-earner unable to provide adequate medical care for himself and his family", if left to his own resources.

To approach the problem comprehensively, it is important to recognize that there are actually four major aspects of health and sickness contingences rather than one:

    (a) Public health measures.
    (b) Medical care.
    (c) Sickness benefit (cash payments).
    (d) Disability, chronic illness, and other forms of long-term interruption or cessation of earning power.

The latter two are dealt with elsewhere in this

report (Section 11). Public health facilities are referred to only incidentally, but the importance of their relationship with medical care needs no emphasis. There are special questions of administration, including the division of federal and provincial functions, affecting all of these in some degree. But the solution of them for health insurance has crucial implications, with regard to the effective operation and extension of all social insurance, which it is convenient to discuss later (Section 14).

Apart from these, the fundamental matters in the insurance approach to medical care are really only two; (a) the costs involved, including the manner in which doctors' and other medical practitioners' services are secured and reimbursed; and (b) the assessment of the total cost upon the appropriate population.

The first naturally depends on the scope of the care and services to be provided, as well as on rates of fees. A growing number of enquiries and reports from various sources have been directed to this; practically all those emanating from this continent agree that the maximum possible range of medical aid should be available, including general practitioner services, drugs and medicines, access to hospitals, appropriate nursing and convalescent care. Dental care is a matter which may reasonably be somewhat limited in the first instance, because of the large potential scope of dental defects, and also because a good deal of dental attention should conveniently and desirably be provided through other sources, particularly the schools. Diagnostic facilities, such as X-ray for tuberculosis, are so important for the preventive attack on disease that it would be false economy to exclude them. The services of specialists are perhaps in a different category from other medical requisites since the element of personal skill is so important, and it is reasonable to assume that special regulations for specialists' services should be drafted in a health insurance scheme.

There is a growing degree of agreement also in the computations which have been made from time to time, from Canadian and American sources, of the yearly amount which would be required on a per capita basis to provide this standard amount of medical care. Broadly most of the figures range between $16 and $24 per capita. Whether these are to be considered reasonable, low, or excessive can only be judged by reference to the quality of the services rendered on the one hand, and existing scales of medical charges on the other. The difficulty on the latter score is that the range of present fees chargeable by medical men is distorted at both ends, by the number of services supplied gratuitously to clinical and destitute patients, and by the large fees securable from the wealthiest classes or by the most highly-skilled specialists. It may be that nothing except experience will establish what should be the most justifiable and appropriate charges for a national system. The settlement of a scale, to be put into operation subject to review after a stated time, however, should be sufficient for a start to be made on the collective mobilization of the necessary funds. It is relevant to point out that there are two advantages in the insurance method which should influence the calculations, and which will undoubtedly continue to do so in the future development of the scheme: the ease of collecting small periodical contributions from the potential "consumers" of medical service, as contrasted with uncertain and sizeable medical bills; and from the practitioner's point of view, the advantage of a regular flow of income, even if at moderate rates, as compared with a varying range of accounts not all of which are collectable.

At least a little light is thrown on "capacity to pay" by the special survey of incomes and expenditures of representative urban wage-earning families which was made by the Bureau of Statistics

in 1937. This included considerable detail in its
assessment of expenditure practice, and it is of much
interest to note that these families, whose total resources averaged around $1,400, spent sums varying
from $46 to $83 per family on health and medical
costs of one kind or another. The expenditures per
person averaged $15 per year. It is reasonable to
assume that if these expenditures were budgeted on a
periodical basis they could be a little larger without
undue strain. It is clear on the other hand that
some proportion of the costs, especially for the lower-
income families, will have to be found from governmental sources.

The Proper Coverage of a Health Insurance System

The second step is the assessment of the total cost
efficiently and equitably upon the appropriate population: employers, employees, other gainfully occupied persons, children and other dependents, and
governments in their capacity of financial agent for
the citizen body generally.

It should be taken as axiomatic for Canadian
health insurance planning that every endeavour
must be made to include the rural and farm population, and that administrative facilities must be
devised to do so if they are not already existent.

There are certain branches of social risk or need
which it is quite proper to consider only for the
industrial or urban population, the obvious example
being unemployment insurance, which must indeed
be confined not only to the industrial population but
to persons actually or potentially of employee status.
It would be a serious mistake, however, if any idea
from this now familiar piece of social legislation were
carried over unchanged into the field of health
insurance. Health care is needed by all groups, and
it is imperative that means should be sought, no
matter what the initial difficulties may be, to
extend its benefits to the largest possible population.

The employee population has always lent itself to social insurance methods because contributions are easily collected at the time of wage payments. It might seem sufficient to supplement this by arrangements for voluntary contribution from all other categories of persons, who could be expected to desire the benefits of the scheme. Experience in other countries has proved, however, that unless the very strongest inducements are offered, the voluntary system does not secure the required proportion of entrants; and, what is more important in initial considerations such as this, it does not in the long-run eliminate the necessity for some special administrative arrangements which it was hoped to avoid.

A related question of scope is the extent and manner in which the members of the family should be brought within insurance. In the special case of a wife who is a wage-earner, there is no reason why she should not pay her contribution in the same way as any other employed person, as is already done by the insurable classes of female wage-earners under unemployment insurance. In the majority of cases, however, of the wife whose main occupation is the care of the household, there are two alternatives. (1) Every male contributor should be required to pay the same rate, this rate being calculated to cover two persons, which in the case of the married man would be himself and his wife; or (2) the married man might be required to pay a higher contribution than the single man.

On the grounds argued elsewhere (Section 4) it is distinctly preferable that the former principle should be followed, i.e. that in effect every male adult pays into the common fund an amount to cover his wife, actual or potential. This simple and justifiable procedure avoids administrative complications, and double contribution scales which would be particularly unsettling for a system already conceived on a graduated-scale basis. The principle of a single rate of contribution irrespective of marital status has already been accepted in some degree in Canadian unemployment insurance: it is even more important to note that different rates for married and single contributors have not been incorporated in health insurance legislation in any of the countries which possess it. Everything points to the need for promoting easy entrance to health insurance privileges. It is far better to assist this entrance by adjusting contributions to broad income levels than to attempt any further concession to equity which is not in keeping with the major principles of social insurance methods.

In health insurance above all it is necessary, in addition, to provide automatically that the contribution of the male head of the family carries with it the right to medical care for all his children. Once again the only satisfactory and in this case the eminently desirable way, is to provide all the services on the simple condition that the basic contribution is paid. The effects of the insurance mechanism in this form is to distribute the costs of medical care in such a way that persons with smaller families make a contribution to those with larger families—a procedure which no responsible member of the community should resent. (In any case, the distribution is equalized to some extent by such contribution to costs as is made from state funds.)

A major contribution in relating the costs of insurance to the unequal distribution of income, in particular making it possible for the lowest income groups of the community to receive proper medical care, can be obtained through insurance contributions paid by the governments themselves. Given a standard computation of the financing required for proper medical care, the government contribution could be adjusted to make up the balance at each of the graduated levels. At the top range it may make no contribution at all; at the lowest level, of persons able to declare that they have no monetary income or none above a certain minimum level, but who are otherwise insurable, the state contribution to the fund would be the full amount. A system such as this has been suggested as particularly appropriate for health insurance contributions. It may be noted that it is neither strictly a flat-rate nor strictly a graduated scale. (It really requires a separate name, and the term "degressive" has been adopted for ease of reference.) So far as the minimum-income group is concerned, a reasonable device preferable to no payment at all is a token payment or registration fee, such as is applied (at the rate of £1) in New Zealand. This serves to establish the person concerned as a contributor, and ensures his participation in the requirements of registration and other records.

The logical requisite, therefore, for the proper initiation of a Canadian health insurance scheme is an income registration in appropriate form, at least for all regional and occupational classes who are not already registered for unemployment insurance, or more easily covered through the payroll method. The registration or declaration need not be too exacting and certainly does not have to take on the character of a means test such as might be applied to the indigent; but it should be sufficiently exact to permit the assignment of the contributor to certain broad levels of income. These might be somewhat more simplified than those adopted in the present Unemployment Insurance Act, but should be related to them as far as possible.

The other aspects of contribution collection, concerned with administration rather than income-graduation, are so important in relation to other insurances that they are discussed separately at the end of this Part.

10. INDUSTRIAL ACCIDENT AND DISEASE: WORKMEN'S COMPENSATION

Workmen's compensation provisions are the oldest form of collective provision by the insurance or pooling techniques, to which state aid or control has been added later. The method which has now become familiar has evolved from an earlier situation which persisted for a long time after employers were made liable for industrial accidents, the most frequent device to meet this liability being separate arrangements with private insurance companies or the formation of mutual associations by groups of employers. Placed on a mutualized basis, as in Canada, workmen's compensation has become a microcosm of social insurance. The best developed form meeting this definition is characterized by three features:

> *(a)* the establishment of a specific fund, built up from contributions or assessments from employers;
>
> *(b)* administration by a more or less independent government-appointed board (the government being the province, in Canada);
>
> *(c)* the classification of industrial groups according to their degree of danger or hazard, and appropriate gradation of premiums paid.

In Canada this form is best organized in Ontario (where it dates from 1914), and the Ontario system is frequently quoted as a desirable model in literature on the subject. It may be noted that Quebec in first setting up workmen's compensation experimented with private insurance of the liabilities, but changed to the Ontario principles almost in their entirety after a few years' experience.

The most important advantages of this technique

for providing against the risks and costs of industrial accident and related liabilities, are threefold.

(1) Ordinarily the liability of the individual employer is transformed into a collective liability. The payments set aside on industrial accident account are better spread and more easily absorbed into the company's accounting. For every firm the possibility of a crushing bill for a major disaster is removed. Furthermore, "friction between the claimant and his employer is eliminated, since the latter is no longer a party to the case. Participation of workers' and employers' representatives in the management secures that the law is administered in a fair spirit, and justifies the substitution of the fund itself for the courts as the arbitrator of claims".[1] It may be noted in reference to this quotation from an I.L.O. report, that worker's representation is not specifically provided for in all the provincial acts in Canada.

(2) It provides a measure of guarantee for employees on a matter which is of real significance in their working life. This again is brought on to a collective basis so that, for example, no worker is dependent on the solvency of his particular firm. The premiums are paid by his employer but this special instance of one-party contribution is generally accepted as reasonable.[2] "Once insurance is compulsory and is administered by a state fund, it is seen that the insured person is no longer the employer but the worker, on whose behalf the employer pays the premium. With the disappearance of the direct liability of the employer towards the workers and its replacement by the collective liability of employers, discharged through an insurance institution, workmen's compensation becomes a branch of social insurance".

---

[1] *Approaches to Social Security*, I.L.O. Studies and Reports, M.18, p. 24.

[2] In British Columbia and Alberta a small contribution for medical care is collected from all workers under the schemes.

(3) Substantial economies are effected, from various sources. The procedure of the Workmen's Compensation Board is far less expensive than individual or company litigation, which may in certain cases be protracted. Considerable savings have been realized in administration, and result also from the elimination of advertising and selling costs and of profits. It is fair to add that a good deal of the progress which has been made in factory security education and accident prevention measures has been facilitated through the existence of Workmen's Compensation Boards and their power to evoke the co-operation both of the firms covered and of other public authorities.

Present Coverage and Limitations in Canada

Workmen's Compensation Acts apply today in all provinces of Canada except Prince Edward Island, in which there is little industry, and in this province Dominion government workers by special arrangement are covered on the same basis as workers in New Brunswick. Five provinces passed legislation between 1914 and 1918, but it was not until 1931 that the roster of the industrial provinces was completed. All the Acts now conform closely to the same model, since all are derived from the Ontario Act of 1914 and have been amended along parallel lines.

Co-ordination of procedure throughout the Dominion has been much assisted through the operation of the Association of Workmen's Compensation Boards, a body able to bring together the administrators periodically, under rotated chairmen from the various provinces. This Board has undoubtedly had influence in restricting what might otherwise have been a wide opportunity for anomalous divergences. Standardization has been brought nearest to completion in the rate schedules for permanent partial disability, and such matters as first-aid equipment specifications for factories. Unfortunately, the Association now meets much less frequently than in the earlier years when schemes were first being inaugurated. Considering the expansions of coverage in war industries, the disparities which still exist in respect of some Dominion government liabilities, and the need for improved and co-ordinated statistical analysis—to mention only three topics—it would be very desirable to resume some early meetings, to consider a wartime and post-war agenda.

All the more hazardous and heavy industries are now covered. Special concern (such as the utilities, municipal governments, etc.) who can handle their cases through the Boards have largely taken advantage of this.[1] All appropriate classes of Dominion government are covered, the cases being dealt with usually through the Board in the particular province concerned. This is apt to lead to variation in assessments, and there may be room for more uniformity of practice. But in general the situation is regarded as satisfactory. Workers in war industries, also persons operating under Dominion-provincial training schemes, were included by Order-in-Council under the War Measures Act.

It is not possible, however, to determine the precise coverage of workmen's compensation in Canada in terms of actual workers, so as to compare these with the number who should reasonably be regarded as needing this protection. The statistics of the various Boards are not only defective in this matter, being confined only to payroll quantities, but vary in classification in several provinces. Statistics have been well developed to measure accident incidence

---

[1]For some occupational groups, such as the employees of municipal, police and fire departments, there are special provisions because they may be covered by other arrangements. In other cases the operation of permissive clauses (sometimes revocable by employers or workers, sometimes only by the former) serves to extend coverage desirably; but it is questionable if this expedient should be relied on for more than minority groups and special cases.

and the record of claims, but not of total scope. The roughest of estimates, which is alone possible, suggests that the number insured through Compensation Board funds in 1940 was about 1,500,000; and this number has probably been augmented with the progress of war production. If the coverage of the Unemployment Insurance Act (which excludes several important groups) is taken as a measure of the proper scope, at least 2,500,000 workers should come within the boundaries of this type of protection. The expansion of war industry has, of course, added abnormally not only to the size of the industrial population but to the hazards of industry itself. But it is reasonable to assume that some portion of this expansion will be carried over into the postwar future. Broadly speaking, therefore, it is possible that security measures for industrial injury and disability (more particularly so far as income-maintenance guarantees are concerned), do not yet apply to more than two-thirds of the desirable total.[2] Further statistical analysis would be desirable to check this possibility.

The Canadian schemes correspond substantially well to the terms of International Labour Conventions, which may be taken as expressing the desirable minimum standards accepted by all the principal countries. They fall short mostly on some points of coverage. Stores, restaurants and other commercial establishments are not covered in any provinces except Alberta and New Brunswick. Clerical workers are not always included in industries whose industrial workers are covered; a more important omission, in the light of their closeness to the poverty line, is that of casual and irregular workers in many industries. Perhaps the most serious discrepancies are the exclusion of agricultural workers, and of seamen.[3] Since many of the latter may be

---

[2]A survey instituted by the Building Trades Council in British Columbia indicated that less than half of all construction workers were covered by workmen's compensation. Part of the building industry, of course, is particularly characterized by small units.

[3]Some fishermen (where readily identifiable as employees) are covered in British Columbia.

regarded as outside provincial jurisdiction, Dominion legislation would probably be required to ensure their protection.

Extension to agriculture, though clearly desirable on the grounds of the small wages of agricultural labourers and the heavy effect of serious accident, is admittedly difficult. Workmen's compensation is essentially a special extension of employers' liability, with the cost assessed on industry on the assumption that at least some of the risks are within the employer's control. The continued record of success in the reduction of factory accidents is proof of the validity of this view in many fields. But there is no close comparability between the agricultural and industrial situation. The farmer cannot conduct safety campaigns nor can he employ safety devices and procedures to any measurable extent. A partial answer is that the agricultural worker will be better provided for if *(a)* there are comprehensive health insurance provisions and *(b)* disability pension schemes. On the other hand, workmen's compensation systems have completely accustomed themselves to operation at different levels of risk and premium. It should be possible to set rates which would not be very burdensome for farmers; presumably, as in other occupations, compensation rates would be scaled appropriately to wages, and these are among the lowest of all occupations.

Accident and Disease Liabilities

An estimate which is frequently quoted (from an extensive sample survey made in the United States) is that "non-industrial disability of workers themselves is about fifteen times as large as industrial disability."[1] This presumably includes domestic

---

[1] I. S. Falk, "Mobilizing for Health Security", in *War and Post-War Security;* American Council of Public Affairs, 1942. S. J. Williams, in the Encyclopedia of Social Sciences (quoted in *Labour Legislation,* p. 145), gives an estimate that industrial accidents cause only "one-third of all non-fatal injuries", but this computation evidently rests on a differently defined base. Much depends on whether "disability" includes short periods of sickness, minor accidents, etc. (some of which, under social or private insurance, would not qualify for cash benefit).

accidents within its base; and these from the social viewpoint should be brought within coverage, at least for all cases in which they may seriously affect the family income situation. But it is hard to set any exact ratio for Canada. The total loss of working time specifically attributed to accident was returned in the 1931 Census as 227,500 weeks, distributed over 19,350 wage earners. The total incidence, represented by the number of workers who lost one week, was 58 per 1,000; but this average compares with 384 per 1,000 in mining and related industries, 139 per 1,000 among construction workers and 133 per 1,000 among unskilled workers and labourers, and 129 per 1,000 among forestry workers. Manufacturing industries (unless a proportion of unskilled workers, whose industries are not all specified in census figures, are included) show relatively low rates, of just under 100 per 1,000, taking male wage earners only, and 86 per 1,000 for female workers.

What is of particular interest in interpreting all these statistics is that the average duration of lost time due to accident is relatively high and remarkably constant throughout the various industries, ranging between 10·2 weeks and 15·1 weeks around a national average of 11·8 weeks (male wage earners only). The inference would seem to be that only important accidents were reported to the census enumerators; and since unemployment in the year 1930-31 was heavy there was less opportunity than usual, statistically speaking, to record long periods of lost time. The average duration of lost time, per person affected by an accident, was only fractionally less in the group made up by trade, finance and services (largely uncovered by workmen's compensation) than in the group made up of manufacturing, mining, construction, and electric power plants. In the first-named group, therefore, while the aggregate need for insurance provision is distinctly smaller, the need of the particular individuals suffering accidents may be just as great as for a factory worker. A great many trade and service workers have no guarantee of continued wages if they are absent from work.

The rates of fatal accidents to all accidents of a certain kind (e.g., traffic, domestic, industrial) is fairly constant; but it is markedly different from one kind to another. It is worthy of note that the workmen's compensation statistics (if the 1930's may be taken as representative) record about 150,000 industrial accidents a year, of which about 700 are fatal. The total register of fatal accidents, occurring in all industrial fields, as recorded by the Department of Labour, yields figures of about 1,200 a year during the 1930's. This would appear to indicate that at least one-third of industrial accidents are not yet accounted for under workmen's compensation schemes. In addition it may be noted that the authority quoted in the Sirois Report study, *Labour Legislation*, estimates that industrial accidents cause only one-quarter of the total number of accidental deaths. If this is true it indicates a large area still to be covered before we can be sure that the disruption of the family budget by this particular kind of hazard is provided against. Automobile and traffic accidents are, of course, a special section of this field where efforts have been made to enforce protection. Another part of this area of personal or non-industrial liability is, of course, covered by those who take out private accident insurance policies or who participate in group-medicine schemes; but these usually reimburse immediate expenses only and few provide for maintenance during the period of disability. Moreover, this particular type of private insurance is admittedly expensive.

Industrial disease today is probably the best covered. In Canada, the extension which recommends itself as valuable, and easy to put into effect, applies to the scope of industrial diseases scheduled as proper subjects for inclusion in workmen's compensation. For some medical recognition ought to suffice. Certain forms of cancer of the skin which result from contact with tars and oils are covered only in Ontario, certain mineral oils poisons only in Alberta; pathological conditions due to radioactive substances are covered only in Ontario, Quebec and Saskatchewan. It may at first sight seem unreasonable to suggest that the schedule of industrial diseases recognized should be uniform throughout the country, on the ground that the distribution and types of industry between the provinces is a variable matter. It is in fact true that some special diseases peculiar to the industries located in particular provinces (e.g., frostbite, and nickel poisoning) are included in their legislation, and that these are additional to those prescribed in the I.L.O. Convention standards. The *ad hoc* character of workmen's compensation procedure, however, is one of its disadvantages. It is reasonable to assume that if a particular disease is recognized in one province, it should automatically be included in the provisions of all other areas. There may be only a few cases arising in those provinces which have no particular industry of this form; that is not to say, however, that a worker from the main industrial province may not suffer some inequity because the onset of the disease appears after he has moved elsewhere. The costs arising from the inclusion of the newer diseases in provinces other than the one most concerned would obviously be so few that there should be little objection on the score of added financial liability. At present the provincial lists, while explainable in considerable degree by the industrial character of the particular provinces, would appear to contain some unjustifiable differences. In the list compiled in the Sirois Report appendix, (which showed the 1938 situation), 38 diseases were specified in all. But only 5 were covered in the legislation of all the

provinces; 15 were covered in one province only
and 11 in two provinces each; and the remainder
showed a variety of geographical combinations.
There has been no movement towards unification
since this date.

Benefit Levels

Details as to the amount of compensation granted
in the eight Canadian schemes are listed in Appendices I and II. In a majority of cases the
procedure, which takes around two-thirds of the
previous wages as a standard, is in accord with the
recommendations of I.L.O. Conventions, and is
favourably commented on in most studies of the
subject. In some provinces, however, a maximum is
placed on the figure of annual earnings (e.g. $1,500)
which may be reckoned as the base, a limitation
which is of doubtful validity.

In 1925 the International Labour Conference
recommended that the dependents of all persons who
died as the result of industrial injury should receive
allowances sufficient for their support up to the age
of 18 years. This has not been fully implemented
in all the provinces in Canada, though the principles
are recognized. It is an important question to
consider how far the need for payments to dependents
in compensation cases would be obviated in the event
of the establishment of a system of childrens' allowances; or whether payments in the particular case of a
fatal industrial accident is to be regarded, like the
pension of an ex-service man, as a sum additional to
maintenance, which is specifically compensation.
But levelling up of standards should not, of course,
wait on the introduction of a children's allowance
system.[1]

---

[1] The Sloan Commission appointed to review the workmen's compensation system in British Columbia reported in September 1942 in favour of
increasing allowances for the children of workers killed in industry from
$7.50 to $10 a month, and "in order to provide some incentive for children
between the ages of 16 to 18 years to remain in school", allowances of $12.50
a month during these two years provided the children were at school.
(Cf. p. 90). It also recommended that the maximum annual wage on
which any benefit might be calculated should be increased from $2,000 to
$2,500.

In a few respects or in some provinces, there are some improvements which might be made with regard to the medical side of workmen's compensation provision. A few do not supply medicines and drugs; some do not provide adequately for the repair and renewal of artificial limbs and surgical appliances, but standards of routine medical care are invariably good. It is to be recommended that the Association of Workmen's Compensation Boards be requested to undertake a national review of the type and quality of medical care applied to industrial cases. The experience in this respect would be a particularly valuable aid in the consideration of future extensions in the territory of non-industrial disability; but a careful report on the whole field would also be very timely in view of the fact that health insurance is in contemplation.

Relation of Workmen's Compensation to Social Insurance Plans

Workmen's compensation, or industrial accident insurance, is well established in Canada, and provides for those whom it covers a substantial range of benefits including medical care, and payments in the event of temporary incapacity, permanent disability, and death. It is properly restricted to employed persons as a category, but still restricted to a specified range of industrial accidents and diseases. It must be noted that the social need occasioned by industrial accidents and diseases is actually no different from that arising from non-industrial causes, but better provision is made for meeting it, since the number of cases is relatively small, and the cost, despite the fair level of benefits, is not a substantial burden. That the situation is somewhat anomalous should not be ignored. There is so much other ground that remains to be covered in Canada, however, that reform or absorption of industrial-accident insurance is not the most pressing item on the agenda. It would be more reasonable indeed, as is suggested elsewhere, to seek ways and means by which the experience of Workmen's Compensation Boards is put to fuller use in the future. Two features in its favour at present are its good record in organizing medical services and physical rehabilitation; and the value of merit-rating, so far as it can be practised, as an effective encouragement to industrial safety work.[1]

In general, while there is a presumption in favour of not disturbing a scheme which is long established and giving general satisfaction, much will depend on the proposed level of benefits for non-industrial incapacity and death if these are covered by social insurance extension (under health insurance, disablement pensions, and otherwise). If benefits are about the same as those of compensation, (they are not likely to be higher), the case for the retention of a separate compensation scheme is weakened. Under the proposals which seem most likely to permit a comprehensive and nation-wide scheme for Canada, the pension amounts would probably be smaller than compensation rates, except for the very lowest wage-groups.

In the interests of keeping higher standards in view for the future, it might be argued that the existence of a more generous though somewhat privileged unit outside the regular social insurance structure might not be undesirable. Contributory disability insurance would of course in some degree buttress the existing schemes. There should be a diminution in the doubtful or marginal cases where the accident or disease is alleged to be of industrial origin, but may possibly be of extra-industrial origin. The difference between the levels of compensation and benefit would determine the extent to which

---

[1] It may be noted, however, that the most recent inquiry into workmen's compensation (in British Columbia) reported the need for a much more comprehensive rehabilitation programme, and recommended also that present accident prevention services should be simplified and unified, and related to a provincial bureau of industrial hygiene. The first point is perhaps specially affected by the heavy casualty rate in the logging industries.

there would still be some preference for acceptance through workmen's compensation if it could be secured. In recognition of these factors, the existence of social insurance provision should not be allowed to prejudice the extension of workmen's compensation, to e.g. agriculture or trade, particularly where prevailing wage rates are relatively low.

11. DISABILITY AND INVALIDITY

The present coverage of disability as a factor in social security and loss of income, is fullest in those fields of industry covered by Workmen's Compensation. Apart from this still comparatively limited field there is only a fragmentary recognition in a few pieces of social legislation. Pensions may be secured by blind persons, subject to the limitations examined elsewhere (Section 12) which apply to old age pensions. In a few provinces permanent incapacity which prevents the husband from working is recognized as a situation requiring assistance on a similar basis to that of mothers' allowances; contrasting with these are the substantial and well co-ordinated series of provisions for disabled ex-service men, both with regard to monetary pension, and with regard to medical care, the latter extending along almost every avenue of physical and vocational rehabilitation. This comparison is not intended to be invidious. There is no need to justify the special provisions which should be made for men whose future earning-power is impaired or destroyed as the result of military service. It is proper, however, to recognize that widely varying standards of treatment as between different classes of the population, will appear as anomalies after the war when many men now in uniform will have become ordinary citizens again; they would demand attention also if, after the institution of comprehensive health insurance, medical needs were brought prominently into view without any provision for disablement and the crippling diseases.

What should be the systematic attack on this large field of non-industrial disability, and to what extent should it be covered? The key to understanding the logical place of disability insurance and pensions, and the proper way to proceed to the extension of facilities that will provide for it by collective means, is to make two important distinctions. The first, *(a)* temporary disability and *(b)* permanent or at least long-term incapacity, is fairly familiar. It is a feature of almost all health insurance schemes, though this universality has often resulted in the distinction being taken too much for granted. The second distinction is that between *(a)* medical care and related rehabilitation services, and *(b)* income maintenance, the special significance of which in relation to the construction of social security systems has already been pointed out.

So far as medical care is concerned, everything depends on the existence and scope of health insurance. If health insurance were confined, like unemployment insurance, only to the urban or industrial population, this would mean—apart altogether from the inequity to the rural population— that the coverage of non-industrial disability would still be only partially improved. If the population coverage of health insurance is practically complete, however, this part of the problem does not confront us. The main decision would be whether, medically speaking, a limit should be set beyond which disability treatment rather than ordinary or short-run medical service should be given. Over a fair range, there is a recognizable difference in the type of medical care; as between, for example, treatment for influenza and treatment of fractures or operations. But there are many other matters in which no clear line can be drawn. The probability or even certainty of disability may be evident at once (e.g., in the case of the loss of an eye or a limb); or it may emerge only after a period, prior to which there was a possibility of complete cure.

There is no difficulty on the point of initial treatment, i.e., at the time of the injury or immediately afterwards, if the medical service coverage of the scheme is comprehensive: if, to be specific, hospital care, surgery, nursing, and provision for convalescence are all included. It is in fact in keeping with the strongly-held views of the medical profession that the services contemplated should be as complete and integrated as possible; and there is little doubt that Canadian health insurance, when it is launched, will accept the wisdom of this view.

A question which might be posed by some, however, is whether the privileges of ordinary medical care should cease because a man is declared disabled. If the health insurance were drawn up as if it were a parallel to unemployment insurance, some such principle might be applied. It might be argued that the status of the disabled man in relation to health insurance is somewhat comparable to a status of a man who has been in insurable employment, but who exhausts his right to unemployment benefit after the maximum period to which he is entitled (e.g., 26 weeks). It should need but little examination, however, to perceive that the analogy is a false one. It is still necessary for the unemployed man to find employment. It is equally necessary for the disabled man to receive the privileges of ordinary medical care. It is the unemployed man's right to *cash benefits*, not his need of appropriate treatment, which has expired.

This point may seem too obvious to those with knowledge of health insurance operation. But it is worth stating because of the confusion between cash benefit and medical benefit which superficial acquaintance with established schemes has created. It may seem reasonable to seek some provisions in a health insurance scheme which would protect the fund against too heavy a demand on medical services in the case of the disabled man. There should be careful consideration, however, of the impact of any such provisions. Limitations might serve to impede adjustment, at least psychologically. Moreover, if the right to receive ordinary short-term medical care were unduly restricted, there would be a strong incentive to secure it in some other way as part of the service required for the specific disability. Such a tendency would seriously detract from what is a most desirable situation, namely, the evolution and improvement of services specialized for the constructive treatment of disability as such.

It is important to note that the attack on the complex field of disability is greatly helped to the extent that free treatment is extended for sufferers from disabling diseases, which is already given some attention through public health and related facilities. If we could be sure that all cases of tuberculosis, venereal diseases, mental patients, etc., could be cared for in appropriate institutions, and that our facilities for better recognition of these diseases at early stages were as complete as we could make them, we should at the same time be reducing very considerably the residual categories of disability patients; and also at the same time reducing the portion of costs which has to be covered by contributors through the social insurance mechanism. It is hardly possible to overemphasize these fundamentals, of adequate health and treatment institutions.

(a) Sickness Cash Benefits for Temporary Invalidity

The second aspect of disability is that of the loss of earning power. It has already been stressed that full social security is not provided by securing medical care alone. From the point of view of the family budget, more especially if the sick person is the chief earner, temporary disability or sickness may be completely equivalent to unemployment.

There is little question that by far the greater proportion of illnesses are of comparatively short duration. Even for industrial accidents and their consequences, it is the experience of Workmen's Compensation claims that only about 10 per cent last more than thirteen weeks. The problem of sickness, therefore—from this particular viewpoint of family income—is much the same as that of unemployment; namely, that a great proportion of the spells of unemployment are comparatively short. Experience in social insurance administration has increasingly supported the suggestion that sickness or disability benefit should be assimilated as closely as possible to unemployment benefit. Putting the situation from the viewpoint of the worker concerned, (a) he should be able to draw unemployment benefit if he is unemployed, in the sense of being able and willing to work, but not at work because he has no job; but (b) he should be able to draw sickness benefit of equal amount if he is away from his work through illness, and his job is of the type which does not provide him wages when on sick leave.

This proposal may seem to raise formidable administrative difficulties. The need of the worker —in the income sense—it is true, is the same in both cases. But the function of the Employment Service Office is specialized to certifying that a man is available for work, not of certifying the contrary, that he is *not* available for work. There is no real difficulty, however, in establishing the fact of temporary illness, or of the undesirability of the man's being at work (e.g., in the case of his having a mild but none the less infectious disease). If it is certified by a doctor, properly authorized to do so, the Employment Service office has no further obligations to perform, provided that a system of health insurance exists. In other words, this part of the procedure becomes almost automatic.[1]

---

[1] What must be added, is that the experience of placement and of the labour market generally should be brought to bear on the situation of the temporarily disabled man if the cause of his disablement becomes prolonged. It is particularly important in the case of the man whose illness or injury may threaten to develop into permanent partial disability. If contact is established at an early stage, there is much more likelihood of some kind of partial employment being sought in advance for the future, to say nothing of the advantage of the psychological preparation of the worker whose full earning capacity has been impaired. This however would not be a sickness-benefit situation.

There is a strong case, therefore, for a system of sickness cash benefits being organized as soon as possible in relation to a health insurance scheme. The latter may well be confined only to medical services; and there is no particular reason why a contributory system for sickness cash benefits might not be devised separately. There is equally no particular reason why such a system should be provincial in operation, and there are good reasons for its being federal, so as to be effectively co-ordinated with unemployment insurance and the work of the national Employment Service. Certification of sickness, however, should proceed desirably from the health insurance system. The administration of the benefit could be handled through unemployment insurance mechanism, or more strictly, the Employment Service offices, provided suitable arrangements are made for extra staff, so as not to overload them beyond their existing resources. Some administrative details would have to be settled, dealing with the collection of contributions, and their transfer to whichever fund is appropriate (to which the discussion in Section 14 is relevant). And there should probably be provision for the checking of infirmity certification, which under the proposals suggested here, would be by federally-appointed medical officers.

Assuming the equivalence of scope between sickness and unemployment benefits recommended, there are very desirable relationships between the health and unemployment administrations which should be noted. Unemployment insurance benefits, if no cash benefits for sickness are existent, are likely to be sought by sick persons if there is any possibility of gaining them—a considerable one particularly for categories in the remoter areas who are obliged to register only once a fortnight, for example. If they are really sick, yet making such appearances at employment offices as are necessary, this may be detrimental to quick recovery. From the point of view of securing the best utilization of the national manpower it is better that the security of the cash benefit should serve both to ease their minds and keep them home for rest or treatment. On the other hand, the payment of sickness cash benefits in the absence of a health insurance scheme which is able to validate the applicant's claim that he is sick would open the way for serious difficulties and abuses. If any warning is needed, the unsatisfactory experience of Ireland, in which this system obtains, offers convincing evidence of its handicaps.

Maternity Benefit

For gainfully employed women the proper counterpart for sickness cash benefit is maternity benefit. Most customarily it is made payable six weeks before and six weeks after the birth of the child, absence from work being the condition of payment. Applied in conformity with other scales proposed, it would presumably be payable at a rate approximately half the wage level of the normal earnings of the recipient. It might be worth consideration, whether the rate for cash maternity benefit should be somewhat higher than this as a special case. Maternity benefit as a complement to health insurance and cash sickness benefit is almost universal practice in all countries with social insurance legislation.

One limitation on the scope of cash benefits for sickness, if it is not already obvious, must be made clear. Cash benefits are not appropriate for non-wage-earner groups, i.e. for the self-employed and most rural and agricultural classes. There is no real equivalent, in the case of the farmer, the farmer's son (as distinct from the paid farm labourer), or the store proprietor, to the loss of wages which is suffered by most employees (at least after a certain minimum period) if they are not able to go to their workplace. Sickness benefits should therefore be confined to the main industrial groups. Their most desirable coverage is the same as that set as proper for unemployment insurance (assuming that this is itself comprehensive for the employable population).

It is obvious also that some allowance has to be made, firstly, for very temporary periods of indisposition that would not justify payment of sickness benefit; and, secondly, the fact that many industries and occupations provide for limited periods of sick leave with pay. The device for this purpose incorporated in all sickness benefit insurance is the "waiting period". The I.L.O. conventions for sickness benefit set this at three days. In setting the period much would depend on the rate at which sickness benefit is payable. If it is very high in relation to the normal wage, there is more justification for a long waiting period; and *vice versa*. Sickness benefit in Canada, on the assumption that it were assimilated to present unemployment insurance, would be approximately only half the normal wage, and a relatively short waiting period would, therefore, be in order. Another aspect of the matter, however, is the general priority of attack. If it is sought to meet the more serious problems of sickness and disability first, and this is the understanding on which steps are taken to get the scheme started as soon as possible, a long waiting period, perhaps of two or three weeks, might be justifiable. On the other hand, it must be noted that the full benefit of a health insurance scheme (i.e., the resort to medical care, including readiness to take the doctor's advice) will not be secured by wage-earners who are unable to be absent from work without losing pay. Health insurance would provide for the sick man, but would do nothing for his family's maintenance.

Substantially reliable statistics are now available of the pattern of duration of most disability covered

by sickness benefit insurance.[1] It is an important
fact that by far the greater proportion (well over
90 per cent) of the illnesses known to the records of
health insurance are terminated within less than
26 weeks.[2] If the extension of benefit beyond
this period is left to the discretion of the doctor,
therefore, there is a very desirable possibility of
certain patients being brought to cure or recovery,
returning thereafter to ordinary employment. The
other alternative would be, in the event of a rigid
limit being applied, that the patient had no means of
support and might have to cease treatment at a
point when continuance would promise more than
proportionate benefit. The better course would be
to allow certification by a doctor at or near the
26th week. If the patient were declared to have
possibility of full recovery within a reasonable period
(say, another 13 or 26 weeks) benefit could be
continued; or alternatively, a temporary disability
pension at a standard rate could be made payable.
The desirability of this type of procedure in cases
such as those of tuberculosis is very clear. (In
the first instance, the provision might possibly be
qualified by limiting it to certain specific diseases or
disabilities, of which tuberculosis is probably the
most outstanding). The effect of this provision
would be to increase the cost of the scheme dis-
proportionately for a small percentage of cases,
though not greatly in terms of averaged per capita
costs. It would on the other hand reduce to some
extent the amount liable to be paid for permanent
disability or even survivors' pensions.

To sum up, sickness cash benefit (or temporary
disability benefit), and its special complement for

---

[1] *The Evaluation of Permanent Incapacity for Work in Social Insurance*,
I.L.O. Studies, Series M. No. 14. The experience of sickness insurance in
Germany during 1928-1937 may be worth quoting: on the average, 43
persons out of every 100 insured fell sick every year, for a typical period of
24 days.
[2] *Ibid*, p. 187.

working women, are not only the logical supplements of unemployment insurance, but necessary for the long-run efficiency of unemployment insurance administration. There can be little doubt that the scheme would fit well into the conditions of those employments which permit regular or statutory sick leave. Adjustments would be called for in those industries which already provide cash benefits as well as medical care for some or all of their employees.[3] But, as in the parallel case of nationally-organized retirement pensions, the direction of the adjustment would probably be towards a supplementary arrangement rather than substitution. Firms wishing to establish or maintain sickness privileges could do so at higher than bare minimum standards, and would still have much to gain from this as from other enlightened personnel practices.

It must be pointed out, finally, that the constitutional position on this matter is by no means clear. It might seem on the one hand that, since sickness benefit is so similar to unemployment benefit in certain respects, that it might be covered in the amendment to the British North America Act made in 1940. On the other hand, it might be regarded

---

[3] A considerable number of industrial firms maintain arrangements for medical care for their employees through (a) insurance for hospital, surgical and related expenses, (b) mutual benefit plans, financed entirely by the employees, or (c) the provision of actual service, e.g. a hospital, with equipment and staff, which is often necessary in an isolated community. Fewer make provisions for some income for (wage-paid) employees in lieu of earnings, other than limited sick leave. Typically, arrangements are made (a) through private insurance, (b) mutual benefit funds, and (c) disability wages provided by the industry.

Cash benefits are usually not more than half normal earnings, but disability wages are apt to be a full equivalent of earnings. The latter are not usually available unless the employee has been with the firm for at least one year. Most frequently medical aid and sick benefits are provided for a maximum period of three months, and the waiting period is typically one week. Benefits in schemes financed entirely by employers are sometimes extended to a six months' limit, and one or two companies continue to pay part-earnings for a maximum of two years.

Salaried employees are usually treated, in regard to sickness provisions, as a separate category and on considerably better terms, though often without any predetermined arrangement. The continuance of salary to the employee is usually a matter of the employer's discretion, depending on service, type of illness, his past and potential value to the company, and his prospects of return.

as on all fours with health insurance, in which case
the method of implementation would be of primary
importance, and subject to resolution of the same
constitutional issues as are emphasized in Sections
14 and 22.

(b) Permanent Partial Disablement: Disability Pensions

It remains to clarify another aspect of provision
for disability. Workmen's compensation schemes
have made familiar the distinctions between partial
disability and total disability, and have developed
standard assessments for various categories of
disablement or impairment of employment-capacity.
The administration of pensions for ex-service men
has, with some justification, worked out and maintained in operation even smaller refinements.
Should this type of classification be carried over into
contributory insurance when this is applied to
disability? It must be remembered that the application contemplated in this instance is to be not
primarily for industrial accident and impairment,
but for a much wider range of non-industrial types
of incapacity. Furthermore, disability pensions,
the appropriate provision for this risk, are a long-
term commitment; and also a benefit which should
be available for all gainfully occupied persons and
not wage-earners alone. Finally, as argued below,
the decision as to permanent disability (which is
one form of unemployability) must be absolute—
though not necessarily irrevocable—if it is to be
administratively workable, more particularly for
pension recipients who were formerly wage-earners.
All of this calls for a much simpler pension assessment than special or limited schemes permit.

So far as the service branch of provision, i.e.,
medical care, is concerned, there may be some
special problems, though they are not problems
which should be beyond the capacity of health

insurance and related public health facilities (e.g., in the case of tuberculosis) to handle. Whether an individual is to be regarded as totally or partially disabled should not raise any major question with regard to his right to receive ordinary medical care: the chief matter for decision is this respect is the appropriateness of such routine future care or special rehabilitation measures as are best adapted to his case. His ordinary medical care rights should be retained whether he is receiving cash benefits or a pension. But the difficulties of determination or certification would be much greater in some cases than in others.

The status of the man whose degree of disablement is in doubt is of most consequence if he is normally a wage-earner and eligible for unemployment benefit (or unemployment assistance). If he is in the category which, under workmen's compensation principles for example, would be recognized as partially disabled, should this be allowed to affect the test applied to him by the administrative agency, namely, the employment exchange? If he can work *at all*, i.e., in an employment not requiring altogether special working conditions, he satisfies the test of being "available for employment": the principal function of the employment office is then to find him a job. Since he has suffered at least some impairment, there is a likelihood that he will be in one of the lower wage classes of the unemployment insurance scheme. This being so he will be under no special disposition to remain unemployed on the calculation that his unemployment benefit will be more adequate than any wage he could earn. It seems clear that such an individual should be certified, *for unemployment insurance purposes*, as employable—not as "partially employable". He will retain his rights to unemployment benefit but will not be admitted to eligibility for a pension.

The justice of this situation as compared with

workmen's compensation is that the responsibilities
are different, though there may be a few marginal
cases. The industrial benefit is compensation, a
species of damages for harm suffered at the hands of
industry. The debtor to the non-industrial invalid
is the community of other insured persons: they
expect the invalid to do his best to get along without
a pension, and conserve the funds. In terms of the
detail of physical handicaps, the differences can also
be illustrated. Industrial permanent disability consists typically of obvious mutilations, the effect of
which on earning-capacity can be assessed according
to tables which are reasonably systematic. But
non-industrial permanent disability consists typically of internal disease—of the heart, lungs, etc.—
for which no objective methods of assessing the
degree of reduction of earning-capacity have been
devised. It is possible in such a case to offer the
man a job: if he can hold it down, he cannot be
regarded as totally disabled though, if he is earning
less than before, he is undoubtedly partially disabled
in this sense. The general practice in non-industrial
permanent disability insurance, accordingly, is to
consider a person totally disabled if his earning-
capacity in any occupation reasonably open to him
is considered to have been reduced by at least two-
thirds; such a person, as long as his physical condition does not improve, is allowed to earn whatever
he can, but he is excluded from unemployment
insurance. Once the degree of disablement is
established as really serious, there is in fact little
that can be gained in the long run by allowing a man
to be classified as employable. It is far better that
he should become adjusted, psychologically and
occupationally, to the situation. Given comprehensive social insurance, it is reasonable to make the
receipt of a permanent disability pension the *quid
pro quo* for the waiving of rights to unemployment
insurance benefit.

The proper implication is that in the consideration of all such cases, every man should be given the fullest benefit of the doubt. If he has any reasonable hope of being self-supporting in some degree, he should be classed as employable. Every endeavour should be made through employment office machinery to develop special canvassing and placement procedures for these cases—much as employment offices are already charged to do, with the co-operation of special Veterans Welfare Officers, for ex-service men. Everything possible should be done also to give this kind of man access to physical and vocational rehabilitation facilities, orthopaedic training, etc.; reiterating on this point that rehabilitation is a task which particularly demands collaboration between the health insurance and unemployment insurance administrations.

In general, it is clear that disability pensions require assimilation to (contributory) old age pensions, in the same way as sickness cash benefits should be related to unemployment insurance administration. They must be available to the gainfully occupied persons besides wage-earners; and are thus presumably, under present Canadian conditions and trends, for a collection-basis as well as certification and payment, dependent on a successful scheme for health insurance being worked out.

12. EXISTING OLD AGE PENSIONS
AND RETIREMENT PROVISIONS

In all or nearly all the problems of security discussed thus far which involve provision for maintenance of income for the chief earner and his family, one common characteristic prevails. It is assumed that the breadwinner will sooner or later be able to return to remunerative employment. Only in the case of permanent disability is it necessary to accept the fact that the earner has reached the end of his employment trail. The problems of security during old age and retirement for other reasons are therefore more closely allied with the problems of providing for permanent disability than they are with the plans for short-term security during unemployment, ill-health, accident, etc. The universality of old age automatically means that the nature of the problem concerns all peoples in all lands. This is true of Canada, as is evidenced by the fact that only in the case of old age pensions is there a full acknowledgment of social responsibility by all nine provincial governments and the federal government as well. The nature of the problem, however, is sometimes not so thoroughly considered. There is nothing in old age, of and by itself, which requires that social security provision be made for it. If, for example, medical science were able to discover some secret by which the active work-span of men and women could be prolonged to one hundred years of age, no one would think of suggesting old age pensions at seventy. It is only because increasing age associates with itself the increasing incapability to perform useful work that we have to consider the problem at all. This point of view, which makes of old age a disability, permanent and increasing to the extent that the prospects of eventually returning to employment are practically nil, reinforces the point made earlier that the nature of provision for old age and for permanent disability should be similar, if not identical. Old age is, in short, a specialized aspect of permanent total disability so far as the employment market, the wage structure, or the ability to earn and maintain a level of income, are concerned.

Having thus pointed to some of the characteristics of the problem of old age and retirement, its importance should next be considered in terms of size. The age at which it is assumed that the ability to carry out useful employment begins to diminish is usually set somewhere between sixty-five and seventy for men, and somewhere between sixty and sixty-five for women. Whether or not there is any scientific basis for this, it is certainly true that nearly all provision of old age assistance or insurance centres around these ages whether it is non-contributory state assistance, contributory state insurance, or private and voluntary provision. The facts with regard to Canada are that in 1941 there were 460,000 persons aged seventy years or over in the country, and 767,000 persons of sixty-five and over. The following table shows how the population of these ages has varied in Canada from one census year to another. One-time immigrant groups, a youthful element prominent in the population in the first instance, are now growing older. Moreover, it is a well-established fact that with medical science, public hygiene, maternal welfare and other related developments prolonging the life span, the numbers of aged persons who have passed beyond the years of useful employment in Canada will increase decade by decade, as they are in fact doing almost universally elsewhere. The number aged 65 or over to-day comprise 65 of every thousand of the population: by 1971 it is estimated that the proportion will be 94 per thousand.

When with this is coupled the fact that the birth rate in Canada is declining steadily, it will not be

TABLE 7.—POPULATION OF BOTH SEXES AGED 70 AND
OVER IN CANADA

(Census years 1901-41 and estimates for 1951-71)

Year	Number	Year	Number
1901.............	163,715	1941...........	459,582
1911.............	202,614	1951...........	620,000
1921.............	247,094	1961...........	822,000
1931.............	344,697	1971...........	920,000

Sources: Census 1931, Vol. III, pp. 17, 31; data for 1941
supplied by courtesy of the Dominion Bureau of Statistics; and
A. E. Grauer, *Social Insurance and Public Assistance.*

difficult to see that the problem of provision for
old age will become one of increasing importance
in future years. This is shown graphically in the
following table, which shows that in the next thirty
years the population aged seventy years or over,
and the expenditures on non-contributory old age
pensions in Canada, even assuming that no changes
whatsoever are made in the present Old Age Pension
Act, will almost double.

TABLE 8.—ESTIMATE OF COST TO PROVINCES AND
DOMINION OF OLD AGE PENSIONS IN 1941, 1951,
1961 AND 1971

Year	Population		Estimated Cost of Pensions
	20-69 years	70 years and over	
			$
1941............	6,879,000	463,000	46,300,000
1951............	7,799,000	620,000	62,000,000
1961............	8,410,000	822,000	82,200,000
1971............	9,222,000	928,000	92,800,000

Source: Department of Finance Report on the Administration
of Old Age Pensions in Canada, 1938.

The indications are that if the birth rate continues to decline and our working-population deficiency is not supplemented by immigration, the result will be fewer and fewer people of working age being obliged to carry, in one way or another, the burden of support for more and more persons who have passed the span of useful employment. The problem is not therefore one that can be disregarded or tossed lightly aside. Even if we do nothing at all, the fact will still face us that thirty years from now our old age pension bill will be approximately twice what it is to-day. Sir William Beveridge's statement that "the problem of the nature and extent of the provision to be made for old age is the most important and in some ways the most difficult of all the problems of social security", applies with equal force to Canada. On the other hand, one should not be too pessimistic. If Canada, with children's allowances and other social services, is made a more desirable place for children to live in, the fall in the birth-rate may be checked. In any case, the population in most countries shows a fairly constant proportion of persons in the dependent ages, i.e. children and aged combined.

Canadians have not, of course, ignored the problem of permanent retirement from work occasioned by age, as is evidenced by the fact that every province in Canada has an Old Age Pensions Act conforming to the Dominion legislation passed in 1927, and providing pensions under certain conditions on a non-contributory basis to persons seventy years of age and over. Nor is this in fact all the provision that has been made in Canada for the contingencies of disability due to age. One special feature of the Old Age Pensions Act, in fact, recognizes the principle that some persons should be considered as eligible for permanent retirement through disability at an earlier age than others. The amendments made with respect to blind persons, for example, say in effect that a person under this disability is prematurely aged and eligible for retirement from the labour market as having no prospect of further employment when he is forty years of age. Likewise, the principle adopted in the federal War Veterans' Allowance legislation recognizes the fact that one class of persons—namely, veterans—may be considered as prematurely aged at sixty, fifty-five, or even lower, and therefore as eligible for maintenance of income when they retire from the employment market. The need for further consideration of the flexibility here indicated will be referred to again in the succeeding Section.

Present Provisions in Canada

Various provisions are made in Canada under public or private auspices for the maintenance of income in the case of aged people retiring from the labour market, other than the provisions already referred to. Alternative provisions fall into four main categories:—

    (a) Governmental or semi-governmental superannuation schemes such as federal, provincial and municipal employee plans (including firemen, policemen, school teachers, on the municipal level);

    (b) Industrial retirement schemes;

    (c) Government annuities;

    (d) Private commercial annuity or pension insurance.

It is difficult to make any reliable estimate of the total number of aged persons over a given age (whether sixty or sixty-five or seventy) covered in these different ways. So far as superannuation and retirement schemes sponsored by private industry are concerned, their contribution to the coverage of the total population which might reasonably be regarded as in need of them is much smaller than is often assumed, according to the facts assembled in the only quantitative surveys which have so far been made. The most relevant parts of this information (from *Industrial Retirement Plans in Canada*, published by the Industrial Relations Section of Queens University in 1938, which also summarizes the data secured by the National Employment Commission in 1937), have been reproduced in Appendix V. The first-mentioned report concludes that "at least 70 per cent of the wage and salary earners of Canada would seem to be working in establishments which make no definite formal provision for the retirement of their employees . . . . Moreover, the adequacy of the actual provisions varies greatly under the different plans". The covered 30 per cent is sizeable in itself, but the individuals concerned who have good superannuations to look forward to are comparatively privileged members of the working-force.

This does not mean that further development by Canadian industries of provisions for the retirement of their own employees is not desirable. On the contrary, it may be particularly helpful at certain stages of the post-war labour market. It may be useful, accordingly, to refer to the conclusions reached, in the survey already referred to, on the merits and defects of present schemes, and on the principles which should guide the formulation or reformulation of new ones. These are also reproduced in the Appendix.

So far as state pensions are concerned, it is known that old age grants in force today under the Old Age Pensions Act represent about forty to forty-five per cent of the total population of Canada aged seventy and over. To this there would have to be added the figures for war veterans' allowance cases aged seventy and over, for persons covered by government superannuation schemes and annuities, and the

annual number who actually take advantage of
industrial and commercial retirement provisions
(which is not known with any exactitude). A small
number of additional cases might be picked up
through a variety of other channels such as workmen's compensation, or even, in a few scattered
cases, mothers' allowances. All in all, however, it is
doubtful whether these provisions would cover much
more than fifty-five per cent of the population of
Canada over seventy years of age. If the lower age
levels of sixty-five and sixty were taken it would
certainly show an even smaller percentage of Canadians with any form of secured income to look
forward to, other than perhaps small sums in savings,
in the event of their having to retire permanently
from employment.

The question may well be asked: What is the
position with reference to those persons who have
reached the age of retirement from employment
and who have not at their disposal, in the event of
need, any of the above-mentioned resources for a
secure income? Can it be assumed that a third to a
half of our aged population have the means to support themselves in comfort from accumulated
income set aside during working years in one form or
another? Alternatively, can it or should it be
assumed that all those people are adequately provided for through the fact that they have relatives
in a position to look after them? That this is true of
a certain percentage of aged people cannot of course
be denied. But any one who has had even brief
experience in the administration of old age pensions
will be quick to point out that there is ample evidence
that a large percentage of aged people in need of
assistance to maintain them on a minimum level of
subsistence apply for pensions but are refused,
because of relatively narrow interpretations of the
law, the regulations, or the administration of eligibility requirements. These people who are thus

refused old age assistance in Canada at the present
time do not, of course, literally starve. Some of
them—many of them in fact—find their way to the
doors of public welfare agencies. Other "get by" on
what little they have. Still others find themselves
an uneasy welcome in the households of relatives or
friends who may themselves be struggling to maintain a dubious living standard. Others again find
their way into hospitals, homes for the aged, refuges,
hostels of various kinds, and even, in increasing
numbers, into mental hospitals. The bulk of
evidence clearly indicates that aged people who do
not come under coverage of any of the schemes
mentioned above face the prospect of retirement
from employment, in the great majority of cases,
with no security whatsoever—rather the certainty of
insecurity.

In Britain just before the war, two-thirds of all
people over sixty-five, and about four-fifths of all
people over seventy, were in receipt either of state
pensions or public assistance in some other form. In
Canada it is unlikely that much more than fifty to
sixty-five per cent of all persons over seventy are
similarly dependent upon the public treasury. While
it would be tempting to assume that this is an indication of the greater comfort of the aged in Canada,
and their greater ability to provide for themselves
with savings or through their families, independent
of the state, such an assumption is hardly sufficient
to reconcile the entire difference. When one turns
to examination of the old age pensions administration
in Canadian provinces, one finds a major portion
of the answer to this discrepancy between British
figures and our own; an answer which is a good
deal more realistic and less to the credit of the
Canadian people as a whole. Examination, for
example, would reveal written into the Act itself, and
especially into the regulations—but most of all

practised in the administration—a rigid system of eligibility requirements set on a very low level, which makes it difficult for many aged persons, genuinely in need of some form of assistance on a permanent continuing basis, to qualify for allowances. These provisions include:

1. Citizenship;

2. Residence restrictions, both Dominion and provincial;

3. Means testing in terms of the applicant's personal income, personal property qualifications, and even the assumption of income from property where in fact such income does not exist;

4. The principle, zealously adhered to in certain provinces, of the responsibility of the children, to the point of assuming that income is actually forthcoming from children for the support of the applicant, even in cases where it is not;

5. Scaling-down of allowances below the amount permitted by the statute, on the grounds that the pensioner does not require even that amount of pension which is found to be the arithmetical maximum payable after the exhaustion of all statutory, regulatory and administrative means-test procedures.

The result of the application of these restrictive procedures is, first of all, a relatively high percentage of rejected applicants; and second, in some provinces especially, a relatively low average pension even compared to the maximum that the Act calls for. The *Canada Year Book* shows the average pensions payable in the different provinces of Canada during 1941, as follows:

Prince Edward Island..................... $11.25
Nova Scotia............................ 15.04
New Brunswick......................... 14.81
Quebec................................ 16.04
Ontario............................... 18.62
Manitoba.............................. 18.70
Saskatchewan.......................... 17.08
Alberta............................... 18.62
British Columbia...................... 18.97

The administrative agencies chosen for old age pensions have also, for the most part, tended to reinforce a legalistic type of approach based on calculations from the maximum down, rather than the social administration approach which would endeavour, so far as the restrictions of the Act itself permit, to relate the income payable to the living needs of the applicant. Illustrations of this point are to be found in the fact that in two of the provinces most outstanding otherwise for their relatively enlightened social approach to the problems of security—namely, Manitoba and British Columbia—the administration of old age pensions is turned over to the relatively mechanical administration of the Workmen's Compensation Board instead of to the government department concerned with other phases of social welfare administration.[1] The tendency in workmen's compensation administration is to *assess* eligibility on relatively hard and fast lines and then to apply the eligibility schedule strictly. Scaled to different earnings levels and to a variety of accident cases, this is less apt to produce harsh results. Scaled to what is supposed to be a minimum and to a need which is relatively equal for all cases, it can only produce inequities. Unfortunately, federal supervision reinforces these tendencies, through the fact that the old age pensions

---

[1] In British Columbia provision was made, by an amendment passed in 1942, for the transfer of the administration of old age pensions from the Workmen's Compensation Board to the Department of the Provincial Secretary which administers the social services. At the time of writing, it is understood that this transfer (which required the approval of the federal authorities) is now in process of being made.

authority on the federal level is located in the
Department of Finance. The supervision of provincial administrations consists almost exclusively
of audit and financial control, the result being a
restrictive influence on provincial administrations
which is easily reflected in a repressive attitude
towards the applicant.

Possible Improvements

In no province can it be said that the old age
pension administration carries out an adequate
social treatment of the problem of assistance and
service to the aged person. This raises the question
as to the possibility of improving the present system
of non-contributory old age pensions by removing
the restrictions on eligibility, and carrying out
certain other improvements which would make it
possible to deal adequately with the problem of
retirement under the present arrangements. Is it
possible to reform the present old age pension
machinery to the point where it will meet this
responsibility in a socially satisfactory manner?

First of all, much could be done in the way of
improvement to make the present assistance programme for the aged more acceptable and more
socially constructive. Many of the unjustifiable
restrictions as to eligibility could be removed. It
is seriously to be questioned, for example, whether
insistence on the responsibility of children for their
parents is socially sound, and it is certain that,
socially sound or not, insistence is impracticable.
Britain has found this to be the case, and as a result
has abolished the household means test, which is
comparable to the principle of the Parents' Maintenance Acts and similar legislation found in the
Canadian provinces. There is no reason why the
old age pensions' authority, in considering the means
of an applicant for pension, should *assume* income
and support from children of the applicant when such

income does not actually exist. No objection can be taken to a social approach to the children which will limit itself to encouragement and persuasion of parental support; but it is utterly unfair to penalize, by refusal or reduction of pension, the aged applicant merely because a son or daughter, now beyond his control, is unwilling to offer support. Equally it is unsound to assume income from property of the pension applicant when such income is non existent. The present Act provides that a calculation shall be made on the assumption that a pension applicant's equity in property is producing for him five per cent interest per annum.   As long as this income, together with any other income the applicant possesses, is not greater than $125 per annum, the pension is reduced by the amount by which the applicant's income—real or assumed—exceeds $125.

Again, the insistence that a pensioner must be able to prove in extreme detail his continuous residence for twenty years in Canada immediately prior to application, and likewise continuous residence in the province of application for five years immediately prior to application, represents an unreasonable complication which has only the effect of making it necessary to refuse assistance with one hand and give it, in some instances, on a poor relief basis with the other. The basis for such a residence principle is presumably the assumption that a man, by virtue of the fact that he has spent a considerable portion of his life in the country, has contributed to the development of the country, and therefore deserves in old age some special form of security not accorded to every individual. If this is the case, it does not seem to make a great deal of difference whether the applicant has lived the last twenty years of his life in Canada continuously, or e.g., for two separate ten-year periods, as long as he spends the required amount of time during his constructive working span. Similarly the provision regarding provincial residence is a restriction at the expense of the individual applicant, regardless of his merit, for the sake of a particular governmental authority. It is assumed to prevent the movement of aged people to certain parts of the country, thus avoiding the creation of a disproportionate burden in particular areas. It may be doubted whether this endeavour to restrict the mobility of the aged is in any degree effective; and even if it is effective, it is to be doubted whether it is socially sound.

Even the provision regarding citizenship may be called into question. There are plentiful illustrations from depression years, of persons of alien citizenship being maintained on relief rolls until they reached seventy years of age, when it became the business of the local relief authority to help the applicant to take out his citizenship papers; not for the purpose of showing his pride in Canadian residence, but for the purpose of commercializing his citizenship to the extent of raising his pittance from relief rates to old age pension. This surely places a low value on Canadian citizenship. The citizenship provision, moreover, loses all point if it does not restrict effectively. It becomes merely an annoyance, and on these grounds should be removed from the Act.

Incomes Provided

These minor repairs to present legislation, if made, would not remove the entire range of difficulty. The fact is that, as shown by the average pension paid in many of the provinces, the supplementary income which the pensioner may have, or is assumed to have, is very small indeed. In spite of the restrictions, the average pension paid is still close to the maximum in many of the provinces. This raises the question of the adequacy of the present allowances for those persons who are completely without supplementary resources. Three provinces, British Columbia, Alberta and Ontario, have already recognized the inadequacy of the present pension as a minimum for decent living on a permanently retired basis. The first two provinces have done so by an addition of $5.00 monthly from provincial funds to the pension allowance—technically as a cost-of-living bonus. The province of Ontario has given similar recognition to the inadequacy of the allowances by provision of supplementary medical services to persons on old age pension. Further improvements are promised in statements made at the opening of the legislative sessions this year, in Ontario and in Manitoba.

It is true, of course, that the Old Age Pensions Act is theoretically more generous than it appears from the simple statement that the maximum pension payable is $20, in that it allows the pensioner to supplement his maximum pension by as much as $125 per annum, making a theoretical maximum of $365 annually, or $1 a day, without deduction from the pension. This provision, however, is misplaced if it discriminates in favour of persons with supplementary income, while, at the same time, it provides less than a basic minimum for those who are reliant solely on the pension itself. It would be much more adequate as a scheme of social assistance if a higher maximum pension were possible, and less generous provision made for supplementary income and resources. A maximum $30 monthly pension, with means-testing and income-deduction more rigidly applied than at present, would be fairer to the completely destitute and dependent than the present scale of assistance.

Reconsideration of Age Limits

One other item is deserving of special consideration as a possible means of improving the coverage and adequacy of non-contributory old age assistance. This is the question of the age limit. What age should be set as the age of eligibility for old age assistance? At the present time Canada has an age limit of seventy. Is it meeting the retirement problem to leave this age limit where it is; or should it be reduced to sixty-five, or even to sixty? In this respect, as in others already enumerated with regard to old age pensions, Canada has leaned to the side of caution, at the expense of the person prematurely aged whose working years are over before seventy, and whose security is not provided for. No country with a non-contributory system of old age pensions has a higher age level than Canada, although several ¹ave the same. Some of the non-contributory systems, such as in Australia and South Africa, provide for non-contributory pensions at sixty-five for men and sixty for women; while nearly all of the twenty-six or more countries having compulsory contributory systems set the age level at sixty-five for men and sixty for women, and in some cases, lower. Review of the forty or more systems of old age assistance—contributory and non-contributory— effective in the world today clearly shows that the generally accepted view as to the proper age when consideration should be given to retirement from work and provision of security is sixty-five for men and sixty for women.

Before this trend is accepted, however, it is important to consider certain reflections which full-employment experience now occasions. The shift to a younger age for retirement was highlighted particularly in the depression period, and gained wide acceptance as a consequence of the fact that there were not enough jobs to go around. Hence the solution was thought to lie in terms of siphoning off the relatively aged population who had completed a fairly large stint of employment during their lifetime, thus making way for the younger generation who, under depression conditions, were being frustrated in their search for employment. It was perfectly natural that such a defeatist point of view should develop during the depression years, when there appeared not to be enough employment for all, so that therefore the older workers should be pushed on to maintenance and retirement, while the younger workers took up the responsibilities of gainful occupation, and along with it, support of the aged in one form or another.

The Beveridge Report sounds a salutary note of warning against the wisdom of attempting to pension off too hastily, men and women who are of mature years but not by any means, in all cases, at the end of their productive powers. It is true of Canada, as it is of Britain and Australia, among other countries, that with declining birth rates and increasingly aged populations, we should use all the working forces we can muster to carry the burden of maintaining the economy of the country on a high level. Security maintenance is essential only for those who have genuinely exhausted, through age or other reasons, their employment possibilities. To the extent that workers are retired at sixty or sixty-five when they still have useful working years ahead of them, the country is being wasteful of its resources. Lacking any compensation in increased technical productivity, this might have to be reflected in lower benefits for those genuinely retired, along with heavier burdens for the younger working generation.

The conclusion to be derived is that, while it may be necessary to fix a definite age level as a standard for retirement, either in a non-contributory or a contributory system of old age assistance, provision should be made for two modifications. On the one hand, a premium should be available, as of right, to every person reaching the prescribed age level who chooses to defer the commencement of his pension, the premium varying with each year of deferment. On the other hand, there should be provision for admission to benefit, either under the contributory or non-contributory system of old age pension, or persons who, before reaching the age of sixty-five (or sixty in the case of women), can show on competent authority that they are permanently unemployable, "burnt out", or for some other reason unlikely ever again to return into the employment market.

The latter principle has already been intelligently applied in Canada in the administration of War Veterans' Allowances. Among other things, it would result in less haggling over the age of the person where there is no satisfactory record, if that person is shown to be obviously and permanently beyond consideration as far as the prospects of any future employment are concerned. The procedure would, of course, be in line with the principles discussed for disability pensions in the previous Section. The first-mentioned principle would be easier to apply in an insurance system. But even for an assistance pension some modification of the upper level, through higher exemptions for supplementary income, would be desirable.

13. CONTRIBUTORY RETIREMENT
INSURANCE

Considerable attention has been given in the preceding pages to the possibilities which exist for improving in various ways the present system of non-contributory old age pensions. Enough has been said to show what these might be if the present legislation were amended to permit the beginning of pensions at sixty-five with a premium on deferment, and discretion to admit for disability or for other reasons at a lower age. If residence and citizenship restrictions were modified; if assumed but non-existent income were left out of calculations of resources; if the maximum allowance were set at $30 (or even at $25), accompanied by full or more rigid deduction of surplus income—if these statutory changes were implemented, and in addition the administration were transferred to a social service basis, giving help to the aged person on his housing, clothing and other personal problems—much of the repressive and unsatisfactory character of non-contributory old age assistance, as it exists in Canada now, would disappear. But assuming that all these things were done—and they should be done, whether a contributory or non-contributory pension system is to continue—would there still be a need for a transformation in principle from non-contributory to contributory pensions for the aged and retired?

The answer that modern industrial society as a whole is giving with singular unanimity to this question must be taken as having application to Canada as well. The trend is clearly in the direction of compulsory contributory insurance against retirement and old age. Non-contributory old age assistance schemes are giving way more and more to contributory insurance schemes. No country which has ever adopted old age insurance in any form has ever abandoned it and gone back to the non-contributory arrangement. Likewise the trend is clearly in the direction of compulsory insurance as against the voluntary type of state insurance, and there is no record of this trend ever having been reversed. Individuals prefer to get their retirement income as a right, on a basis consistent with their idea of human dignity. Means-test procedures, however lightly applied, violate to some extent this conception of the right to retirement income. But it does not seem possible ever to abolish means-test procedures and income limits from non-contributory plans for old age assistance. Under an assistance plan, even if better rates were granted, they would still be granted subject to a certain amount of investigation into the personal affairs of the applicant which is usually resented.

The Case for the Contributory Form

It is now ten years ago since one Canadian body of enquiry, the Quebec Social Insurance Commission, declared itself in favour of the contributory approach to the problem, stressing its acceptance of the existing scheme as an inadequate transitional measure; and some of its striking passages are worth quotation:

> "The Commission does not claim that the province of Quebec has found an ideal solution of the problem of protection for the aged, and that the system which has always worked will be satisfactory in the future. What the province has done up till now[1] is simply to offer charity, and charity necessarily restricted to a certain privileged group, still more limited if we take into consideration the large number of desolate old people who here, or elsewhere, have their last days saddened by poverty. Other countries have adopted a similar policy, assisting their aged either directly by means of their public services, or indirectly by means of institutions, until it became necessary to consider whether they were to continue this policy or

---

[1] Quebec did not pass legislation bringing the province within the terms of the federal Old Age Pension Act till 1936.

whether they were to institute a system by means of which the individual of advanced age, having paid for years to an appropriate organization a certain sum, should become the beneficiary of an income which would permit him to live until death. This is old-age insurance. The Social Insurance Commission is decidedly in favour of instituting, in the province of Quebec, a system of old age insurance, which is contributory and obligatory. Reasons of justice and of logic, a desire to awaken the conscience, the sense of responsibility, the love of independence, the habit of thrift among our people—all this has helped to create this conviction.''

There can be little doubt that there are important psychological considerations which weight the scale on the side of a contributory scheme. Each person who makes his contribution, however small, during his working years to the future need of his old age is learning and practising the discipline of thrift and foresight. Contrary to the impression which prevails in some quarters that social insurance will destroy these qualities which go to make good citizens, the fact is that old age insurance in particular is a means of ensuring that saving is practised on at least a minimum basis during the entire earning period of the average citizen. The fact that all persons stand together in the over-all state plan —each contributing what he can to the needs of the future, both for himself and for his fellows—enhances a concept of community solidarity which can be a strong feature in democratic civilization. Contributory insurance combines the best features of the individualist and of the collectivist approach, in that it binds every citizen of the community to the need of providing some measure of security for himself in the future, and at the same time signalizes certain responsibilities which the individual carries to help meet the pooled risks of his fellow citizens.

In addition, certain financial considerations are

frequently advanced, supporting the idea of compulsory contributory old age insurance as against non-contributory old age assistance. It is pointed out —and rightly so—that the latter policy is a form of locking the stable door after the horse has been stolen, and places a dead weight of increasingly large proportions on the shoulders of the community. The insurance approach, on the other hand, is constructive in nature; it not only protects the individual by forcing him to save against his declining years, but also protects the state's financial structure by helping to lift from the public treasury some of the burden of old age assistance payments which must be met entirely from taxation, shifting this burden to the individual citizen during that citizen's working years. In certain types of old age insurance, especially those which have a limited coverage and which operate on lines closely similar to commercial insurance, there is much in this argument on financial lines.

But it is fallacious to pursue the idea of accumulating reserves for old age pensioners too far. To the extent that old age insurance plans contemplate coverage of the whole population, it becomes increasingly less useful for detailed and intricate records to be kept up over a long period of years, showing the amount that each individual contributor has built up as his own insurance right. Likewise it becomes less useful to maintain the fiction of setting aside insurance reserves and keeping them separate from the current income of the state, if all members of the community are under the contributory scheme. The public finance arguments in favour of compulsory contributory insurance weaken in strength as the insurance coverage becomes more and more comprehensive, to the point of eventually covering the entire population. This trend towards universal and non-discriminating coverage seems inescapable. Nevertheless, to the extent that cover-

age under the old age insurance scheme does actually
fall short of the entire population, there is an argument in favour of maintaining a contributory basis
of providing security for old age—for insured groups
only—as against the out-right non-contributory
form.

Methods of Attainment

How is Canada to meet the problem? There are
several methods of approach, each of which deserves
consideration. They are singled out for brief
review here, to clarify their main features.

Under all methods, the basic pension rate, and
provisions for adult dependents or survivors are the
same. There is, of course, an important choice
between a single standard rate, and graduated
pensions dependent on the level of earnings or income
of the contributor. The suggestion of this report
(further reviewed in Section 20) is that a number of
considerations weigh in favour of a standard rate for
Canada. The first of these is that graduated pensions, more particularly if they are regarded as
requiring a long period of contribution accumulation, involve a complicated and costly series of
records. Secondly, old age insurance is inescapably
expensive. It must be faced on a national scale; and
it will certainly be easier to attain if administration is
simplified, and if costs are reduced by making a
maintenance minimum the first objective. Thirdly,
there is something to be said in its own right for the
principle of regarding a retirement pension as a small
nucleus to which private and industrial provisions
may be added. It is not necessary to regard this as a
primary determinant, but it is a very important
incidental.

On these lines the basic rate should be an amount
sufficient for minimum maintenance, with a distinction drawn between an individual (man or woman)
and a married couple. The rates which suggest
themselves both by reference to the minimum assist-

ance standards examined earlier, and in relation to present pensions, are at least $30 a month for a single person with $15 a month as the supplement for the spouse; or possibly $25 and $20 respectively. If any minor children of dependent status existed, these extra needs would be cared for by means of children's allowances. In the event of the death of the insured person, it would be reasonable to follow the practice, which is common, of converting the supplementary benefit for the dependent spouse into survivors' pension. On the other hand, if the dependent spouse were able to find accepted employment, the supplementary pension might be made subject to reduction or possibly to elimination.

These arrangements would correspond exactly with the provisions made for permanent disability, the only difference being that the person permanently disabled would be eligible for retirement under the retirement scheme at an earlier age than the person retiring solely on account of age. In the same way persons reaching retirement age and choosing to remain at work for one or two years more should be encouraged to do so, and would have their retirement income increased by a corresponding amount.

The problems of transition which arise once the decision to proceed to an insurance basis is taken, rest on the supposition that a minimum number of years of contribution should be accumulated before eligibility for an insurance pension is established. Strictly speaking, this qualifying period, particularly if it is a number of years, is not essential for the purpose of building up an accumulation of funds. Pensions or assistance for the aged in any given year must be chiefly financed out of the current revenue of the same year. If a sufficiently large government subsidy were available it would be possible to pay pensions to persons above a given age limit immediately, drawing more on contributions and less on state revenue in ensuing years. Transitional arrangements, however, are usually necessary *(a)* to move the total disbursements gradually from the present level to the new level at which the full complement of persons would be on pension; and *(b)* to meet the equities of the situation in which some contributors will have long records of payment and others little or none.

1. *Age Limit Method*

The first method is to limit the availability of insurance pensions to persons under a given age (say fifty-five). Older persons would in effect be regarded as having an insufficient working span left in which to build up any satisfactory insurance protection. Under the age limit as many persons as possible would be brought under the compulsory insurance scheme, and during the course of the remaining ten years or more of working life, they would be expected to build up an insurance right which (together with other funds which might come from employers or the state or both) would be sufficient to provide a minimum pension. This would not be subject to means test but obtainable as of right; and it would necessarily have to be more ample in its terms than the assistance pension.

The complementary part of this plan would be to continue the present old age assistance plan with as many improvements as possible. This alone would be available to persons over the age limit at the time of inauguration. A few others who might not be able to come within the contribution provisions would also depend on old age assistance of the preexisting type. In effect, the state would say to these people, as well as to people under fifty-five who could not be reached by any compulsory method of collection: "You are not really insurable, either because your age leaves an insufficient time in which to build up any adequate insurance protection, or because the way in which you make your living renders it impossible for the state to reach you for regular contribution. We will do our best for you by maintaining a more generous non-contributory old age assistance scheme, under which, subject to the means test, you will receive, on the basis of need, such assistance as the community can provide through straight taxation."

This is one of the most common methods, and the one which would probably be the least disruptive of present arrangements. Its weakness, however, is that it does not remove the need for the non-contributory system for many years. A number of persons who contribute to the scheme may find it necessary to retire from employment, or for some other reason may fail to build up the required amount of contributory time. They might be dealt with through refunds, or possibly by partial retirement pensions. But a majority would probably find their way eventually to the old age assistance scheme. If their lump-sum refund were exhausted, they would require assistance as full pensioners. If they possessed partial insurance pensions they might require partial supplementation on a means-test basis. A considerable expenditure of administrative effort—elaborate record systems, calculations to show that the minimum length of the contributory period has been complied with, the procedure of lump-sum settlements in some cases and the assessment of partial pensions in others—will have been wasted. Assistance will still be necessary outside the insurance scheme; and this will require the maintenance of the second system involving means test procedures and the other details of operation.[1]

2. *Qualified Benefit Method*

The second method is to provide subsidies making it possible to deal with all persons in the transitional stage as equivalent to insured persons on a full-coverage basis. This is clearly a more straightforward alternative to subsidizing non-insured and partially-insured persons outside the insurance scheme. It would make it possible for the insurance scheme to begin almost immediately instead of waiting for ten years (or some other period) of accumulated contributions. And the residual or assistance scheme would be limited only to those persons with no records of contribution at all.

The main problem to be encountered by this alternative is the extent to which persons with, say, one year of contribution should be placed on a parity with persons having up to ten years of contribution. If no differential is made at all, the stand might very well be taken by contributors that there was no point in making contributions. At least three expedients offer themselves for resolving this question.

> (a) The first would be to introduce within the insurance scheme partial means-testing for that portion of the pension not ensured by insurance contributions. The person with a ten-year record of contribution would thus get his pension entirely free from means testing. The person with a five-year record would have one-half of his pension free from means-testing, and the other half subject to means-testing. And so on, down the line. The problem of means-testing would be com-

---

[1] The United States system, which endeavours to preserve all the features of annuities graduated according to the income of recipients, encountered many of these difficulties. "The scheme will not...... provide for all the aged or even all the needy aged. For many years to come annuitants will not have built up sufficient reserves to cover their needs after the age of sixty-five; many low wage groups of workers and part-time workers will probably never accumulate sufficient reserves to carry themselves in old age even when the scheme is operating in full, and in general owner-workers are exempted from the contributory scheme. Thus, although the scheme covers about one-third of the nation and, therefore, spreads widely the promise of some measure of security in old age, it has not removed the necessity for non-contributory pensions, or for contributions by the federal government to the annuities of those with small reserves and in need." (Report of the Royal Commission on Dominion-Provincial Relations, Book II, p. 37).

paratively large at the outset, but would constantly diminish until at the end of ten years it would be almost completely unnecessary.

(b) A second expedient would be to raise the minimum age level of eligibility for contributors with less than a certain period of contribution. Persons with less than five years of contribution might not be eligible, for retirement of full pension until ages between sixty-seven and seventy; persons with five to nine years premiums might have to wait until they were aged between sixty-five and sixty-seven; or some more refined schedule might be set down.

(c) The simplest arrangement would be to set an arbitrarily reduced pension (say $25 a month) to those persons who have met some contributions, but retire before having completed the full qualifying period. Such a reduced pension need not be subject to means test as such; but means-testing would enter into the situation if they were forced to seek supplementation of these reduced pensions.

3. Qualified Contributions Method

The third alternative worthy of consideration in the planning of an old age retirement scheme is one modelled similar to the New Zealand plan. The unique feature of this scheme is that it provides means testing during the contributory stage of the scheme rather than at the end, upon retirement. Every person in New Zealand above a certain age is obligated by law to pay a social security tax which is, in effect, a contribution to insurance, including old age insurance. There are heavy penalties, and it is regarded as an offence just as serious as income tax evasion not to comply with this requirement. Provision is made, however, for those whose means do not permit them to pay the tax to make special application for exemption from the tax; if, on enquiry, the facts seem to justify it, exemption is granted and the applicant's status is taken to be exactly the same as if he had actually made the contribution. Where exemption is granted from contribution, this case must be reviewed periodically in order to establish the fact that further exemption is justified. If, on reaching the age of retirement, the record shows that an individual has a full record of compliance with the provisions of the insurance scheme, it does not matter whether this record is a continuous record of contribution or a continuous record of exemption, or a combination of the two. In any case full pension is granted. It is only the person who has flouted the law by neglecting to contribute or to apply for exemption, who finds himself in difficulty when the question of retirement pension arises.

Even here, such cases can be kept to a remarkably low minimum because of the simplified record system which is possible under such a scheme. It should be pointed out that the New Zealand system makes it completely unnecessary to maintain records for old age insurance in great detail over a long period of years. At the end of each year the insurance book can be called in for examination, and as long as that year can be completely accounted for, either by periods of contribution or periods of exemption stamped in the book, the detailed record can be destroyed and a simple notation made that the individual's record of compliance for the year in question has been completely established. At the end of each year, therefore, it becomes possible to ascertain the identity of those persons who have not

complied with the law and have not completed their
record for the year.   Proceedings for non-compliance
can be taken immediately against such individual,
the appropriate penalties can be meted out and the
individual's record can be re-established, thus avoiding the accumulation of a large number of difficult
cases at the end of the contribution period when
application for pension is made.   This means that it
is practically impossible for a case to arise where a
man on reaching the appropriate age applies for
pension only to find that he is ineligible because of
failure to comply with certain provisions of the insurance act, ten, fifteen, or even twenty years before.

The New Zealand system, it should be added, is
only possible because of the fact that the revenue-
collecting side of the insurance administration is
completely divorced from the pensions administration.   An individual's eligibility for a pension, as of
right, depends in no way on the amount or even on
the fact of his contribution.   It depends entirely on
the record of his compliance with the provisions
either of contribution or of registration for exemption.   The fact should not be overlooked, however,
that the New Zealand plan does contain the elements
of means-testing in respect of contributions.   Even
with this, however, it is probably the simplest and
most satisfactory type of provision for old age
retirement to be found anywhere.

Whether or not such an advanced scheme would
suit the temperament of the Canadian people is a
question on which there is no ready answer at the
present time.   The most obvious difficulty would be
administrative in nature in view of the large area of
Canada and the scattered population, with the con-
sequent difficulties that arise in enforcing universal
compliance.   Obviously, the fact that New Zealand

has a small area and a compact population renders administration measurably easier than in Canada.

The possible arrangements may be compared somewhat more easily if they are presented in the following schematic fashion, indicating broadly the groups who would be eligible for the insurance pensions, and those who would remain dependent on assistance. The proportions would, of course, be considerably different in each case.

Eligible for Insurance Pensions	Assistance Basis
1. *Age Limit Method* All males below (say) 65 All females below (say) 60	All persons over 55 (Persons who fail to complete 10 years' contributions)
2. *Qualified Benefit Method* All persons with (say) 1–10 yrs'. contributions	Persons with no contributions (not till age 70)
Differential arrangements: (a) Exemption from means test for proportion of pension (e.g., $\frac{1}{16}$ for 1-yr. contributor, $\frac{1}{4}$ for 2-yr. contributor. etc.)	(Partial means tests corresponding to proportion in first column)
(b) Schedule of retirement ages. (e.g., 69 for 2-yr. contributor 68 for 4-yr. contributor 67 for 6-yr. contributor 66 for 8-yr. contributor 65 for 10-yr. contributor)	
(c) Lower rate (e.g., $25) for non-completed contribution	(Partial assistance if unable to supplement reduced pension)
3. *Qualified Contribution Method* All persons with record of (a) payment of all-inclusive social security premiums, or (b) certified exemptions	(Persons with record of non-compliance, subsequently unadjusted)

If the principle were incorporated of making higher rates available to pensionable persons who deferred their retirement, a simple formula would have to be found to apply to the basic rate, over and above any adjustments made in accordance with the above schemes. There would be least difficulty in applying this formula to method 3, and probably most to method 2b.

Contributory Pensions in Relation to Industrial Retirement Schemes

A few points may be noted, in conclusion, on the way in which a comprehensive old age plan would fit in with existing provisions made by industries for the retirement of their employees. One of the undesirable features of company retirement plans (when they are limited, as at present, to a minority of firms) is that a prejudice is set up against the hiring or re-employment of older men. If these retire after a comparatively short period of employment, the superannuation to which they would be entitled would be small or negligible. Their going would seem to cast a slur on their employers; or else occassion a special subsidy to enable them to receive superannuation comparable with that of employees with long terms of service. This problem would be removed almost entirely with the advent of universal old age insurance. The older worker would be more welcome. The pension available to everybody would, it is true, supply only a basic minimum. There would still be complete freedom for industrial schemes, but they would be able to act more clearly and more effectively as supplements. For the better paid workers they could help to provide substantial retirement incomes. (There would, of course, be no means test applicable to the insurance pension).

In the survey of industrial retirement plans previously referred to, it was frequently stated that the firm was ready to adapt its plan in the event of a national retirement or old-age plan being established.

(Appendix V, paragraph 22.)   In the longer run a
further advantage would accrue.   It is possible that
with the greater extension of industrial schemes, a
man could carry with him from one employment to
another his industrial pension rights.   In either
event, mobility would be assisted much more than
it is at present.

14. HEALTH INSURANCE AND OTHER
SOCIAL SECURITY PLANS

In the last part of this report the outline of a comprehensive system of social security will be reviewed as a whole. The relation of health insurance to other branches of social security legislation is so important in itself, however, that it is necessary to pause here for an interim summary of some of the matters most relevant to the administration of protection against the universal risks. (Widowhood and survivors' insurances will be dealt with in the next Part; sickness cash benefits, maternity cash benefits, and workmen's compensation, as already explained, belong to the special group of "employment risks.")

For two related reasons, considerable importance attaches to the methods adopted for the administration of health insurance in Canada. The first of these is the desirability of making the benefits available as widely as possible. This has already been discussed. It involves special consideration of methods—a combination of methods if necessary—for the collection of contributions from at least the whole gainfully-occupied population. Once this is achieved, there is no particular difficulty in extending coverage to other members of the family: the principle of a standard contribution, to provide for two persons, and in the special case of medical care to extend to all children in the family, has been explained in previous sections.

The second reason, in the long run, is even more important. For substantial sections of the population the health insurance system can be the basis for the collection of contributions for other types of insurance: it may in fact be the only possible basis for certain groups, more particularly farmers. The complexities of a health insurance scheme are such that there is a danger that attention may be concentrated on the adequate provision of medical care, and not enough on the way in which health insurance may be fitted most efficiently into a total social security system.

For wage-earners there is no particular difficulty, from the administrative point of view, in extending insurance schemes to cover disability pensions, survivors' insurance and contributory old age pensions (and, for that matter, sickness cash benefits and related benefits specially appropriate to the wage-earning group). To begin with, the method of collecting contributions through industrial pay-rolls is comparatively easy, and already established. Secondly, unemployment insurance, the basic measure for the wage-earning population, is now a going concern with a nation-wide administrative mechanism under federal control. Extension of social insurance to rural and non-wage-earner groups, however, is a new venture; though none the less a necessary one. For disability, survivors', and old age insurance, as for medical care, there would be no justification for a Canadian scheme which did not extend to agricultural and other non-wage-earner groups as well as to the industrial population.

It is of first importance, therefore, to realize that health insurance and unemployment insurance between them may be the two basic administrative systems for Canadian social security. Health insurance will, of course, extend to wage-earners, and contribution collection could conveniently be organized through payroll deductions. But there is no reason why the two systems should not be more closely integrated, at least so far as forming part of a national system of contribution collection is concerned. The possible "division of labour" is not exactly between urban and rural areas, but rather between wage-earners (or employees) and other gainfully-occupied persons.

The important point is the distinction between the mechanisms of collection, and the mechanisms of administration or service. There is no inherent reason why these should be synonymous. It is possible to visualize two major collection agencies for a variety of insurances, each dealing with separate sections of the community. The health insurance basis—in effect, a method of assessing contributions—would provide for the collection of all contributions for the universal group (medical care, disability, survivors and old age) from the self-employed, rural, agricultural and other non-wage-earners. The unemployment insurance basis —in effect, payroll deductions—could be used for all of these insurances plus unemployment insurance and any other subsidiary provisions such as cash sickness benefit, for wage-earners. This side of the total transaction would simply be concerned with payments and transfers into particular funds; there would be no inherent difficulty even if there were both federal and provincial funds. Obviously, if all the collectors (employers making payroll deductions or affixing stamps, the income tax authorities, municipal assessment boards, provincial licence offices, or whatever there may be) act as the agent for the federal government *so far as collection of social security premiums are concerned,* the whole procedure is simplified. Some individuals, incidentally, will have the possibility of making their payments in more than one way, and can choose the one which is most convenient, and the possession of the appropriate card or book, duly stamped, will be all the evidence necessary to prevent double assessment.

On the other side, there would, of course, be quite distinct divisions for the two sets of services. Only the health insurance authorities, established appropriately throughout the country, with whatever was considered the most effective liaison with provincial and federal Departments of Health, and, of course, with both urban and rural units, would supervise the actual provision of medical care and the payment of doctors and other practitioners. Only the employment offices would administer unemployment benefit, sickness cash benefit if this were established, and a series of related placement facilities. The payment of pensions of all kinds might use a different mechanism, such as the post-offices; though co-operation should probably be effected with the other existing service agencies (health authorities, or employment offices) for the purpose of registration, certification, etc.

Legislative Aspects

In these circumstances, the method of implementing health insurance legislation is particularly important. A basis for the insurance of the universal risks on contributory principles which is to be satisfactory for Canada must be comprehensive; it must be administratively efficient; and it must be constitutionally free from dispute. If the set-up of health insurance is to offer this basis, the same canons apply. It is not merely a matter of avoiding overlapping or of securing economies in administration, but of ensuring national coverage and at least a reasonable degree of uniformity.

There are presumably three methods by which health insurance might be implemented in Canada. The first would be straightforward amendment of the British North America Act in the same way as was done for unemployment insurance to give the federal government full jurisdiction in the matter. A second method might be the utilization of a procedure such as seemed to be contemplated in Section 94 of the Act, providing for action and uniformity through concurrent legislation, and ensuring recognition of Dominion priority in cases of conflict between the terms of the statutes. The third method would be to depend principally on provincial initiative, providing for national co-ordination through grants-in-aid, the various procedures associated with audit control, and methods of consultation such as are employed, for example, in the Dominion Council of Health.

To take the third alternative first, the main issue in this context is not really the efficacy of this method of co-ordination and control. The possibilities of the constructive administration of grants-in-aid have not always received the attention they deserve in this country; and they are referred to in another connection in a later section. The primary difficulties so far as social security is concerned are twofold. There would be no guarantee that some provinces would not lag behind, and the transition period before national coverage was obtained might be indefinitely prolonged. Apart altogether from the undesirability of this situation in so important a matter as medical care, it might not be possible to institute, for example, a Dominion scheme of contributory old age pensions, until the several provincial health insurance schemes provided the necessary collection arrangements. So far as disability pensions are concerned it would in any case be unwise to set up a Dominion scheme until health insurance were functioning. It is true that the federal government might set up appropriate offices in the tardy provinces (it would not be feasible to use the employment offices for non-wage earners), but this would simply postpone problems of rationalization of administration for some later date.

The second difficulty is the danger of considerable divergence in scope and type of coverage, contribution scales, etc., apart altogether from differences in administrative practice within each province, and problems which would arise when, for example, contributors move from one province to another. The experience of this process has been most sharply illustrated in the United States with the evolution of fifty differing State unemployment compensation systems. All authoritative observers have freely predicted a movement towards national reconstruction of the system "either by the evolutionary process or by drastic revision in time of stress".[1] It is conceivable that the Canadian unemployment insurance scheme might not have been unitary in form. If not, it would certainly have run into similar difficulties. But Canada escaped the United States dilemma by the British North America Act amendment of 1940.

The method of straightforward amendment recommends itself as being the most direct and unequivocable. It would assure uniformity in a field which is of vital significance for all future social security planning; and it would undoubtedly offer some economies in terms of administrative expenditure. The nature of health and medical care administration is such, however, that the federal authority would undoubtedly have to set up a series of regional boards or offices. In view of the interests of active Departments of Health in each of the provinces (and of other important auxiliaries in some provinces, such as Health Units, municipal doctors and hospitals, etc.) this might easily produce unnecessary duplication. There is not the same parallel between local health insurance administration, and unemployment insurance, in this respect. The need for a Dominion Employment Service, with a network of regional and local offices, is justified by the nature of the problem with which it must deal and the fact that comparable facilities were not previously in existence. In addition, a

---

[1] E.g., Bryce M. Stewart *et al: Planning and Administration of Unemployment Compensation in the United States.* (Industrial Relations Counsellors, Inc., 1938).

considerable degree of adaptation to the special circumstances of their regions has been evolved by most of the provinces. It was for this and other reasons that the Rowell-Sirois Commission saw value in a division of labour between federal and provincial governments in the health field.

Whatever method is followed, there is clearly room for a distinct measure of decentralization in the administration of medical care. However, there is not the same argument for the decentralized administration of funds. It is a matter for serious consideration as to how far federal government machinery might be used, if not as the chief method, at least as one of the participating methods for the collection of contributions for health insurance and other purposes, even in rural areas.

The appropriateness of a combination of payroll methods, voluntary contributions, and collections through income assessment has already been discussed. The mechanism of the income tax naturally suggests itself, more particularly since its scope has been so widely increased during the war. At least potentially, it applies to all the gainfully-occupied of the country. On the other hand, a considerable proportion of farmers have incomes too small to render them liable to tax, while also there is still a substantial percentage of non-compliance. It has therefore been suggested that the income registration required (Section 9) might for some groups be best obtained through the mechanisms of property-tax payments, which, for example, involve all farmers at least once a year. It would be necessary to ensure that careful definitions are applied at the time of the initial registration so that, for example, figures of property value and of normal yearly income are not confused. It would probably be necessary also to strengthen the staffs of the municipal assessment authorities for the first period of registration in which the bulk of the contributors would be established. It seems fairly evident that the services of the Dominion Bureau of Statistics and of the provincial Departments of Municipal Affairs would be required in setting up a standard procedure.

These and other considerations suggest that the most desirable arrangements would be a co-operative agreement between all three parties, federal, provincial and municipal governments, to assist in the establishment and future collection of insurance contributions. There could hardly be any question that the effort and expense, for so important and far-reaching an objective, would be worthwhile. Given the announcement of comprehensive social security objectives, it may be added, the value of the income tax machinery may be enhanced. If health insurance and other benefits (including children's allowances, if these were made contingent on having paid the universal-risks contributions) existed as an inducement to pay social security contributions as well as taxes, the rate of compliance would rise. As noted elsewhere, tax payments are being successfully utilized in New Zealand, although the administrative conditions there are substantially simpler.

On the same grounds, of the need for inter-government co-operation for successful health insurance establishment, the method of concurrent jurisdiction suggests itself as particularly appropriate. Whether it is constitutionally available at present, and whether it is equally appropriate for the other insurances is a matter for separate consideration; further reference is made to this in the concluding Part.

Some Other Aspects of Administration

This report does not concern itself with any examination of the best method of organizing medical service itself; but it endorses the view which has been frequently expressed in Canada, (1) that Departments of Health, both federal and provincial, would be effective media of supervision, allied with appropriate advisory bodies. It is assumed that on these advisory bodies the representation of medical men would be prominent; but it is highly desirable, and in accord with the experience of all countries in which health insurance has been long established, that citizen and "consumer" groups should be strongly represented as well.

These are familiar matters. A less obvious suggestion, which is worthy of serious attention in this country, is (2) that use should be made of the organization and experience of Workmen's Compensation Boards. The procedures adopted by the Boards in the realm of disability treatment, relations with doctors, specialists and hospitals, the sympathetic handling of claims, and progressive work in physical and vocational rehabilitation, are widely regarded as having measured up to good standards. While the Boards deal solely with industrial beneficiaries, a considerable proportion of their administration extends to small towns. It is evident that advantage could be taken of the functioning of the Boards most directly and immediately in the field of disability insurance. None the less, Workmen's Compensation administrations are accustomed to handling a great deal of routine and short-term medical care. They have, at least in this country, established good working relations with the medical profession, and they are one of the few going concerns in the social security field with a viewpoint transferable to the exigencies of health insurance.

(3) The pros and cons of establishing a separate federal Department of Social Security are deliberately not entered into here. This is a matter which can hardly be elaborated until it is known how extensively and rapidly the outlines of a comprehensive social insurance system are to be filled in. It does seem relevant, however, to express the view

that, from the moment health insurance is given the
sanction of any federal legislation, there should be set
up a strong interdepartmental Social Insurance Committee, with a mandate to effect co-ordination on all
matters requiring co-operative action between the
Department of Health and the Department of
Labour on all matters relating to these two basic
insurances. The scope of their work should extend
as rapidly as possible, not merely to the dovetailing
of collection agencies for the various occupational
groups, as indicated above; but to the constructive
services complementary to social insurance; such as
research and development of administrative information, and rehabilitation facilities for cases which
require both medical and placement service.

PART IV

FAMILY NEEDS

15. CHILDREN'S ALLOWANCES

It has been strongly maintained that the best
augury for the future of Canadian social security
legislation is a clear understanding of the logic both
of social needs and the methods by which they are
met through the insurances. The special place of
children so far as family income levels are concerned
has been reviewed in relation to present areas of
inadequate wages, to the legislation of social assistance type which already exists in the Dominion, and
to present a possible social insurance legislation if it is
predicated on the two-person unit contribution. It
has been recognized throughout that the maintenance
of children—the need of income sufficient to give
them health, proper food and clothing and desirable
conditions of family life—is not an unpredictable
risk or contingency in the same way as unemployment, sickness or the death of the husband. Nor is
it a special, non-recurrent expenditure which may
put sudden pressure on the family income, like birth
or death. It is a continuous requirement, at least
for the period of infancy up to adolescence; changing
in character and size, it is true, but continuous none
the less in times of prosperity and times of depression,
and whether the chief earner, if his occupation is
irregular, is earning his full income or not. If wages
and incomes were everywhere sufficient to provide
properly for the children of all our families, there
would of course be no case for children's allowances
at all. There would be no case for them in the form
in which they are here analysed, but only in the partial
sense of applying them to the insurances designed for
income maintenance in times of need, if children
were a contributing cause of poverty, or the source of
inability to make both ends meet, *only* when one of
the emergencies like unemployment or sickness or
widowhood struck the family.

But the fact is that there are large areas of inadequacy not only at times of nation-wide depression or personal misfortune, but in normal times. Children's allowances are a clear part of the policy of a national minimum— of the direct attack on poverty where it is bound up with the strain imposed by a large family on a small income. Quite irrespective of whether the right parents have the most children, children should have an unequivocal place in social security policy. If we are concerned about the quality of parents and their children, the proper approach is not to condemn the children to hardship or inadequate conditions because their parents happen to be poor. The child has no choice. His opportunity in the modern community does not depend only on such advantages as he receives by inheritance from his parents, but on their income level, and on the children with whom he must grow up. The needs, of course, are greatest among the lowest income groups, but there are narrow margins for the families of many parents whose earnings by labour market standards would be regarded as reasonable or moderate.

An unqualified recognition by the state of the needs of parents, and of the national value of healthy children, already exists in well-established form in the deductions allowed for income tax; moreover, these have now been stabilized at a figure ($108 per year per child) which applies universally to all liable to pay the tax. The groups and classes subject to tax have moved far down the income scale. It would not be correct, however, to present this income tax deduction as if it were a children's allowance already in operation. For many in the lower categories, it means that they pay no tax at all, not that their income is supplemented; while those heads of families whose earnings are so low that they do not come within the provisions of the tax, are precisely those who need an allowance most.

Methods of Approach to Children's Needs

There are three avenues along which we can approach a readjustment consistent with the objectives of social security. It is possible that we may achieve the net result desired along all three; but it is not possible to reject one of them without a proper appreciation of the limits of the others.

1. *Social assistance, negative and positive.*—First the provision, mainly in the form of income maintenance, can be left to social assistance methods, as these have been defined herein. In the light of what has already been reviewed, it is unnecessary to emphasize that there is a radical difference between social assistance if it means only relief of destitution, and constructive service which supplements certain minima already achieved through some social insurance provisions. The anomalies in the recognition of children in the various types of existing legislation, even where standard monetary rates are set, have already been pointed out. The uncertainties and other drawbacks of the budgetary assessment where this is actuated by relief standards have also been described. Even if these deficiencies are overcome, the problem would not be met on the proper plane because social assistance will be extended to the children only when the family is in primary need. The probabilities are that the need will be urgent, for the family may delay application for aid while it has any resources left, and after that because of the unwillingness to swallow the bitter pill of asking for relief or charity. Aid should be immediate or almost automatic if it is to have the best chance of being constructive, materially and psychologically.

If social assistance can be made positive instead of negative—if its purpose is supplementary income in the appropriate case, and the services which will smooth the transition from the previous state of self-support, or promote rehabilitation later—the situation is different. Voluntary social work and public welfare administration alike will come into their own, only as some of the basic social security areas, particularly health and unemployment, are covered by legislation. The possibility of special concentration on child welfare, concerned not only with basic maintenance levels for children, but its special application or maintenance when the family is under misfortune, would be something to welcome.

It is still reasonable to ask, however, whether the best programme of public and private co-operation can do all that is required, as a normal continuous programme as well as for periods of emergency. Even if this could be competently organized for the future, a further consideration remains. Canadians believe not only in the family, but in a strong measure of individuality. There must be reasonable leeway for parents' decision in the expenditure of the budget for their children. It is an impossible situation to imagine that all guidance and all services should be provided by non-family authorities. The virtue of a standard endowment or benefit in cash is that it becomes part of the normal family income, which it is left to the parents to expend.

2. *Provision in kind.*—A second method would be to leave provision for children to take the form of public services in all the types which are appropriate. That there are broad and constructive measures to be taken in this field will not be denied. The many forms of education, not forgetting educational guidance and scholarships; health services, not only for sickness but for normal care, as in the examples of the well-baby clinics and regular medical inspection through schools; free school lunches and other nutritional supplements; recreational services: all these build up the social minimum as it applies particularly to children. None the less, there are certain

limits. A child cannot take full advantage of public services if he has poor shoes or inadequate clothing, if there is insufficient fuel in his home to warm the house, if his home is in such an environment that good educational work is undone or he has no desirable place to play. In other words, the approach through the income of his family must go at least part of the way to meet whatever may be done in strengthening some of the most constructive features—those applied to children—of all social welfare programmes. The margins are of course adaptable. If, for example, a vast programme of re-housing were undertaken in which special arrangements were made to subsidize the rents of large families (a procedure which has been followed in Sweden), it might be reasonable to reduce such children's allowances as were in vogue. If the basic allowance decided upon is itself small, however, it might be better social policy to look rather to an augmentation as national wealth and wage levels improve.

3. *Cash allowances as part of a social security system.*—The third method is to recognize children's allowances in forthright fashion, as a specific social security measure justified on its own merits. What is envisaged in this report is a children's allowance system considered as a unit along with unemployment insurance, health insurance, disability insurance, and other measures in the social security system, but geared into them at every point where they belong. Not only is this logical, but it will contribute immensely to administrative simplicity and efficiency if this plan is adopted. This has now been indicated at many points in preceding sections, and requires no further emphasis.

Allowance Scales

It is significant that the scale at which children's allowance rates should be fixed is not under the same necessity of being related to wages in the lowest categories of work, as are the benefit payments of the insurances. The reason is that they are universally available. They cannot in themselves provide any special incentive for a worker to stay on unemployment benefit rather than seek employment, because the allowance goes on whether the man is employed or not. They are uniquely open to adjustment, therefore, in relation to the total national income of the country and other considerations affecting public recognition of welfare standards. In the first instance it is undeniable that they must be calculated with some relation to what the nation as a whole can afford, recognizing always that to a substantial degree they are only a redistribution, on better principles, of existing income—whether secured from tax revenue or contributions, or both. Minimum budget standards based on authoritative statement of dietary and other needs, are directly relevant; but these ought to be computed not on the assumptions that successive children in a family are automatically more economical to rear, but on a specific determination of the desirable minimum requirements at each age or age-period. The more adequate the rates finally set, the more definitely it may be assumed that present expenditures under existing legislation and assistance measures of various kinds can be eliminated; and this enters into the calculation of the net cost to the nation of the scheme.

It is quite possible that on account of total costs— since there are 3,500,000 children (under 16) in Canada—the allowances might be inaugurated on a fairly low scale. The assistance minimum reviewed in the early part of this report would set the average amount for full support at $14.50 a month, though there is evidence that in small towns and rural districts lower rental costs create differentials (Appendix VI). Children's Aid Societies, which have extensive experience in the maintenance of children, both in cities and on farms, allow rates in various provinces ranging between $14 and $20 a month. It would be better to start with small rates, subject to adjustment, than to have none at all, or to compromise the social security system by applying them partially in the form of allowances attached to insurance benefits. Rates comparable with those proposed in the Beveridge report would be about $8–$9 a month; which also corresponds to the present average allowance deductible for income tax purposes (though this latter is not based on any specific computation of needs).

Various suggestions may be made with the object of economy in view; but they should be evaluated against the advantages of a universal scheme at comparatively low rates as well as on their own merits.

It might be suggested, for example, that children's allowances should be granted only for the larger families, e.g., those with four or more children. This of course would result in reduction of costs. But it does not close the gap; particularly because the families with one to three children are by far the more numerous.[1] Their anomalous situation which has already been depicted, would remain unchanged. The economy would be too great, and the remaining gap too wide.

Following from this it might be suggested that an effective compromise is to attach to those among the insurances which involve monetary payments, extra allowances for children up to the first three in a family; thus permitting the insurance and the children's allowance scheme to meet half way. This recourse, however, would introduce more problems than it resolves. It brings complications to the insurance system which the whole plan of this

---

[1] There were between 450,000 and 500,000 families in 1931 with four or more children, or 20-25 per cent of all families (according as to whether all families, or "normal" families, with both parents alive and living together, are taken as base).

exposition has been seeking to avoid; and to the children's allowance system it brings the complication of extra difficulties of investigation and administration. Moreover, it becomes doubtful how far the new distribution of income, affected by drawing more from insurance contributors and less from taxpayers generally, is either a more desirable redistribution or resultant in substantial economies, when the net balance (including extra administration costs) is struck.

The one variation from a completely unqualified system which would be least likely to vitiate the principles explained in this report would be (a) to pay allowances to all families in respect only of children other than the first, (b) to pay allowances to first children only when the family concerned was in receipt of benefit from any of the insurance schemes, or some form of public assistance, and for the duration of such benefit or assistance. The extended allowance for dependency periods would of course be, like the regular family allowances, an outright state grant, not charged to any of the insurance funds. This procedure would reduce very considerably the cost of the allowances schemes, since first children are a large proportion of all children; it would constitute a special recognition of family needs in the event of misfortune from any of the social and economic hazards. On the other hand, particularly since the first child would receive one of the higher rates, if these were graduated (see below), it would raise some possibility of a dependency income being higher than working income, among the lowest-paid and poorest groups.

The method of graduation which recommends itself on entirely different grounds for universal application is one which scales the benefit according to the age of the child. This method is the most economical in the sense of scaling amounts paid to a more precise assessment of need; and it might even

take account of such publicly-supplied services as
are available for children, *e.g.*, during the period of
school life.   The age at which children's allowances
should cease fairly clearly defines itself.   It might
be the recognized age at which compulsory attendance at school ends (16 in most provinces) or the
age at which the young worker comes under other
appropriate forms of insurance (particularly unemployment insurance) in the case of the juvenile
wage earner.   These two ages should, of course, in
a properly articulated system be synonymous.   A
scale such as that presented below for illustrative
purposes, would average about $7.50 a month:

Age	Rate (per month)
Up to 4 years	$ 5.00
5– 9 years	6.50
10–12 years	8.00
13–14 years	10.00
15–16 years	12.50

Rural-Urban Differentials

A suggestion which invites consideration is that
children's allowances might be set at different rates
for urban and rural areas.   The grounds for the
proposal are, of course, differences in costs of living
as well as in income levels, which have been referred
to elsewhere (Section 4, and Appendix VI).   It is
clear at the outset assuming that the differential is
a valid one, that administration would be difficult
if it were based on a distinction between "urban"
and "rural" as such.   Determination would, in fact,
have to be made arbitrarily, by zones concentric to
the main cities, as, for example, for wage regulations
in Montreal and other districts of Quebec.   This
would undoubtedly create a number of unreasonable
cases; for example, that of an agricultural labourer
working within a main suburban area of a metropolis,
as compared with an agricultural labourer in more
remote districts.   The distinction might be more

appropriate and more flexible if, conforming with principles suggested for other purposes, the boundaries were determined by unemployment insurance coverage. Theoretically, the scope of unemployment insurance defines the wage-earner group, which is not entirely urban but works under conditions and has a status such that certain extensions of social insurance are desirable. This solution would be effective if unemployment insurance were completely comprehensive. The case of the agricultural labourer, for instance, would be resolved, because it would be determined solely by his status as an insured employee, not by reference to the district in which he worked. In point of fact however, many of the sections of the working force not yet covered by unemployment insurance, and sections where there are administrative difficulties in extending this coverage, are precisely those who are marginal between rural and urban areas. The proposal would place an added premium on the completion of unemployment insurance coverage, and, of course, would increase the desire of various categories of workers to be brought within the scheme; but some arbitrary demarcations would seem to be inevitable.

So far as the differentials themselves are concerned, such experience as is available is not conclusive. In Canada the Children's Aid Societies have special experience in the boarding of foster children on farms as well as in the cities. In one major area which includes both urban and rural districts the C.A.S. has considered the difference in rates between farm and city families, but doubts if there is justification for more than a small margin of difference (*e.g.*, $18 as compared with $20 a month).

On the one hand, the difference in the situation so far as children's maintenance is concerned is easily exaggerated. For example, different and simpler clothing is required for children on a farm, but the experience is that it comes to be substantially equivalent in cost. Food is not necessarily measurably cheaper if proper provision is made for variety and adequate nutrition. The most measurable difference is undoubtedly in respect of rent. Country accommodation may not be always superior in construction and general facilities, but it is invariably a better environment as compared with low-rent housing or slum situations in the town. There is also less hazard, broadly speaking, in respect of contagious diseases.

On the other hand, if a differential were set up certain consequences must be envisaged. A higher rate of children's allowances for urban families would strengthen the tendencies already evident for families to move from country to town. In practice, the higher rate obtainable would be of doubtful advantage: relative to most farm situations, the urban family would secure poorer environment for a higher rent. The advantage, apparent or real, which would swing the balance towards migration, is the greater scope and variety of job opportunities.

Putting the point the other way round, if a universal flat rate did in fact give an advantage to rural dwellers in terms of the actual purchasing-power of the allowances, it would have two merits. It would act as an incentive to remain in rural rather than move to urban areas. It might furthermore be regarded as a fair compensation for some of the admitted deficiencies in rural services (*e.g.* health facilities, schools, job opportunities).

These considerations would suggest that a single rate for the Dominion as a whole is desirable. If a concession had to be made to low living costs in certain areas, it would be a preferable alternative to set the national rate somewhat low rather than to invite the difficulties of a differential system.

There would remain some areas of difficulty in

which earnings or standards might be so low that the children's allowances for a large family would offer enough by themselves for family maintenance. This would be less likely the lower the standard rate. On the other hand, if poverty were so pronounced as this, the general argument for children's allowances would presumably be strengthened rather than weakened. The positive approach towards such cases, which would almost certainly be cases of backward areas or of personal deficiencies, is to focus on them the attention of all the constructive agencies and services possible: the Children's Aid Societies and adult education movements, for example, so far as private agencies are concerned; and training and special assistance projects (as suggested in Sections 6 and 8), so far as public programmes are concerned. It is true of all social insurance that it may be put to improper use in a minority of special situations. But this is another way of saying that it brings into a stronger light the fringes of personal or economic inadequacy which can only be removed by other appropriate action.

Contribution Possibilities

The possibility of a contributory basis for children's allowances, in whole or in part, is perhaps not to be regarded as entirely out of court under Canadian conditions, although it is rejected after careful consideration in current British proposals. The graduated scale used for unemployment insurance, and the "degressive" method proposed for health insurance both involve at least a limited recognition of the principles of the personal income tax, *i.e.*, of assessment according to capacity to pay. If this principle is appropriate at all, however, it is far better applied through the national revenue as a whole. The measure is so universal in application, and there are such positive virtues in its being universal that it would be better implemented as an outright state grant. This would be the logical

corollary of tax-financed contributions to child
welfare generally.

It would be simpler, and probably desirable, to
link children's allowances to the contributory insurances in another way. It could be made a requirement that children's allowances would be paid only
to those families in which all current social insurance
contributions (assuming the appropriate members
of the family to be insurable) had been paid. From
another angle, on the advent of the scheme, it would
be reasonable to eliminate or at least to modify
substantially present income-tax exemptions for
children. Another administrative feature has less
point. If any income ceiling were attached to the
combined social insurances, it would be reasonable
to apply it also in the payment of family allowances.
The imposition of an upper income level has perhaps more justification for this measure than, for
example, health insurance. But the more the
validity of an income ceiling is explored the less it
recommends itself. The cardinal fact is that an
income ceiling of, say, $3,000 would serve to exclude
only some 3 per cent of all families. A universal
application is in this light much more sensible than
it may appear.

A final point worthy of some consideration is
whether, as the basis of a national children's allowance system, some division of labour might be
organized as between federal and provincial authorities. If the provision of services for children in kind
were mainly left to the provinces, the federal complement might be the monetary allowance, in somewhat similar form to present old age pensions. It
might even be desirable to pursue the integration
further by the federal government's making the payment of family allowances in a particular province
conditional upon a desirable minimum of children's
welfare services being provided in that province.

16. WOMEN'S NEEDS IN THE SOCIAL SECURITY SYSTEM

A special note on women's needs and benefits is called for, not only because the place of women in a social security system has commonly been given little systematic analysis, but also because women have become more and more important in the nation's working force. The greatest reserve of labour power on which all the war industries have drawn are hundreds of thousands of women who in normal times do not seek gainful employment. The great bulk of these, of course, have been single women; but one of the important phenomena of the wartime labour market is the greatly increased number of married women who are now serving in the ranks of the employed. Younger and unmarried women who can fairly easily break their family ties were absorbed comparatively rapidly; it is possible that 200,000 unmarried women have entered wage-earning employment for the first time as a result of the war. But, as a recent review of the situation in a bulletin of the Dominion Bureau of Statistics states, "If the war is of long duration, involving the absorption of more and more men into the armed forces on the one hand, and, on the other, an increasing tempo of war production... the ranks of married women under 35 years of age, not gainfully occupied, which in 1931 numbered 678,700... will have to be heavily drawn upon." This will not be easy, for married women have family obligations. They cannot be immobilized without active development of services for children's care, meal preparation, etc., such as now flourish on a large scale in Great Britain.

Experience in these fields, it should be noted incidentally, may be of some relevance in the future in the recasting and improvement of public welfare functions generally. But particularly in the post-war world women are vitally important as home-makers and as rearers of the nation's children, whatever role may be reserved for them as gainfully employed workers in the post-war occupational structure. It is unnecessary to emphasize also that, on the farms, women have always played a special part and are still likely to demand that the major share of their consideration be for services which affect them in the home rather than as employees.

This section does no more than give a brief indication of the ways in which a comprehensive social security system could or should apply to women. There are many details which require further study before the precise scheme of social security as it would relate to women can be set down, but it will be helpful to assemble the main heads.

1. In her capacity of housewife, the adoption of the two-unit principle advocated at several points in this report would ensure that she is brought in automatically to the most important benefits, particularly those of medical care, which would be available in a comprehensive scheme. There should be no difficulty about medical attention for invalidity and permanent disability, but the pros and cons of pension payments in the event of the latter misfortune should be carefully evaluated. Provision for disability of the husband, if it were from industrial causes, would already exist. In cases of non-industrial disability, it is proposed that a married pensioner should receive a larger pension than a single man, to provide at least the "assistance minimum" for two persons, the scales being in general in conformity with the scales for (reformed) old age pensions. At all stages in the family cycle, the

income minimum would be buttressed at its most vital point, i.e., the varying claims of children up to (presumably) the age of sixteen, through family allowances.

Proper provision for maternity is a special matter. It will be unquestioned that the fullest arrangements for medical care should be woven into any health insurance scheme that is to be devised, and that this should be available for all women, whether they are the wives of wage-earners or of other gainfully occupied persons in either urban or rural districts.

The mother who is normally a wage-earner, however, should have every inducement to refrain from working during the periods immediately prior and subsequent to the birth of her child. If sickness cash benefits are instituted for the employee section of the population, therefore, the establishment of maternity cash benefits for working women would be a desirable corollary.

It may be noted that the new Beveridge proposals (based on flat rates) seek for an equitable arrangement in specifying that cash rates for ordinary sickness benefits should be lower for women than those for men, but maternity cash benefit higher than the standard unemployment benefit rate, to run for a period of thirteen weeks before and after the birth of the child. The Canadian situation, assuming the retention of graduated scales, would not call for such an adjustment. It might be appropriate, however, to set a minimum for maternity benefit rather than to allow wage scales to rule for the lowest-paid workers.

2. It goes without saying that the institution of comprehensive children's allowances would be a feature welcomed by all mothers. This part of the social security structure would mean ease of mind as

well as of budget, because it would remove all doubts as to at least minimum provision for the welfare of children over a considerable period of years. It is not unimportant to add, however, that both in recognition and in monetary effect, allowances granted specifically for children and not in some generalized fashion for dependents' needs contribute towards treating a mother as an individual in her own right. The procedure accepted by most advocates, furthermore, is to make the allowance (in normal cases) payable in the name of the mother only.

3. As a wage-earner, if her employment is reasonably continuous, a woman whether single or married would have access to unemployment benefit and cash benefit for periods of sickness on the same terms as male workers in comparable wage classes. It is to be noted that, assuming the present principles of graduated scales are retained, as in the unemployment insurance administration, the benefit rates will be very low for the youngest and least skilled workers. Much would depend upon the extent to which training facilities for the increase of skill are desirable and adaptable to the post-war environment. For the most part, however, this problem is not special to women but to all younger, partial, or inexperienced workers. If it still remains true that women will look forward to industrial careers in only small proportions as compared with men, it will be equally true that securance of the best available employment conditions cannot depend on an unemployment insurance scheme alone.

4. It is to be expected that large numbers of the female workers in Canadian industries will, in effect, retire voluntarily from the labour market through marriage. The suggestion has been made in several

countries, and is embodied in concrete form in the Beveridge Report, that this trend might be encouraged by a general marriage grant or bonus. If this is not considered desirable for unqualified application, a special and appropriate variation might be made in the form of allowing to a previously employed woman, on marriage, a commutation of all unemployment insurance contributions paid into the fund during her period of employment. Marriage grants, however, are not an essential element in a social security scheme[1] and no recommendation is made in this report.

Experience has suggested in Britain that if a woman decides after marriage to continue as a wage-earner certain modifications should apply. Because she has other definite sources of support, her registration as unemployed must be attested by strict interpretation of genuine availability for employment; and it is proposed in the British projections that unemployment and sickness benefits should be lower than the standard rate. Whether the latter provision would be necessary under Canadian conditions is open to question, in view of the graduated scale which would already be in operation. It is possible that no more than an upper limit would require consideration.

5. Provisions necessary for widowhood, and also the deficiencies of present mothers' allowances, have been examined elsewhere. Existing provisions for the wife of an industrial worker who is covered by workmen's compensation would still remain; there

---

[1] It should be noted that commutation arrangements would be an exception to the general principles of *social* insurance under which no contributor has an individual claim to the return of the contributions (or excess contributions) which he or she has paid. The arrangement would really be an expedient to graduate the bonus according to length of previous employment.

would, however, be a question as to the proper adjustment to the fact of the existence of children's allowances, if these were in effect. This is not a question to be answered simply, since the relation of principles followed in respect of ordinary widows' pensions to workmen's compensation principles must also be taken into account. For the widow who takes up gainful employment, it will be necessary to give attention to the conditions most appropriate for eligibility to benefits, as in the somewhat comparable case of the woman who resumes employment after marriage. The important division of principle between what the Beveridge Report has called guardian's benefit (for the woman who remains in the home) and training benefit (for the widow with no young children), has already been referred to, and merits further study.

6. There remains provision for old age. This also, in terms of existing measures and through contributory improvements, has been examined elsewhere. The desirability of relating it more systematically to disability applies equally for men and for women, but possibly with some adjustments in recognition of the husband as the chief wage-earner. It is a matter of general agreement that if old age pensions can be improved they should become available for women at an earlier age (e.g., at 60 as compared with 65 for men). It is reasonable to balance such an improvement, provided the standard rates are higher than those at present set by the Old Age Pensions Act, against a lower rate for the pension payable to the female partner if husband and wife are both pensionable and living together. It would also be desirable to provide that the double pension should be payable to a married couple, whatever the age of the wife once the husband had reached the pensionable age.

17. WIDOWHOOD: MOTHERS' ALLOWANCES

It might be assumed that if health insurance and employment security follow the gainfully occupied to the end of their lives, this would completely cover the main insurance needs of individuals. Such an assumption would only be partly true, for it would apply only to unattached men or women who go through life without acquiring by marriage or parenthood any family responsibilities. For those who do marry and raise a family, the problem of security for the parent and children who survive the death of the bread-winner can be a growing cause of anxiety. What provision exists in Canada to-day to meet the needs of these survivors whose mainstay of support has been taken away? What better plans can be devised for the future?

There is no integrated programme of widows' or survivors' insurance under government auspices in Canada. Extensive coverage is provided through commercial life insurance companies to the minority of Canadians who can afford such insurance; but even there, in most cases, the settlement for the family on the death of the breadwinner is on a lump-sum basis which is inadequate to meet the continuing needs of the family, helpful as it may be to tide over the transition period. Workmen's compensation, of course, provides survivor's benefits to the families of those who die as a result of industrial accident. The compensation varies between provinces—from a low of $30 to a high of $40 to the surviving parent, and a range of $7.50 a month to $12.00 a month for children, the latter payments usually extending to about six-teen years of age. Very wisely, the workmen's com-pensation laws provide, for the most part, for settle-ments on the basis of maintenance of income, rather than for lump-sum payments. Finally, many of the industrial retirements schemes, as well as municipal, provincial and Dominion government superannuation schemes for civil servants, provide in their plans the option of joint survivorship pension for married wage-earners whose husband or wife is still alive and dependent upon the wage-earner at the time of retirement.

All of such plans put together, it is fairly certain, do not go far, for the low and moderate income families of the country as a whole, towards meeting the security needs of those members who survive the death of the breadwinner. While the number of breadwinners who make some provision for their survivors is probably a good deal larger than the number who make provision for their own old age, the problem in this present instance is the inadequacy of the provision rather than the complete absence of it. It is a tribute to the quality of Canadian family life that most men prefer to buy insurance protection that will benefit their families after they are gone, and take a chance on what happens during their own declining years. At the same time it is a tragic fact that most men are simply not in a position to provide enough in the way of survivor's insurance to maintain their families for more than a very short period of time.

It has already been said above that no state plan of survivors' insurance exists in Canada. That is not to say that the state has taken no cognizance of the situation at all. The federal government has made special provision for one class—namely, the widows and children of military pensioners. It has not, however, assumed any responsibilities for other classes of widows and children, comparable to the responsibility which it has recognized for aged persons under the Old Age Pensions Act. For the most part the matter has been left entirely with the provinces; and, in most cases, these governments have dealt with the question through mothers' pension or allowance legislation, without the co-ordinating influence of federal grants-in-aid or a Dominion statute.

Mothers' Allowances

Mothers' allowances in Canada, *i.e.*, the payment made to widows with dependent children, are a special example not only of the divergencies which arise in a situation in which there is no Dominion legislation or co-ordinating arrangements between provinces[1], but of the complexities and anomalies which arise when a particular category of need is administered on a poor-relief or charitable-grant basis.

One of the difficulties is that of securing Dominion-wide coverage itself. Legislation in this field was passed first by Manitoba and Saskatchewan in 1916 and 1917; other provinces have made provision at varying times up to 1940, the year in which legislation in Quebec (passed in 1938) was brought into force. New Brunswick and Prince Edward Island still have no statutory provision for mothers' allowances at all, although the former province has had an unproclaimed enactment on its books since 1930. A residual of the endeavour to insist on municipal responsibilities in relief matters still remains in the province of Alberta, where 25 per cent of mothers' allowances paid are charged back to the municipalities or residence; elsewhere the provincial governments have assumed all the cost.

There are thus seven separate systems of mothers' allowances in Canada. The needs which they are intended to meet are presumably identical, i.e., the care of dependent children in the event of the death of the main wage-earner. The considerable variation in qualifications for the receipt of the assistance is, therefore, anomalous, and at least some of

---

[1] British Columbia is the only province which has general provision for co-ordinating arrangements with other provinces; Saskatchewan and Ontario have joint arrangements confined to the two provinces.

the qualifications which hinge upon the condition of the parent, rather than the status of the child, are illogical. It is to be noted that widowhood as such is not covered. Widows without children are not eligible for assistance, and assistance where it is granted is really granted to them because they have children. The systems in operation, of course, are not social insurance at all. There is no uniform rate related to contributions previously paid, nor is there contractual or statutory right to benefit. Application has to be made on the ground of insufficiency of income, and the grant is subject to a means test, which itself may also be subject to variation. In six of the seven provinces allowances may be sought by widows who have only one child; in one province allowances can be payable only to a woman with two or more children. In one province the amount for additional children is a flat rate, in some there is a sliding scale, in others adjustments are made on a budget basis, each family being considered more or less separately. In five provinces a maximum amount has been set to the total allowance receivable, and this maximum is $50 in Alberta, $89 plus winter fuel allowance in Manitoba, $80 in Nova Scotia, $75 in Quebec, and $48 in Saskatchewan.

The maximum amount which may be paid to any one-child family is subject to even greater variation. one family is subject to even greater variation. In British Columbia it is $42.50, in Alberta $45 or $47.50 according to the age of the child. In Ontario the maximum is $35, with lower rates set for the small towns and rural areas[1]; in Quebec the figure is $25, with a similar scale according to locality. In Manitoba the maximum is $33 plus winter fuel allowance, but the allowances are sometimes paid

---

[1] In a statement to the Ontario legislature on March 23, 1943, Premier Conant announced the intention of the province "to increase all mothers' allowances after April 1 by twenty per cent.... This means that a mother with one child now receiving $35 a month will... receive $42 a month, and a mother with three children, considered average, now receiving $45 will receive $54 a month."

in kind. Nova Scotia sets a minimum of $15,
whereas in Saskatchewan the maximum is $10.
Saskatchewan's system is really a children's allowance, not a mothers' allowance at all, for no payment
is made on behalf of the parent.

Even with regard to the age of children covered by
mothers' allowances provisions, there is variation
as between the provinces. In Manitoba the allowance ceases at 15, except in special circumstances.
In most of the provinces, the age limit is 16. In
Quebec, provision is made for continuation of the
allowance beyond the sixteenth birthday of the child
to permit completion of the school term, while in
British Columbia by reason of a recent amendment
provision is made for extension of the age limit to as
high as 18.

Some provinces have definite regulations as to the
amount of earnings which the mother may have and
still be eligible for allowances; in others the matter is
left to the judgment of the administrator.

Largely because the facilities have already been
organized to deal with the needs of the unemployed,
medical care within certain limits is available to
mothers' allowances recipients in British Columbia,
Manitoba and Ontario, and in some cities in other
provinces. No special provision either for the
mother or the children is made in other provinces,
except in so far as they would be eligible as non-
paying patients at hospital or outpatient clinics.
There is in fact an indeterminate amount of supplementation to many of the recipients of mothers'
allowances.

Administrative Deficiencies

It is obvious that under these conditions a great
deal depends on the methods and adequacy of
administration. A means test or budget system
may be the vehicle of a rigid and restrictive sub-

sistence payment, a rule-of-thumb assessment, or a careful and desirable adjustment to particular needs. Whatever may be done in the direction of statutory change, the need for competent personnel for the investigation and administration of mothers' allowances will always remain important.

It will be seen from the above that many of the same disadvantageous features which have been noted as attaching to non-contributory old age assistance apply in the area of mothers' allowances. Provincial legislation is full of the same type of restrictions concerning citizenship, residence, property, ownership, income limits, etc. In some respects mothers' allowances show even more limitations. Provision is made almost everywhere for moral judgments as to the suitability of the woman to raise her children. Restrictions are frequently provided through administrative practice, if not through legislation, on the payment of allowances to women who are judged immoral. In one respect, namely, the lack of legislative uniformity within the provinces, the situation is worse than with respect to old age pensions. On the other hand, in the field of administration, it can be said that this is on the whole more lenient than for pensions; in two or three provinces, a social welfare approach is characteristic. Means-testing is somewhat less rigid, and the same can be said of deductions from the maximum allowances payable due to alternative sources of income. The reason for this greater flexibility is probably due, first, to the fact that the system does not operate within the strait-jacket of audit and financial control imposed by federal authority, and secondly, that the mothers' allowance administration has in most provinces been related fairly closely to the framework of public welfare administration as a whole, rather than isolated under separate commissions, or under Workmen's Compensation Boards.

There is, of course, great need for improving and co-ordinating coverage as between the various provinces. For example, not only the children of deceased breadwinners need the protection afforded by this legislation. From the point of view of the status of children as dependents, serious disability of the husband may have results on income almost as unfortunate as in families where the husband is incapacitated. Quebec and British Columbia are exceptional in providing for special allowances for the husband himself in such cases. If provision for incapacity in this way is desirable, however, it would be reasonable to extend it to cases in which the father is in a sanatorium for tuberculosis, is insane, or the inmate of a penitentiary.[1] In the other direction there is need for co-ordination of the conditions which must be regarded as comparable to widowhood so far as the need of dependent children is concerned. Should deserted and divorced women, therefore, be considered? Should not unmarried mothers warrant some assistance in cases where they assume the full responsibility for their children? This is done in some provinces, but by no means uniformly in all of them.[2]

Presumably there is or ought to be some common principle with respect to these categories of mothers and children which has equal validity in all provinces. This being the case, the objective in an over-all social security plan should be twofold. First, in point of coverage, (1) to extend non-

[1] Allowances are paid to mothers whose husband is in a penitentiary, in British Columbia and Saskatchewan. All provinces now recognize eligibility where the father is confined to a mental hospital. Specific provision for payment where the father is in a tuberculosis sanatorium is made in Ontario, Nova Scotia, and Saskatchewan; and the latter province also recognizes cases where the father is in an institution for incurable diseases.

[2] British Columbia provides for allowances to a mother who has been divorced or deserted for a period of two years and has been unable to obtain support from her husband. In this province also, eligibility is extended to an unmarried mother who co-habitated with the man in the *bona fide* belief that she was legally married to him.

contributory mothers' allowances to those provinces where they do not exist at present, (2) to iron out the inequalities between the various provinces so far as conditions of eligibility are concerned, (3) to eliminate nuisance restrictions on eligibility, and (4) to establish greater uniformity between the provinces as to the variety of categories eligible under the allowance scheme.

Secondly, rates should be revised. The allowance levels, so far as payments of assistance are concerned, should be raised to a point that in all provinces will at least approach a minimum subsistence level. There is a wide variation at the present time in the average allowances paid to mothers' allowances families in the different provinces. The following table, of average allowances, computed per family, is somewhat influenced by differing family composition, but fairly clearly demonstrates inequality of practice:

Nova Scotia	$ 28.55
Quebec	26.64
Ontario	28.91
Manitoba	35.79
Saskatchewan	13.77
Alberta	22.96
British Columbia	39.19

When these allowances, in turn, are compared with those paid to the family of a soldier through the Dependents' Allowance Board (which really establishes a form of wartime mothers' allowance on account of enforced separation from the breadwinner), the margin by which these civilian mothers' allowances fall short of a minimum level of adequacy can easily be seen. For example, a mother with one child under dependents' allowance receives not less than $35 for herself and $12 for her first child, plus $20 assigned pay from her husband. A moment's reflection on these two contrasting scales of assistance will suffice to mark the inadequacies of present provincial mothers' allowance legislation, and the need for a post-war adjustment of the situation.

18. SURVIVORS' INSURANCE

Much can be done, and needs to be done, if we are to bring our present system of assistance to mothers and children, deprived of the support of the bread-winner through a variety of reasons, to an adequate level of maintenance which Canadians can regard as satisfactory. The first point to note, however, is that if the recommendation made in this report with respect to family allowances is carried out, the need for this particular form of public assistance to mothers of children, will be materially diminished. Children's allowances will largely take care of the needs of children in the family unit, both inside and outside of insurance. Their existence moreover would draw proper attention to the plight of the widow if she needed assistance, and make it at least administratively simpler to provide for her.

The remaining problem for the future will be to provide an income on the basis of security main-tenance to enable the widow to maintain herself while looking after her family. So far as provision is organized, in accordance with the proposals in this report, for total permanent disability and for old age insurance, it would not be difficult to extend these insurances in such a way as to provide sur-vivors' benefit when the breadwinner, instead of becoming permanently disabled or permanently aged, passes away. It has already been suggested that for a married couple, or for an aged couple on retirement pension, benefit might reasonably be paid in the amount of $30 for the insured person, and $15 for the dependent spouse. If the dependent spouse, in either of these cases, were to die first, the disability or retirement benefit for the insured person could be continued at $30. Likewise, it would seem to be fair that if the insured persons were to die first, the survivor's benefit should continue at $30.

In both of these cases, the benefits would be supplemented by children's allowances in respect to the number of children under the maximum age specified in the fund. The total ˙situation can be clarified by means of illustration. A married man, under insurance, with two children, who becomes permanently disabled or who has to retire on account of age, would receive his old age benefit of $30, a supplementary benefit for his wife of $15, and a continuation of the children's allowance in respect of each child which he had received during his working years. (It is suggested elsewhere in this report that tentatively the children's allowances might be set at rates varying from $5.00 to $12.50 according to the age of the child). If death intervenes in this family, the survivor in either case would continue to receive $30 a month—the man as a continuation of his disability or retirement pension, the wife as a replacement of her supplementary benefit by survivor's benefit.

To the extent, therefore, that the recommendations made in this report with respect to family allowances and other types of insurance are carried out, the grafting of survivor's benefit on to the insurance programme for disability and old age would very largely make mothers' allowances in their present form unnecessary. Assuming that survivors' benefits are not provided in the manner suggested, but that children's allowances are provided (or, alternatively, assuming that the widow is ineligible for survivor's benefits because of the fact that her husband was not an insured person), there would still seem to be little case for mothers' allowances in their present form, since the proper way to supplement the children's allowances, in order to provide maintenance for the widow, would be through a reformed system of public assistance. In other words, if children's allowances are accepted as a desirable feature of the Canadian social security structure, mothers' allowances, as they exist under present legislation, would wither away and disappear. This can be understood best by consideration of the effect that the inauguration of children's allowances would have, for example, in the Province of Saskatchewan, where the allowances paid under the Mothers' Allowance Act are intended only for the children, and assistance for the mother comes by way of supplementation from the public assistance authority. Likewise, when the aid-to-dependent-children programme under the Social Security Act in the United States was inaugurated, providing money grants to dependent children in their own homes, the structure of mothers' allowance legislation as we know it in Canada soon began to disappear, and any supplementation of the aid to dependent children that seemed necessary to maintain the family budget came through assistance to the mother herself from the public welfare authority.

Widows Able To Take Up Employment

The widow who has one child or more, and whose constant presence in the home is essential for their proper care, would be provided for by a pension which is in effect, to use Beveridge's term, a "guardian benefit". The case of the young widow with no children (or even with a child which she is able to maintain satisfactorily from the income received from her employment) is in a different category. Under the proposals here made, if her husband at the time of his death were an insured person, she would presumably draw the survivor's benefit on the same basis as the widow with children. But it would seem entirely desirable that such pensions are available subject only to attendance at the employment office within an appropriate period to investigate the possibilities of training for gainful occupation. There might be an upper age limit to the condition, e.g., fifty. Other conditions have been suggested, for example, that the rate should be relatively high for an initial period of six months or a year, and at a low level thereafter. The higher rate would serve to ease the shock of the immediate transition; the lower rate would be more of an inducement to enter the labour market. If, of course, the pension rate as a minimum is low in amount, there will be less scope for adjustment; and equally little incentive to live on the pension in idleness.

The problem of a pension for a widow of potential earning age being relatively high is actually only likely to arise if the pension for the woman is generous, and children's benefits are also available. This is the situation, for example, with regard to pensions for the wives of casualties in the present war. The civil case under ordinary social insurance would be provided for, so far as their children are concerned, through children's allowances. But these would not be additions to the income, but a carry-over from a previous status. There does not seem to be any valid reason for exempting the pensions for ex-servicemen's widows from the adjustment which would be called for in the event of a national system of children's allowances being paid.

Provision for Orphans

Finally, there is the case of the child where the mother has predeceased the father, and on the father's death the child becomes a full orphan. The question arises as to whether or not, in cases where the father is insured, a survivor's benefit should be paid in respect of the child, on some basis similar to that provided under workmen's compensation laws in Canada. This would be a logical procedure to suggest if children's allowances were not provided in accordance with the recommendations of this report. If children's allowances are provided, however, the question arises as to whether or not the allowance thus paid should be supplemented by survivor's benefit at the rate of $15 per month per child.

There are arguments on both sides of this question; but the balance of the argument would seem to justify payment of survivor's benefit of $15 a month to orphaned children of insured persons where there is no surviving parent. This benefit, together with the children's allowances which would be continued, would be sufficient to provide full maintenance to the provincial or local child-caring authorities (in most provinces the Children's Aid Societies) which would, under provincial legislation, assume guardianship of the child in most instances under prevailing child welfare laws.

If the orphaned child's parent was not an insured person, the child welfare authorities would have to supplement the children's allowance through payments which, under existing legislation, come from the municipalities or the province concerned. The payment or non-payment of survivor's benefit to orphaned children of insured persons in the circumstances described is perhaps not actually very important, because in many provinces the existing arrangements are already adequate to provide financial security for such a child. In some provinces, however, this is not yet by any means the case. Regardless of this fact, there is little question that payment of survivor's benefit to orphaned children of insured parents would greatly reassure the working man who is left with the responsibility of young children on the death of his wife, and is concerned that they should be properly provided for in the event that he too should die. Whichever method is adopted, there would be little difference in the total burden on public funds since the question involved is really whether payment shall come from

public funds of the province and municipality, or
whether it shall come through the insurance as part
of social security. In the long run, probably the
latter is preferable.

19. FUNERAL BENEFITS.

In any family group in which relationships have been at all happy, the death of any member means a social separation which requires a major adjustment on the part of those who remain. But it is in addition one of the heaviest of the emergency expenditures for all families whose means or savings are not large.

Even the death of a small child, especially if there has been any previous illness, may dislocate the family budget which is marginal or near-marginal. The death of the mother is of course much more serious. In purely economic terms it brings problems of wrestling with the household and clothing budget, besides direct funeral expenses. The difficulties for the father in making adequate plans for supervision and training of his children may be acute. A housekeeper adequate to take the place of a mother may be securable only by heavy additional family expenditure.

If it is the husband who dies, this means to the wife and children the loss of the family's mainstay; a mainstay in both the social and economic sense. The more completely the man has carried his responsibilities, the more at a loss his family is to plan without him. It is all too frequent in low-income and even moderate-income families that debts are contracted over the period of illness. The mother may be forced to move to cheaper quarters, to delay medical care to members of the family for whom this was planned, perhaps to move to another home with changes in schools, churches, separation from friends, or alternatively to face the dislocation of the family through the inclusion of boarders or roomers. On top of all this may be the necessity to apply for help from some source, and the prospect of some years of substandard living for herself and her family.

It is in the context of these special anxieties that funeral expenses as a drain on the budget must be viewed. It is true that many families strive hard to take out insurance policies, or make small periodical payments through industrial assurance schemes, against such events. But it is also unfortunately true that most of the policies thus secured are comparatively small; with the result that the greater part of them may be swallowed up by the costs attendant on a funeral, and debts and other expenses which may come to light at this time.

There can be little question, therefore, that if it were possible to include a moderate funeral benefit in a social insurance scheme, even if scaled to meet only the most immediate undertaking expenses, it would be a decided contribution. The need to consider this is strengthened by the doubts which are very widespread as to whether funeral expenses in Canada are not excessive in relation to the services rendered.

It is possible that the heavy strictures which have been placed upon reliance on private life insurance policies as applied to wage-earner groups in Britain, are not valid in the same degree for this country. Even if the case for adopting the alternative of a comprehensive national scheme were only one-quarter as strong as in Britain, however, it would still recommend itself. There have been many inquiries into the deficiencies of British industrial assurance, and the two most recently made agree in criticizing (a) the excessive proportion of administrative costs, and (b) the excessive number of policies which clients are forced to allow to lapse.

According to a sample covering all the main companies, costs including collection management, dividends and income tax amount to 37·5 per cent of the total premium revenue. A substantial part of this is undoubtedly due to the high cost of collection through the retention of a great number of

household-visiting agents, a system which is far
less extensive in Canada, where collections are much
more commonly made through industrial payrolls.
The survey showed also that as many as two-thirds
of all policies which were issued lapsed before completion; and of these more than one-half were
forfeited completely (because of interruption in
payments, etc.) without any cash surrender value.
This is evidence, of course, not necessarily of any
unscrupulousness on the part of the companies but
of the fact that at the rates prevailing most families
attempted to take on a provision for the future
which was too great for their incomes to bear.

The Beveridge Report recognizes that "the business of industrial assurance could not have been
built up without collectors" of this type, but adds
that "it cannot be admitted that weekly collection
of premiums is a permanent indispensible requirement for securing regular voluntary contributions
from persons of limited means". At another point
the report states: "As compared with this, the
cost of administering a funeral grant as part of
social insurance would be negligible. On the contribution side, it would mean adding one or two
pence to the value of the insurance stamp, which
would have to be affixed in any case to the insurance
document; on the benefit side it would mean paying
one claim only for each person in respect of a fact
in which there could be no doubt and which must
be formally recorded by the state for other purposes . . . there can be no justification for requiring the public who need insurance for direct funeral
expenses to pay the heavy tax involved in industrial
assurance."

Similar considerations undoubtedly apply in Canada. Funeral-expense benefits are not the most
urgent of all social insurance requirements; but they
would be one of the simplest and cheapest to add
to almost any scheme of wide coverage. The

contributory basis would be widely welcomed.

It is comparatively easy to work out their cost under a national contributory scheme. It may be assumed that the basic rate, as in Workmen's Compensation allowances for fatalities, would be $100. For children and juveniles rates would be lower, say $25 and $65. A projection of existing death rates at appropriate age groups indicates the total number of funerals to be provided for in a representative year (say 1945) as 121,500 in all. The benefits would total $10,600,000 at the rates mentioned, or less than one dollar per capita of the population. On this basis, the rates for insured contributors would not need to be more than seven to ten cents a week.

If economies had to be considered for this addition to social insurance, it might be feasible to limit the grant to adults only, while for children arrangements might be made for the commutation of a few weeks of children's allowances before they ceased. It might be decided to exclude older persons over 60 for some time after the commencement of the scheme. There is no particularly strong case for extensive limitation of coverage, however. Funeral benefit would be economical because it is easily administered, proof is automatic, and the contributions required very small.

One final point should perhaps be made. At the time of death of a respected member of a family, both convention and genuine sentiment combine to make this an occasion for generous expenditure on funeral arrangements. The rate set for the funeral benefit should not be interpreted as setting the limit for these expenditures or condemning families to routine standardization. Families would still be free to spend more than the grant if their resources and desires dictated. But some indication from the size of the grant that undertakers' charges are frequently exorbitant should not be regrettable.

PART V

OUTLINES OF A COMPREHENSIVE SYSTEM

20. OUTLINES OF A COMPREHENSIVE SYSTEM

To draw together the various threads of the report it will be helpful at this stage to review the broad outlines of a comprehensive scheme such as might be constructed in Canada. It will be understood that this is necessarily tentative, and that some of the rates and procedures referred to are illustrative rather than recommendations. It will be easier, however, to see the relation of each part to the whole, and also the main administrative requirements, in terms of such a projection.

Set forth in somewhat the same way as schemes of other countries were summarized in Section 4, a possible Canadian system would include the elements shown in the schedule on the next page. An important distinction running throughout the whole scheme is that between the universal risks, which are applicable to all persons, or to all persons of working age; and the "employment" group of risks, which are applicable and insurable for wage-earners only. The national investment programme (dealt with in Section 5) is of course not a part of the ordinary social security structure, but it is included in the schedule to complete the post-war employment picture.

The "employment" group of insurances are the most familiar for Canada because unemployment insurance is already established, and workmen's compensation has an even longer history. It is assumed that workmen's compensation will be substantially unchanged, though subject to extension and probably a greater measure of standardization as between provinces. As proposed in Section 7, unemployment benefits would be raised for claimants with adult dependents, and the upper categories would measure up to the assistance minimum standard. Sickness cash benefits would be closely assimilated to unemployment benefit scales; as also would maternity benefit rates, subject to the possibility of a minimum rate being established for this class of benefit as a special measure. The employment group of benefits would thus be largely related to prevailing wage scales. Whether special "training benefits" should carry a maintenance grant for some or all classes of recipients, or should merely be free training, has not been submitted to any decision in the present report. Nor has any limit been placed on the duration for which unconditional or unemployment assistance should be payable, although it has been suggested that this grant should be lower, possibly ten per cent less, than the benefit categories to which formerly insured persons belonged. If special "assistance projects" are instituted, it is assumed that wages will be at a low maintenance level, and might vary according to regional conditions.

It is proposed that the income-maintenance benefits payable under the universal insurances would be principally at a standard rate, rather than dependent on past income or wages, or the actual amount of premium or contribution paid. Pensions for permanent disability, for widows, and for old age retirement would be assimilated in rates and conditions. If these were based on the assistance minimum standard, a feasible rate would be $30 monthly for the breadwinner, $15 for his wife, in the case of permanent disability or old age retirement, the two persons together securing a minimum income of $45. (A single woman or widow would of course receive the standard-unit rate.) A variation on the standard rate in the case of widows has been suggested (e.g., of $40) for the first year only. For old age retirement pensions it would be possible to introduce the feature of making somewhat higher rates available if the claim is deferred beyond the minimum pensionable age. This would be sixty-five for men and sixty for women; but with a wife's pension becoming available

Risk or benefit
I. UNIVERSAL RISKS
A. *All insurable population*
Medical care (services).............................
Child maintenance (allowances)......................
Funeral benefits...................................
B. *All gainfully occupied* (and adult dependents)
Permanent disability (pensions).....................
Widows, orphans (pensions)..........................
Old-age retirement (pensions).......................
II. EMPLOYMENT RISKS
A. *All normal gainfully employed*
National investment programme......................
Training and guidance facilities.....................
Unemployment assistance projects....................
B. *All employees*
Unemployment insurance (benefits)...................
Sickness benefits (cash)............................
Maternity benefits.................................
Industrial disability...............................
Fatal accidents, etc., (industrial).................

(on the husband's reaching sixty-five) no matter what her age. For funeral expenses, a standard rate of $100 has been suggested, with rates of $65 and $25

Source of funds	Mode of administration
ributory...........	Dominion-provincial co-operation (contributions) Provincial administration (services) Appropriate techniques for provincial co-ordination.
revenue...........	Dominion administration.
,ributory...........	(Related to one or several of the other insurances).
;ributory...........	Dominion administration.
;ributory...........	Dominion administration.
,ributory (Tax revenue r transitional deficits)	Dominion administration.
revenue...........	Dominion direction, co-ordinated joint programme
revenue...........	Dominion, and federal-provincial schemes.
revenue...........	Dominion and provincial schemes.
tributory...........	Dominion administration.
tributory...........	Dominion administration (related to unemployment insurance).
tributory...........	Dominion administration (related to unemployment insurance).
tributory (employers)	Provincial administration (Workmen's Compensation Boards).
,tributory (employers)	Provincial administration (Workmen's Compensation Boards).

for juveniles and infants. Children's allowances
complete the scheme, assuming a variation according
to the age of the child. Sub-minimum rates, as a

concession to the difficulty of setting too high a rate at the outset are recommended as superior to any alternative which would involve deferment; with one proposal for variation left optional. This latter would be a restriction of payment in respect of the first child to families which were in receipt of one or other of the insurance benefits, or of public assistance, the allowance still being in this case a wholly tax-financed grant.

The net effect of these benefits would be to lay the foundation for a national minimum, which would be particularly welcome for rural areas. For urban and employee groups, some insured persons would face a reduction of income in the event of disability or related contingencies; a few would move up to the minimum standard. Some further commentary on the relevance of the flat rate as distinct from the graduated benefit may be helpful, and this is undertaken below.

Applying to the "employment" benefits, there would be a waiting period (e.g., of three days for sickness cash benefit) where appropriate; and qualifying periods (which have already been strictly laid down in the case of unemployment insurance). For the universal risks it is an important decision as to how soon benefits should be payable; but not a question dependent purely upon actuarial considerations as has been presumed in some countries. Whatever contribution arrangements are made, in any comprehensive system of social insurance, the current aged and disabled and others receiving benefits are in effect supported by the current population of working age, subject to such supplementation from government funds as is considered desirable. Whether or not benefits can be made payable immediately depends on whether the nation as a whole is prepared to contribute and vote the funds for the purpose, not on a prolonged period of accumulation. To ease the transition period, however, particularly as regards the transformation of old age pensions, there are several devices, including the gradual removal of the means test, and the gradual reduction of the pensionable age, which may be applied, and the alternatives in this respect have been reviewed.

Standard vs. Graduated Benefits

The system thus resulting would contain three elements: graduated scales and benefits for the "employment" insurances, flat-rate or standard benefits for the long-term insurances, and a special arrangement, christened "degressive," for medical care. The latter would involve subsidy, according to capacity to pay, at the contribution end; equally, there would be neither limited nor graduated benefit, but in effect distribution according to need, for the medical services made available. Especially if separated altogether from the income-maintenance insurances, i.e., leaving sickness benefit to be provided by a separate scheme (preferably integrated with unemployment insurance), this would be a logical arrangement.

One of the arguments for the retention of benefits graduated according to income or wages, rather than reducing all income-maintenance insurances to a standard basis, is that these alone are appropriate for the proper handling of temporary situations. The purpose of unemployment benefit, and of sickness benefit which is similar, is to tide over a period of interrupted earning-power which is supposedly short. The supposition is that the insured person will return to employment at more or less his former earnings level. He will not be able to change his standard of living (e.g., secure different housing accommodation) in a short time. Even a graduated rate is lower than full earnings (commonly half): a flat rate would probably be too low for the higher

earning groups, and the object of protecting the
family budget from too severe a blow would not be
attained. In Canada, however, this argument is
reinforced by a different consideration. The multiple
regions which make up the vast territory of the
country are characterized by several wage differentials, and these are difficult to change. In considerable degree, it is true, regional differences are
themselves a reflection of difference in wage levels.
Costs or standards of living in a particular area are
lower than elsewhere because there are more of the
lower-paid occupational and industrial groups in this
area. It is of course desirable to raise the standards,
or to increase the productivity and income of all the
poorer areas. But it is not reasonable to attempt to
do so wholly through a social insurance system.

From the administrative point of view, a single
flat rate is beset by difficulties unless or until these
regional and occupational variations can be smoothed
out. It may not be high enough to offer real benefit
to the upper wage groups: whereas incomes close to
or above minimum subsistence standards would not
be far from the level of earnings of unskilled workers.
The result is that, particularly as applied to unemployment insurance, there may be an incentive
for the unemployed man to remain on benefit rather
than to take a job. A graduated scale of benefits
insures automatically that for all wage classes income payments from the unemployment insurance
fund are less in amount than normal earnings—provided that no dependents' allowances for children
are paid as part of regular unemployment benefit.

It should be clear that accepting a benefit scale
thus graduated to a series of wage levels does not
condemn the country or the social security system
to perpetual low standards. Anything that can be
done to raise wage levels generally, or the wages of
the lowest groups, will react favourably throughout
the whole system simply by bringing more insurable

persons into the upper levels, an eminently desirable
event.   Indeed the existence of a scale is more of a
safeguard in a progressive situation than a single
rate would be.[1]

In contrast to most of the employment risks,
those of the disability group are relatively long-
term. Payments in respect of disability, widowhood, old age, are essentially continuous. Since
they are continuous, they are relatively costly, and
from the national point of view it is not possible to
set an objective higher than the maintenance of the
minimum. (So far as child dependents are involved,
children's allowances are the best method of introducing some flexibility.) Moreover, they relate to a
situation in which it is reasonable to expect some
adjustment to be made. Something of a transition
towards a more common standard as one traverses
the life cycle, ought to be justifiable. The situation
is perhaps clearest for the group (an exceptional
rather than inevitable group) who become disability pensioners. These persons do not pass to
this particular status without careful certification;
incidentally, they have less chance of changing their
status in some way detrimental to the insurance
fund than a normal wage-earner. This is even more
clearly evident for the person whose claim to old age
insurance rests on the test of being 60 or 65. It is
arguable of course that for these classes of risks,
more liable in later life, there is greater individual
opportunity of making extra provision to supplement the minimum that insurances will provide.
For wage-earners and rural groups, however, these
possibilities must be deflated by reference to the
limitations of their incomes. The straightforward
case is that a minimum, obtainable as of right and in
the company of all other citizens, is immeasurably

---

[1] It is equally true that a graduated scale would not prevent a downward movement in all incomes. But as has been reiterated before, the
frontal attack on depression or low productivity, whether nationally or
regionally, must be made by policies outside the insurances.

better than uncertain aid from relatives, charitable
institutions or the state. For those dependent only
on the insurances, regional differences may still mean
that some persons with e.g. retirement pensions,
secure a somewhat greater purchasing-power if they
happen to reside in relatively low-cost districts, but
this circumstance will be of much smaller or negligible importance in affecting the mobility of labour
than would be true of e.g. unemployment benefits.
The exceptional case is that of a widow's pension
receivable by a younger woman without children
(Section 13).

The Cycle of Coverage

As a form of summary, some of the main features
of the scope of a comprehensive social insurance
system can now be visualized as they might apper-
tain to particular individuals or families in the
working population. To do so is, among other
things, to appreciate better the coherence of relationship which must be sought for an efficient set of
legislative measures, whether conceived as being
placed on the statute book together, or developed
over a period of time in ordered sequence. Taken
in conjunction with the qualifications considered in
other sections, it will help to make clear also the
functions of social security legislation—what social
insurance may reasonably be designed to do, as
well as what it should not be asked to do.

Perhaps the most important point from which
to start is the situation under health insurance,
if this is placed on the comprehensive basis argued
herein as the most desirable. Practically all classes,
whether of employee status or not, whether rural
or urban, and all members of the family, whether
breadwinner, wife or dependent, will have more or
less immediate access to medical care. Public
health measures, of course, have always, at least

in theory, been so available; but not the services of the practitioner. What insurance will do is to strengthen the relationship between social insurance in this field and the "social assistance" branch of care, which in this case has already evolved beyond the charitable stage to recognition as a high-standard public service. There would be more room for and more response to health education, early diagnosis, contagious disease prevention, maternal and infant care, more rational distribution of hospital facilities, and so on. Medical relief (in Ontario, British Columbia and some of the larger cities) is, of course, an assistance service at lower level than that of contributory insurance. It might seem desirable to preserve and improve medical relief provision, as a complement to the new coverage secured through health insurance, in much the same way as public assistance is retained as a necessary supplement to unemployment insurance. The parallel, however, is not a true one. Health insurance is eminently adaptable to the broadest possible coverage, and it should desirably replace, or absorb, medical relief schemes as soon as possible. The residual application of assistance principles which might be justified is in the rather more specialized types of medical treatment (and perhaps income assistance) for e.g., disability cases which it is difficult or inappropriate to include under ordinary health insurance and disability insurance, supplementary services of rehabilitation which might be offered to handicapped workers, and so forth.

An important feature of the health insurance coverage would be that the amount of medical service received would have no relation to the wage rate or income of the head of the family. The branch of security provision which would be so related, for all periods of sickness involving absence from work comparable to unemployment, would be the weekly cash benefit paid to the wage-earner families. With children's allowances as an independent (or possibly contingent) part of social security coverage, there would be no problem of income maintenance so far as the support of children during periods of the father's sickness was concerned. If there were no children's allowances, however, it is clear that problems of inadequacy might easily arise if the period of sickness were at all prolonged, in spite of medical care being available.

Unemployment insurance already exists and it is not necessary to sketch in any detail the way in which it operates. Some of the points most relevant to this review should be mentioned, however. Within the insured population certain groups may visualize a different course of events. Young workers can anticipate receiving only very small sums for maintenance if they are unemployed; but they would have on the one hand access to training schemes, and on the other reasonable expectations of improving their wage levels and therefore moving to higher benefit-classes as they grew older and secured more experience. Subject to questions of the basic adequacy of benefit rates, the father of the family whose employment is its main support has assurance that unemployment will not immediately cut off income altogether. The woman who is a wage-earner, whether married or single, is included in the scheme solely by reason of being a wage-earner and not by any definition of dependent status. There is a likelihood that, particularly if she is a married wage-earner, the duration of her earning life may be anticipated as comparatively short. This does not, however, prejudice her right to social security coverage in respect of possible disability or widowhood, and also old age insurance. The normal case would be, assuming her husband is gainfully occupied, that she is automatically insured by virtue of his contributions.

In the event of sickness, for the ordinary wage-earner this temporary disability is recognized as having the same consequences for the family income as unemployment, and the man is entitled (subject to reasonable "waiting period") to draw a cash sickness benefit. Its comparability with unemployment insurance is recognized by its being on the same scale; in other words, there will be a series of possible rates of sickness benefits as there are for unemployment benefits now. If the man is a farmer he will have full medical care; the same would be true of the non-working wife of an insured wage-earner. The married woman in insured wage-earning employment will be entitled to a cash benefit in the event of sickness; which is justifiable on the assumption that her earnings are normally a requisite part of the family income. The rate would again be proportionate to wages. The working mother (in any reasonably insurable employment) would secure special income-maintenance to bridge over the contingency of maternity. The children of all families would be covered for medical attention so far as this was required, through the services of a practitioner (i.e. as distinct from such health and nutrition services as they might receive through schools, health units, public health sources, etc.).

For a considerable part of the population these would be the main hazards encountered. The problem next in importance is that of the possibility of disablement in some permanent fashion. This might strike any member of the family, but it would naturally be more serious if it occurred for the principal earner, usually the husband. While the incidence of permanent incapacity, industrial or non-industrial, is considerably lighter than the incidence of either temporary ill-health or of unemployment, there are no particular limits as to the time at which such an emergency might occur. The procedure which would be favoured for the marginal cases, where the extent of incapacity was uncertain, has been indicated elsewhere. If the disability were finally declared permanent, however, there would be certain important consequences in terms of social security coverage. Whether the person were of employee or self-employed status, medical treatment services would be available, and ordinary medical care would continue after the crucial period of accident (or whatever else might be involved) and the immediate recovery period. The incapacitated man, now fully withdrawn from employment, would go on to a pension at a flat rate. This rate would be somewhere near or above the middle of the present unemployment benefit scales. In conformity with these scales, if he were a single man the rate would be smaller than if he were married. In conformity with these scales also, there would be no provision for child dependents, in benefit terms, but childrens' allowances would continue (or be augmented).

For wage-earner families suffering from this misfortune, there would be a transition stage in the relation between wages and security rates. It would not all be in one direction. For the lowest wage groups it would mean some movement upwards so far as their allowances compared with unemployment benefit. This is justifiable in terms of the attempt to hold a reasonable minimum standard, the pressure against which would obviously be much greater for a family condemned to the loss of the earning-power of its chief member. Workers who had formerly been in the upper wage scale would have to face a lowering of their maintenance rates; this would be a misfortune admittedly, but a much smaller one than having no maintenance provision whatsoever. In practice, a high proportion of disabled wage-earners would probably be beneficiaries under workmen's compensation, therefore securing graduated retirement amounts. Some of them would still be available for employment.   The measure of improvement would be greatest for the poorer rural classes for many of whom a guaranteed minimum would now replace no provision at all.   Somewhat similar conditions would be true in regard to old age retirement.   The arguments from a broad national point of view, for a modest minimum, provided it represented some improvement over present rates, have already been stated; and regional differentials at this stage would not engender any serious inequities.

The economic distress of the family broken by the death of the father, whether an urban or rural worker, would be tempered by pension for the mother, and a funeral grant for burial expenses. Some income for maintenance of children, unlike the situation at present, would continue (through children's allowances) even though the breadwinner's wages ceased to come into the home.   In the agricultural family, if the farm could still be maintained in operation by surviving members of the family, the pension might represent a greater contribution than under urban conditions.   Provision against the effects on the family of the death of the wife is much harder to deal with through insurance since the case in which an income-maintenance problem is involved is exceptional. But many cases of disability could be covered.   And provision for orphans would be measurably strength⁺ ened, both through children's allowances, and arrangements for transmutation of survivors' pensions.

In all of these situations there would remain scope for additional services, and considerable leeway for individual insurance provision.   It might well be expected, certainly in the circumstances of a successful full-employment policy, that habits of thrift and saving would be stimulated, both by better acquaintance with contributory techniques and by the existence of nuclear amounts on which to build annuities, life insurance policies, and the like, for some of the longer-term items. Differences in this respect would remain. It would not be reasonable to expect a social insurance system to iron out all the inequalities of income-distribution except so far as basic minima are concerned. The chances of supplementing income in times of distress are in any case unequal, roughly in proportion to the wage and income scale, whatever may be done in organizing attention to the fundamental family hazards through contributory techniques.

21. CONSTITUTIONAL AND
ADMINISTRATIVE DECISIONS

Adequate provision for social welfare matters in Canada, it has been recognized from the outset, depends not only on legislation but on the machinery of government. In a federal state, these include not only the quality and techniques of governmental activities, but the division of responsibilities and the resources to fulfil them. The Royal Commission on Dominion-Provincial Relations, in exercising its mandate to focus attention on the financial relationships between the federal and provincial governments, was well aware that in doing so it was considering the base for future social legislation as well. Since cities and municipalities depend on provincial authority, the possibilities of reorganization or development of a number of important welfare functions, (particularly, but by no means solely, those concerned with unemployment assistance), hinge in their turn on effective arrangements for federal-provincial division of labour being established. The social insurances are a major part of the social services of public welfare services in the widest sense, setting the broad outlines of the national framework, and as such they are of primary concern to the senior governments. The role of local services, urban and rural is an important subject in itself, which cannot be entered upon here,[1] but their future depends vitally on the existence or absence of a social insurance system. The significance of such a system for the citizen body generally, and the magnitude of the sums involved are so great, however, that a paramount consideration is the constitutional freedom of the federal government to lead and co-ordinate. Implicit in this is realization of the most desirable

---

[1] A memorandum is projected as a supplement to the present report, which will deal particularly with provincial and public welfare services, as well as other matters complementary to social security legislation.

methods of provincial participation. But the need
for clarity of decision on both must not be minimized.

Considerations to be Weighed

To take the constitutional decisions, i.e., the mode
of implementing legislation, first, the proper method
of legislation for social insurance is not merely a
matter of what is good law. It is a matter of administrative efficiency and of building a national structure
appropriate to the needs. This situation has already
been discussed for the special case of health insurance.
It is clearly more important still for the requirements
of all the social insurances as a whole. Even in the
field of unemployment, there is as yet no indisputable
coincidence between requirements or undertakings
on the one hand and constitutional authorization on
the other. The Dominion government might be
willing to inaugurate a sickness cash benefit scheme,
or a programme of unemployment assistance over
and above unemployment insurance. But there is
no certainty in the present state of the law that it
would be fully entitled to do so. Other examples
could be added. The Canadian situation, in short,
is not like that of Britain or New Zealand; it is more
like that of Australia, where, as already indicated,
constitutional clarification is regarded as one of the
first necessities for social security organization as
part of the reconstruction programme.

A system of administration must obviously be
worked out in which the federal and provincial
governments will have clear understanding as to
their respective responsibilities. On the revenue
side the problem is not only one of financial contributions, but of economical collection machinery.
On the distributive side, it is not only the organization of services, benefits and accounting which is
involved; bound up with it are all the possibilities
of development of constructive policies ancillary to

the insurances, and other possibilities of raising welfare standards throughout the Dominion.

Considering only the social insurances *per se* there are two primary needs. It is necessary to avoid the possibilities of overlapping systems, inter-provincial obstacles to the movement of labour, unbalanced incentives to the movement of industry, and pressures or manipulations set up where there are alternatives of provincial or federal benefits. Difficulties of this type were amply illustrated by the unemployment relief experience of the thirties, as presented successively to municipal, provincial and federal governments; and some of the difficulties of division between financial and administrative responsibility have been illustrated in the case of old age pensions legislation.[2] The other need is a basis for collecting and administering contributions, on a nation-wide scale, with maximum efficiency. As already suggested, there should be no difficulty if this basis is a combination of several different methods, if the methods themselves are convenient and justifiable.

The task is therefore to visualize the system as a whole, and to integrate the component units with proper regard for regional and administrative decentralization. It is not essential for every unit to be Dominion-operated. But it would be a catastrophe if all the extremes were represented between, for example, unemployment insurance on the one hand as a comprehensive unitary system, and health insurance on a purely provincial basis, with less co-ordination than applies even to old age pensions at the present. The difficulties of rationalization might be sufficient to delay the advent of the other insurances indefinitely. The view expressed by the Rowell-Sirois Commission is worth quoting on this point.

---

[2] Cf. Grauer: *Public Assistance and Social Insurance* (Appendix 6, Rowell-Sirois Reports), pp. 11-23, 37-39, 50-51.

"If the choice is made in favour of contributory
[social insurance] services the balance of advantage
lies in some degree of uniformity throughout Canada
and, therefore, in the collection of contributions
by the Dominion, though these advantages differ
as between different services. The principal reason
for this uniformity lies in the readiness of industry
in one province to complain if it is taxed for social
services which are provided out of general taxation
in other provinces or are not provided at all in
other provinces. Even if there are offsetting
advantages by way of the better health of employees, or their freedom from anxiety, and even
if in the long run the employer's contribution may
in the course of wage bargaining come to fall on the
employees, the employer is . . . placed in a
position of competitive disadvantage in comparison
with employers in provinces where there are not
contributory social services. . . . A second reason
why uniformity is desirable lies in the probability
of some migration from one province to another.
If one province had compulsory insurance and
another did not, a migrant might be exposed to
losing the benefit of payments made prior to migration. Finally, if one authority, the Dominion, is
making some deductions from wages and imposing
some levies on wage bills it is administratively
simpler and cheaper that it should make all such
deductions and impose all such levies."[1]

Modes of Implementation

One method of procedure, namely, to use concurrent legislation, has been suggested for health
insurance. But it is by no means certain that this
procedure is beyond controversy. Federal leadership without the mechanism of grants-in-aid would
presumably be secured if measures along the lines
indicated in Sections 94 and 95 of the British North

---

[1] *Report of the Royal Commission on Dominion-Provincial Relations*
(1940); Book II, p. 36.

America Act were possible. Section 94 provided
for federal legislation designed to establish uniformity of practice in particular provinces, the legislation to apply in each province only if it is adopted
by specific statute there.[2] Section 95, which relates
specifically to agriculture and immigration only,
covers fields in which both Dominion and provincial
legislatures have statutory powers, but provides
overriding authority for the federal statute in the
event of conflict. To attempt to utilize these
principles without specific amendment, however,
would be almost certainly to enter into a realm of
constitutional uncertainty. Even a matter in which
it would seem both federal and provincial parlia-
ments had legislative authority, namely, agricultural
marketing, has fallen foul of the law, or of constitutional interpretation, in recent times.

There should be no danger, however, if the whole
situation were canvassed and agreed on in advance—
possibly through the medium of a special conference
between federal and provincial representatives, for
the purpose of deciding on the method by which
comprehensive social insurance could be implemented
now or in the future. A statement from the Rowell-
Sirois Report puts this point succinctly: "If unity
and harmony of administration are to be maintained, it must be through voluntary agreement
between Dominion and provincial personnel on the
best means of advancing the policy. And this
agreement must be reached without delay and
without serious compromise watering down the
vigour of the measures employed."[3]

This would seem desirable in any case, since it
does not follow that other units in the social security
system call for implementation in exactly the same

---

[2] However, this applied in its original form only to Ontario, Nova
Scotia and New Brunswick; and presumably its extension could be con-
tested.

[3] Op. cit., Book I, p. 259.

way as health insurance. In the latter, the joint
interest of federal and provincial governments
seems incontestable. But even here, provision
ought to be kept in sight for a future situation in
which income-tax machinery might become the
chief among the various contribution-collection
agencies. So far as disability, survivors' and
retirement insurances are concerned, it seems fairly
certain that these will be handled nationally, probably with contribution from Dominion funds. For
these fields, therefore, it might be most appropriate
to specify complete Dominion authority for these
insurances, it being understood that a co-operative
arrangement with the provinces for collection of
contributions would be organized.

Clearance of the ground in this way would not
remove the possibility of Dominion grants-in-aid
to the provinces being utilized where they were
appropriate. The important point is to distinguish
between grants-in-aid employed as a device to
obtain *uniformity*, or unanimity of co-operation in
an optional scheme; and grants directed to the
objective of *raising standards* in particular areas
where financial or other resources are lacking.
There are a number of fields of public welfare,
many of them important subsidiaries to social
insurance and social security programmes, which
ought to be considered for this type of assistance.[1]
Without a clarification of the statutory situation,
and with only an optional application of grants-
in-aid, there is always the danger that these will be
controlled only by reference to financial and accounting criteria, and not as an instrument for improvement and development.

Since the matter has been mentioned, it may be
added that considerable confusion exists on the

---

[1] Grants-in-aid in relation to local services will be discussed among
other matters in the supplement referred to earlier.

difference between decentralized and provincial administration. Decentralized or regional administration is *prima facie* just as feasible through Dominion as through provincial administration; and incidentally is not a constitutional question. Much depends on practice and personnel, of course, if local administration is to be flexible and sound. But there is no reason why officers of the Dominion government with good local knowledge should not be as effective, and as considerate of provincial rights, as provincial or municipal officers. There are in fact a growing number of examples of this type of regional administration and of co-operation between federal, provincial and other officials. One of the most recent is the establishment of the various offices for unemployment insurance. To take other instances, the Department of Public Works, and the Department of Mines and Resources (through representatives of the Water and Power Bureau and others), have long maintained field staff to considerable advantage. One of the most successful pieces of federal-provincial collaboration for specific purposes is exemplified in the Prairie Farm Rehabilitation Administration, which is a hundred-per-cent Dominion-financed agency with definite regional purposes. It is not as clear in the case of the insurances other than health insurance, as it is for unemployment insurance, that considerable regional staff would be necessary; but at least the need for close relations between employment service functions and various branches of social security provision is clear. The development of administrative statistics and research, and of the machinery of adjudication, are further important examples. There should be everything to gain from making clear room in advance for Dominion interest in improved techniques and development of standards generally, without which a social security system will fail to realize all its value.

Financial Administration

These matters once settled, it is possible to consider various arrangements which would serve to simplify contribution collection. The maximum opportunities would not present themselves unless a comprehensive scheme were in operation, but they should be envisaged in advance. To do so is to help also to break away from the view, which is apt to be prevalent, that there is some inherent virtue in the classic three-party system; (employee, employer, government) or sometimes, a simple modification to the two-party (employer-employee) system. These distributions, however, are matters of expediency; the three-party system, in Britain particularly, being an adaptation to the circumstances of a primarily industrial population and a unitary state which are not reproduced in Canada. Having ascertained what funds are required, there are various alternatives for both citizen and governmental participation.

The arrangements made should not, of course, be decided solely by convenience. There is much to be said for assessing contributions, at least in a broad way, upon the parties most able to do constructive work in reducing the risks; but limitations must be recognized on the extent to which this is possible. It is arguable that employers have responsibilities in the matter of unemployment, so far as they control the stability of their production, industrial personnel policies, and so forth; that the Dominion government, as the strongest national unit, has the largest share of responsibility for dealing with the major types of unemployment (and will have added incentive to undertake constructive or preventive measures, when it is bearing the largest share of the costs); that the provincial governments should have a large stake in health insurance schemes, because they are particularly well equipped for the development of preventive medicine, public health, and other allied medical services which can reduce the incidence of sickness and ill-health.   On the other hand, it is not reasonable to seek or expect risk-prevention work in connection with e.g., disability pensions or old age insurance: the only logical procedure is to assess part of the cost on the potential beneficiaries.

The present contributions for unemployment insurance come from employers, employees and the Dominion government; with the Dominion also paying all the administrative costs.   For health insurance it would be reasonable to establish as contributors only the insured persons and the provincial governments, with or without some Dominion collaboration.   Either a similar arrangement, or a separate two-party system (insured persons—Dominion government) could be applied to old age, disability and survivors' insurance.   And the three-party system already existing for unemployment insurance, could be carried through for sickness benefits, as well as for the universal benefits (health, etc.) for the wage-earner population. Purely *ad hoc* arrangements, however, would invite complications, particularly for those parts of the national working force moving from wage-earning employment to some other means of occupation.

The most straightforward alternative would be *(a)* to use what has been termed the "degressive" system for the whole occupied population (including wage-earners) for health insurance, *(b)* to use flat rates (probably matched by flat rates from government sources) for old age, disability and survivors' insurances, and *(c)* to assess the entire premium for the employment group of risks on employers.   The second group of rates could easily be added to either wage-earners' or other gainfully occupied persons' cards.   As a variation it would be possible, if it were desired to recognize differences in capacity to pay, to apply the "degressive" principle (of making up the standard rate by graduated governmental supplement) to a combined rate for both health insurance and the other universal risks.

In more detail this arrangement would involve something like the following. For health insurance (and if decided, for disability, survivors' and retirement insurance as well), certain broad income demarcations would apply. Insured persons with incomes above a level of say $2,000 a year would pay the entire premium, as already suggested for health insurance, but at an augmented rate. Persons with incomes below this amount and down to a certain minimum level would pay proportions of the standard premium graduated according to their income, the balance in each case being met by either the Dominion or the provinces as appropriate. (It would be most appropriate probably for the provinces to pay the residual contributions for health insurance, and the Dominion for old age, disability and survivors' insurance). Finally, persons below a certain level, e.g., $500, would be formally exempted; but might be compelled to pay a standard registration or token fee, and would be subject also to compliance with certain rehabilitation conditions (involving training, placement, etc.). Whether or not there was need for a further grant to the social insurance fund would depend upon the rapidity with which the disability and retirement provisions were brought into effect.

The following out of this plan would mean that substantial proportions, perhaps more or less equal, would be paid by insured persons and the governments. It would, therefore, be an equitable arrangement to complete the scheme by transferring all contributions in respect of unemployment benefit, as well as new contributions for sickness benefits, to employers. Workmen's compensation, which already assesses contributions solely on the employer, would remain unchanged. The net effect on the distribution of the total costs could only be determined by proper actuarial calculation, given the rates of benefit. But it is entirely possible that a reasonable distribution would be effected between insured persons (employee or assessed), employers, and government.

If this redivision were once achieved it would have many advantages. In particular it would mean that the universal risks, which apply equally to wage-earners and to non-wage-earner groups, rural or urban, could be covered by a single card or book. The individual record of the employment insurances would be an additional card or book retained solely for wage-earners. There would be no difficulty for persons moving from industry to agriculture or from a proprietary occupation to wage-earning employment. Administration also for seasonal and casual workers would be considerably facilitated.

Put in its simplest terms, there would really be only two sets of individual payments. (1) The Dominion, or a combination of government agencies, would collect the contributions of all persons for the universal risks. (2) Employers would pay all the contributions, presumably through stamped cards, for the employment risks. This possibility would, of course, hinge essentially on the inter-governmental collaboration in the initial and subsequent arrangements for health insurance registration which has previously been recommended.

A more orthodox system would be one which (a) grafted on the payments for the new insurance (health, disability, survivors, old age) to the unemployment insurance system, so far as wage-earners were concerned. These would be in the form of payroll deductions, made by the employer. The governmental residuals would be added later. Instead of collecting additional contributions from the employer for the new insurances, however, (which besides being a complication, would have no parallel among the non-wage-earner classes) it would still be simpler *(b)* to transfer all contributions for the employment risks (including unemployment insurance and the new sickness benefit) to the employer. For other gainfully occupied classes *(c)* the Dominion or the province would act as the collector, for contributions in respect of the universal risks only, with or without a flat-rate component. Employed persons who desired to pay their universal contributions direct to the government rather than through employers (e.g., through income tax or property tax) would be able to do so. This system might possibly have to be adopted as a transitional measure, but it would obviously be more complicated.

Possible Priorities

A final decision is whether comprehensive social security should be inaugurated completely or as an ordered series of measures over a period. It is clear that this decision cannot be taken without reference to several considerations, some of which have been the subject of this Section, while an important one is further referred to in the last Section. If there is a case, or necessity, for priorities to be considered, it may be worthwhile to list some suggestions, as a basis for discussion. On the grounds examined at various points in this report, a reasonable order of importance might be the following:

1. Strengthening of unemployment insurance as a necessary framework for all post-war measures.

2. Health insurance, as the most important basic measure additional to unemployment insurance, but particularly because it is applicable to the whole population and is most likely to produce rapid beneficial effects.

3. Children's allowances, as the key measure for satisfactory establishment of all the income–maintenance insurances. (If these were unavoidably to be delayed, it might be desirable to set up a strictly interim scheme of allowances, applicable only to recipients of unemployment benefit, on the same financial basis as the comprehensive scheme to come and therefore separate from the finances of the Unemployment Insurance Fund.)

4. Funeral benefits, as one of the easiest of social insurances to put into effect, and as a small contribution to needs pending the advent of survivors' insurance.

5. The disability-oldage-survivors group of insurances; which depend on both children's allowances and on satisfactorily functioning health insurance, and which also should desirably be instituted together.

6. Sickness cash benefit, and maternity benefit for working women. These are comparatively simple insurances, but delay in implementing them would be tempered in some degree if health insurance, providing universal medical care, were in existence.

If the priorities were to be primarily related to the special exigencies of the immediate post-war transition, it would be desirable to give much earlier consideration to old age insurance. The establishment of a national contributory system would lay the basis for more organized measures assisting the retirement of older persons from the labour market. Funeral benefits, in the same context, have the least direct relationship to immediate post-war problems. Viewed from this angle, therefore, the order of importance might be more like the following:

1. Unemployment insurance,

2. Health insurance,

3. The disability-old age-survivors group of insurances,

4. Children's allowances,

5. Sickness cash benefit,

6. Funeral benefits.

22. FINANCIAL CONSIDERATIONS.

It has not been the purpose of this report to elaborate projected legislation to the point of settling all details of rates of contribution and scales and conditions of benefit. Accordingly, it is not possible to make any close calculation of the total costs of putting a comprehensive scheme into operation. Contributory old age pensions, one of the heavier units of the insurances, is affected considerably by the method and timing chosen to bring it into effect. Children's allowances also, the major tax-financed unit, are subject to a considerable range of variation according to rates and to the decision taken between a universal and a "dovetailed" plan. It might be desirable to undertake a specific actuarial calculation for such a matter as, for example, the recommendation that unemployment insurance benefit scales in the dependent class be raised to a level more consistent with minimum standards; but even this would probably give rise to more than one alternative method of changing the contribution system, if it were decided to raise the extra revenue in this form.

It is possible, however, to refer to the experience and estimates of other countries, and to some comparative figures of Canadian conditions. There are also certain general considerations which should be taken into account in viewing the social insurances and the enlargement of social security coverage as a financial proposition.

The country with the most comprehensive system of social security at the moment, New Zealand, offers some data established by actual practice. If the figures for the fiscal year 1940-41 may be taken, as being not too greatly distorted by the war, the facts with regard to the total disbursement under the Social Security Act (£13,968,000) are of much interest. The New Zealand system, as is well

known, is financed principally by a universal charge
of 5 per cent on all incomes, private and corporate.
The social security contribution from wage-earners
and salaried persons, together with registration fees,
supply more than two-thirds of the total fund (69
per cent in 1940-1941, of which 4 or 5 per cent came
from registration fees). Only one-fifth to one-
quarter is made up by grant from the Consolidated
Fund (23 per cent in 1940-1941) and most of the
balance from the charges on industries and corporations. The proportion of the national income which
is thus directed to social security persons is of the
order of 8 to 11 per cent according to the definition of
national income employed.[1] This is a remarkably
low figure for coverage of such wide scope; though
one or two of the benefits are comparatively low.
(Some increases have been instituted recently).
It is worthy of note that total administrative costs
represented only $2 \cdot 7$ per cent of the disbursements;
and that the Social Security Commission administers, in addition to the social insurances, all war
pension legislation and some emergency or relief
assistance, although ex-service expenditures are
financed by a separate vote. Only work projects
and youth training are separated from the system
centralized under the Commission. The unified
system itself, apart from the simpler administrative
conditions of the country (at least as compared
with Canada) is one of the sources of economy.

It would probably be more reasonable to assume
that the Canadian situation would be more comparable to British or American conditions, or perhaps
somewhere between the two. The provisions contemplated under the Beveridge plan for Britain

---

[1] Figures for 1940-41 are not available.

"Aggregate private income" was computed at £200 millions for
1939-40, but "total value of production" and "goods available for consumption" are considerably smaller totals. (*New Zealand Year Book*,
1942, p. 648). Estimated rates for 1940-41, applied to the two latter definitions, are $9 \cdot 5$ and $10 \cdot 5$ per cent respectively.

would appear to demand about ten per cent of the national income for the first year (on the assumption that the post-war national income of Britain will be in the neighbourhood of £7 billions), and a higher proportion subsequently. The expenditures—estimated at £697 millions for 1945—are due to increase substantially in the course of two decades (about 23 per cent), with state contributions rising from a proportion of 50 per cent to 61 per cent of the total. But even if it is assumed that British national income will rise in post-war years less rapidly than social security requirements (say, less than an average of one per cent a year) the total charge would involve only about 12·5 per cent, or about one-eighth, of the national income. Administrative expenditures are estimated at about 3·8 per cent, including the operation of children's allowances and residual assistance measures.

The United States programme would appear to be substantially indicated by the Elliott Bill (summarized in Section 4)[1], although other developments are still in progress. This provides for joint contributions from industrial and commercial workers and their employers, beginning at ten per cent of the wage bill; and smaller contributions to come from agricultural and domestic workers, farmers and other self-employed. Together they indicate a total fund representing about twelve per cent of the national income. The contributions are arranged so as to increase within a few years (the employer-worker contributions from ten to twelve per cent between 1945 and 1948). A deficit between contribution revenue and total payments is anticipated, particularly with the development of disability and pension insurance, and this is to be made up from

---

[1] This would seem to be confirmed by a recent speech by the Secretary for Labour (Miss Frances Perkins) in which she referred, among other things, to contributions of ten per cent of industrial payrolls.

government funds. A figure of about twelve and a half per cent of the United States national income, therefore, seems a reasonable average estimate. (It should be noted that health insurance, in the sense of medical care other than hospitalization, is not included).

It has been estimated by an insurance executive, Mr. H. A. Behrens,[2] that a full application of the British (Beveridge) programme to the United States would cost $15 billions a year, of which $8 billions would need to be financed from tax revenue. Drawn from a national income of only $100 billions, this total would be heavy; but related to a national income of $120 billions, which is commonly predicted, it would constitute twelve-and-a-half per cent, and less still on the assumption of a $130 billion dollar level which is made by some economists.

Translated into Canadian terms, the British social security budget represents about $3,200,000,000; but this is intended for an insurable population three-and-a-half to four times as large, so that an equivalent sum for Canada would be $800 to $900 millions. A tentative estimate of the principal items (other than employment programmes) reviewed in this report, which would be too rough to have much value without considerably more refinement, nevertheless suggests a figure of about $900 millions. The application of the $12\frac{1}{2}$ per cent ratio to the Canadian national income as a whole would produce $1,000,000,000 or less, according as it was assumed that it will be possible to maintain present levels, or that some reduction from possibly war-inflated figures must be calculated for the first post-war years.

Past expenditures in Canada are not a very helpful guide of capacity to finance social security, partly because the Canadian national income has been lowest in the years in which unemployment expenditures were greatest; but particularly because

[2] As reported in the *Christian Science Monitor*, Feb. 5, 1943.

welfare expenditures apart from unemployment assistance have been comparatively restricted. In the three pre-war years, 1937-1939, which form a somewhat better base than the depression years of the early thirties, the total direct expenditure on public welfare items at all three levels of government in Canada was below $250 million a year. It is estimated[3] that only $18 millions of this total on the average, was public health expenditure. Roughly $100 million a year of the national total came from federal funds.

If social security for Canada involves something approaching a billion-dollar programme, it must be remembered that not all of this amount of collection and disbursement would be tax-financed or state funds; and it must be measured also against the wholly new levels of national production and Dominion budgeting that a war economy has brought into existence. The national income which averaged around $3,800,000,000 in the twenties and thirties is nearer $8,000,000,000 to-day. Even if some temporary reduction is to be anticipated on the grounds that unit-costs of war goods are higher than those of peace goods, it would be reasonable to assume levels of post-war national income which are more than twice as high as those of the years of depression: 10-12$\frac{1}{2}$ per cent of these levels for social security disbursements would be a reasonable commitment.

It is important to add that on a social insurance basis, total disbursements may increase very greatly without implying increases in taxation which are at all comparable in amount. The unemployment insurance fund, for example, calls only for government contributions equivalent to one-fifth of com-

---

[3] H. M. Cassidy, *Social Security and Reconstruction* (previously cited), chapter II. Public expenditure statistics are assembled in systematic form in the Rowell-Sirois Commission reports; the definition of public welfare includes unemployment relief, assistances such as old age pensions and mothers' allowances, and public health; but excludes veterans' services and correctional institutions, etc.

bined employer-employee revenues. If this fund, accordingly, disbursed say $50,000,000 in the first post-war year, only $8,333,000 of this would be federal money. (Administrative costs would, of course, be additional; and the proportions might be made higher to institute adjustments in the scales of benefit.) The case of health insurance is different. Most estimates of the requirements for adequate service on a national plan run in the neighbourhood of $200 million to $250 million, depending on the scale of facilities and of practitioners' fees. It would be more reasonable to expect something like half of this to be provided from governmental sources. On the other hand, medical expenses incurred privately are already very large, and some proportion of the new expenditures under insurance would be substitutes for previous unrecorded amounts. Pensions would require a more substantial contribution than unemployment insurance; and children's allowances would be hundred-per-cent government-financed. The net result might well be (like the Beveridge plan) that half of the revenues should be anticipated from tax sources.

The total Dominion budget appropriation for 1942-1943, comprising both wartime and ordinary expenditures, and including the billion-dollar "war gift to Britain" of last year, amount to the huge figure of $4,428,000,000. Supposing that $500,000,000 from Dominion sources were required (and in practice, some additional or substitute contributions from provincial sources, at least for health insurance, would presumably be forthcoming), this would still be consistent with suppositions that (a) again taking no account of other government participation, $1,000,000,000 were required from Dominion sources to finance an adequate works development programme (this, of course, could be the basis for a considerably greater "induced" general expenditure); and that (b) ordinary government expenditures would require to be continued, at a higher level for peace-time purposes. A generous margin for the latter, of as much as 25 per cent increase, would produce a total Dominion budget of $2,212,000,000; and all of this would still be feasible even though tax and loan revenues were reduced by as much as fifty per cent.

Computations such as these, of course, must not be taken as more than signposts—indeed, as signposts pointing to many still-uncharted ways. Actually, a number of decisions would, and should be interdependent. Among the determinants would be: the tempo at which the war was brought to an end; the manner in which two of the techniques of readjustment should be manipulated—the maintenance of investment, purchasing power and employment by public undertakings, on the one hand, and the stimulus of industrial and investment expansion by tax reduction, on the other; international policy commitments; and other factors. The possibilities of priority inauguration rather than immediate establishment of a total system, referred to previously, are also relative to the same considerations. The broad figures should be regarded only as aid in setting dimensions.

A "residual" amount of the order of $400,000,000, to be met from insured contributors and, for certain appropriate insurance areas, from employers, incidentally gives a preliminary indication of the possible scale of contributions. Assessed on a gainfully occupied force of 4,000,000 of whom 3,000,000 are wage-earners and the others farmers, independent employers, etc., this would permit rates of the order of 75-90 cents a week for farmers and rural groups, 75 cents to $1.85 a week for employees of various wage levels, and an average of about 90 cents per employee for employers.[1] These are deliberately approximate and average calculations: there would be considerable leeway for variation around these averages, through the operation of both graduated and "degressive" scales.

Conclusion: Assessment Factors

In conclusion, and as a guide still relevant when further elaborations of the cost calculations of social security can be undertaken, it will be well to summarize the main considerations which are of general applicability.

1. The first is that a very considerable proportion of all disbursements made under social insurance schemes are no more than a redistribution of existing income. The directness of this is probably more apparent, the greater the extent to which contributions, whether from one or more parties, are raised from the beneficiaries themselves. But even some of the tax revenue, which forms part of the shares provided by governments, may be raised from the insured population either in the form of income tax or from commodity and other taxes. The redistribution will always to some extent be from the wealthier to the poorer members of society; in which case it is a transference on the basis of ability to pay, which is a fully accepted canon of modern fiscal policy. On the disbursement side, much of the redistribution must obviously be according to need, whether the need is that of the unemployed man, who to some extent draws on the fund which has been built up by his more fortunate fellow-workers who still retain their jobs; or the need of large families as compared with small, in the case of

---

[1] Rates under the Beveridge plan vary considerably, for males and females, three age groups, and three classes (employees, other gainfully occupied, and other persons of working age). The most important rates, however, (using approximate Canadian equivalents) are $1.20 and 90 cents weekly for juveniles (girls and youths); $1.80 and $1.40 for male and female wage earners, and $1.00 for (male) non-wage-earners.

children's allowance payments; or the meeting of one of the unpredictable hazards such as accident or disease.

Some transfers might of course be transfers of tax or revenue resources themselves. A special aspect of this matter is involved in assessing the costs of children's allowances. As has already been pointed out, allowances for children and other dependents are already made on a very substantial scale by the state in the form of deductions permissible for income-tax computation. The present rate is $108 per dependent; and this figure (of $9 a month) is not far from the average rate which might be appropriate to put the scheme into effect. Supposing these were the rates in actuality, one of the important implications would be that (assuming war expenditures to cease) a large part of the national cost of a children's allowance scheme could be regarded as already financed. It is not necessary at this stage to attempt an elaborate estimate of the situation, and in any case the necessary statistics from income tax or other sources, are not all available. But a broad estimate is that the deductions are already fully payable in a year such as fiscal 1943 for about 1,500,000 children. In round figures this might mean that well over a third and perhaps half of the costs would be available simply through the abolition (or modification) of the dependent-children exemption.

2. The second consideration is that in several fields which would be more adequately covered once social insurance provisions for the contingencies of income-loss or dependency were made, a number of previous expenditures would be unnecessary. Reference has been made to some of these at various points in the report, e.g., the cost of at least some part of mothers' allowances as these relate to children, the sums already spent continuously for

doctors' bills, medicaments and other health services, some part of supplementary old age assistance, medical relief schemes, at least some of the children's allowance provisions in armed service or ex-service provisions. It is not desirable to push this point too far, because some of the changes would be transfers from one system to another, while better quality of administration and service, or more generous care, usually require greater expenditure. But it is apposite to add that some of these expenditures do not meet their purpose and may be ill-advised or wasteful. One of the most familiar examples of this type is the large sum spent annually by the public for drugs and other forms of self-medication without any guidance from a doctor. That some net deductions would really be reckonable from the vast field of social hazard and dependency, so much of which is at present inefficiently handled, seems undeniable.

3. The most fundamental measurement of social security costs is against the national income as a whole. A computation running to hundreds of millions of dollars for health insurance, or old age security, or whatever it may be, may seem a crushing burden viewed by itself. It is not (more particularly if it includes the multiple contributions of a large part of the population), if it forms only one or two per cent of the total income produced and available year by year. If the scheme is comprehensive, and well designed, there is the possibility that in some degree a "principle of decreasing costs" may be realizable for the expenditure of ten or twelve per cent of the national income. It is altogether possible that more than five times the service and efficiency should be obtainable from an integrated and carefully planned system than from five units, instituted at different times without much relation to one another.

It has already been emphasized that in making computations and commitments for the future, the experience of war production and organization, in Canada as in the United States, raises the expectations which seem reasonable of what our normal national income should be. At high and more stable levels, with the phenomenal demands of immediate war needs removed, there is obviously a much greater margin for the improvement of social security legislation.

A special aspect of this matter has been referred to earlier, namely, the part which organized expenditures in the years of curtailed war production will be required to play. The difficulties in the operation of anti-depression fiscal techniques have already been enumerated; but it is entirely possible that one of the reasons favouring a comprehensive introduction of social insurance rather than a plan to complete it over a long sequence of years, might be the greater mobilization-capacity of social security disbursements, as compared with the difficulties of physical investment projects, which require heavy quantities of materials which may not be immediately plentiful, as well as advanced engineering preparation. This is one of the contingencies, not a certainty: it merely reinforces the wisdom of preparation for post-war eventualities on more than one front.

4. Finally, the obvious but vital point must be made that social security payments are not money lost. The social insurances, and even some straightforward disbursements like children's allowances, are investments in morale and health, in greater family stability, and from both material and psychological viewpoints, in human productive efficiency. They demand personal and community responsibilities; but in the eyes of most of the people who are beneficiaries, give a more evident meaning to the

ideas of common effort and national solidarity   It
has yet to be proved that any democracy which
underwrites the social minimum for its citizens is
any the weaker or less wealthy for doing so.

APPENDICES

APPENDIX I

INDUSTRIAL ACCIDENT (Workmen's Compensation): Provincial Schedules of Payments (January, 1943)

Province	Temporary Disability		Permanent Disability		Maximum Earnings Reckoned (per annum)
	Partial	Total	Partial	Total	
BRITISH COLUMBIA	2/3 of difference in earnings before and after accident. If earnings not substantially less, lump sum may be given.	2/3 of earnings. Minimum $10 per week or earnings if less.*	2/3 of difference in earnings before and after accident. If earnings not substantially less, lump sum may be given.	2/3 of earnings. Minimum $10 per week or earnings if less.*	$2,000*
ALBERTA	Based on impairment of earning capacity.	2/3 of earnings.	Lump sum may be given if earning capacity is not diminished by more than 10%.	2/3 of earnings. Minimum $10 per week or earnings if less.*	$2,000
SASKATCHEWAN	2/3 of difference in earnings before and after accident. Minimum disability ($12.50 per week or earnings if less) in proportion to disability.	2/3 of difference in earnings before and after accident. Minimum disability ($12.50 per week or earnings if less) in proportion to disability.	2/3 of difference in earnings before and after accident. Minimum disability ($12.50 per week or earnings if less) in proportion to disability.	2/3 of earnings. Minimum $12.50 per week or earnings if less.	$2,000
MANITOBA	As above.	As above.	As above.	2/3 of earnings. Minimum $15 per week or earnings if less.	$2,000.
ONTARIO	As above.	As above.	Compensation, both total and partial, to be proportionate to impairment of earning capacity "estimated from nature and degree of injury, but not to exceed 2/3 of the man's average earnings before the accident." The Board may still, if it "deems it more equitable", award 2/3 of the difference in average earnings before and after the accident.		$2,000

QUEBEC.........	2/3 of difference in earnings before and after accident. Minimum disability ($12.50 per week or earnings if less) in proportion to disability.	2/3 of earnings. Minimum $12.50 per week or earnings if less.	2/3 of difference in earnings before and after accident. Minimum disability ($12.50 per week or earnings if less) in proportion to disability.	2/3 of earnings. Minimum $12.50 per week or earnings if less.	$2,000
NEW BRUNSWICK	60% of difference in earnings before and after accident, if earnings diminished by more than 10%.	60% of earnings for duration. Minimum $8.00 per week or earnings if less.	60% of difference in earnings before and after. (If impairment 10% or less, lump sum may be given.)	60% of earnings. Minimum $8.00 per week or earnings if less.	$1,500
NOVA SCOTIA....	2/3 of difference in earnings before and after accident, for duration. If no difference, may be lump sum.	2/3 of earnings for duration. Minimum $8.00 per week or earnings if less.	2/3 of difference in earnings before and after accident. If no difference lump sum may be given.	2/3 of earnings. Minimum $8.00 per week or earnings if less.	$1,500
P.E.I.........	No Workmen's Compensation except for railway employees (Dominion Government), who are treated as in New Brunswick.				

* Indicates that changes have been made since January, 1943.

APPENDIX II

FATAL ACCIDENTS (Workmen's Compensation): Provincial Schedules of Payments (January, 1943)

Province	Widow (or invalid widower)	Children		Other Dependents[2]	Maximum and Minimum (to consort and children)	Funeral Benefit
		Parent living	Orphans			$
BRITISH COLUMBIA	$40 per month	Under 16, $7.50 per month each.* May be paid to invalid children over 16 until they recover.	Under 16, $15 per month each[1]. Maximum in all, $60 per month[2].*	(a) Sum reasonable and in proportion to pecuniary loss. Maximum $30 per month each to parent or parents. Maximum in all, $45 per month. (b) If there is widow or invalid widower or orphans, maximum to parent or parents, $30 per month[1].*	Maximum $70 per month*	125*
ALBERTA	$35 per month*	Under 18, eldest $12 per month, 2nd $10 per month, 3rd $9 per month, others $8 per month each.*	Under 18, $15 per month each[1].*	Sum reasonable and in proportion to pecuniary loss. Maximum to parent or parents, $30 per month. Maximum in all $65 per month[1].*	Not stated	125*
SASKATCHEWAN	$10 per month, plus $100	Under 16, $10 per month each. Payments to children may be made up to 18 years if desirable to continue education.	Under 16, $15 per month each[1].	Sum reasonable and in proportion to pecuniary loss[1].	2/3 of earnings, (maximum $2,000). Minimum $50 per month to consort and one child, $12.50 per week if more[1].	125

				mum $2,000), but minimum $12.50 per week if one child; $15 if more.	125, plus up to $125 to transport body.
	month... 2nd $10 per month, 3rd $9 per month, others $8 per month each.	each.	proportion to pecuniary loss¹. Maximum in all, $10 per month.		
		Payments to children may be made up to 18 years if desirable to continue education. Also to invalid children up to recovery.			
ONTARIO	$10 per month plus $100*	Under 16, $10 per month each.¹	Sum reasonable and in proportion to pecuniary loss¹. Maximum in all, $10 per month.	2/3 of earnings, (maximum $2,000).* Minimum $12.50 per week.	125, plus up to $125 to transport body.
QUEBEC	$40 per month plus $100	under 18, $10 per month each.¹	Sum reasonable and in proportion to pecuniary loss¹.	2/3 of earnings, (maximum $2,000). Minimum $50 per month to consort and child, $12.50 per week if more	125
NEW BRUNSWICK	$30 per month plus $100	Boys under 16, girls under 18, $10 per month each.¹	Sum reasonable and in proportion to pecuniary loss¹.	60% of earnings, (maximum $1,500).	100
NOVA SCOTIA	$30 per month*	Under 16, $7.50 per month each².*	Sum reasonable and in proportion to pecuniary loss¹. Maximum to parent or parents, $30 per month. Maximum in all. $45 per month.	2/3 of earnings, (maximum $1,500).	100
Prince Edward I.	No Workmen's Compensation Act. New Brunswick provisions apply to railway employees.				

*Indicates that changes have been made since January, 1943.

¹In all provinces, compensation in these cases is continued only so long as Board considers workman would have contributed to support.

²Compensation may be paid to others if there is no wife (husband) or child dependent; or maxima apply to total grant made to natural dependents and others.

*Where there is an accumulation in reserve because of lower payments to dependents in foreign countries, this maximum does not apply.

APPENDIX III

Mothers' Allowances: Summary of Main Provisions in Canada (January, 1943)

Province and Legislation	Rates and Allowance	Treatment of Income from Other Sources	Health Services	Provision for Taxes, Etc.
British Columbia Mothers' Allowance Acts—S.B.C. 1937 Chapter 53.	Maximum allowance—$42.50 for mother and one child—$7.50 each additional child, and for incapacitated husband. Until April, 1942, the rate was $35 per month for mother and one child where home owned. If home not owned, an additional $5 per month may be granted for rent. Allowance for additional child or incapacitated husband $7.50 per month. Commencing April, 1942, an additional allowance of $2.50 per month was provided, with provision for a further $2.50 per month in case of need.*	a. *General*—No regulation—amount of allowance dependent on need in each individual case. b. *Contributions from Earning Children, etc.* (a) No specific regulations—nothing expected from married children—earning children at home expected to pay board and a small amount monthly which is deducted from allowance. Earning children away from home are asked for a regular contribution which if paid is taken into consideration when rate of allowance set.	No provision—must be met out of allowance. Doctors often give free service or make a minimum charge.*	No provision—must be budgeted—see regulation *re* allowance for rent but none for taxes.
Alberta Mothers' Allowance Act—R.S.A. 1922, Chapter 215 and amendments.	Maximum allowance $37.50 to the mother, $10 to first child (if over 10, otherwise $7.50), $7.50 to the second child and $5 to each additional child.*	a. *General*—Allowance paid on budget basis and other income taken into consideration. b. *Contributions from Earning Children, etc.* (a)—Included in family budget.	No provision......	No provision—maximum rent allowance is set at $12 a month.

	Maximum Allowance	Regulations	Medical Care	Burial
Saskatchewan Child Welfare Act —R.S.S. 1940, Chapter 278, Part V.	Maximum allowance—mother and one child—$10 per month—$5 each for second and third child and $4 each for subsequent children up to a maximum of ten. Maximum allowance—$48 for mother and ten or more children.	a. *General*—No regulation—allowance based on need. b. *Contributions from Earning Children, etc.* No specific regulation.	No provision.	No provision.
Manitoba Child Welfare Act R.S.N., 1940, Chapter 32, Part III.	Maximum allowance excluding winter fuel—mother and one child $33 up to $89 for mother and 7 or more children. Where allowance is given for food and clothing only, there has been a 20% increase as from Sept. 1942. Maximum allowance for winter fuel—$10 for family of 1 child to $18 for family of 6 or more. Food and clothing allowance for town families is 10% less than the maximum which is for urban families. Rural families get 20% less than urban families.	a. *General*—Rate of allowance is calculated on a budget system. b. *Contributions from Earning Children, etc.*—Earning children are allowed the first $35 and excess paid into the home. Out of the $35 he is expected to pay actual cost of his food. No deduction if child earning less than $35 per month. Children living away from home are expected to contribute but each case decided on its own merits. Married children are not usually expected to contribute.	Hospitalization is covered by Municipal Act. In Winnipeg, City Health Dept. provides nursing and if necessary medical attention. In other areas there is a municipal doctor. No provision for fees in allowance.	Included in budget expenses for which allowance given.

(a) Married children not living in the home may also be considered in assessment of sources of income.

* Indicates changes have been instituted since January, 1943.

APPENDIX III—*Concluded*

MOTHERS' ALLOWANCES: Summary of Main Provisions in Canada (January, 1943)—*Concluded*

Province and Legislation	Rates and Allowance	Treatment of Income from Other Sources	Health Services	Provision for Taxes, Etc.
Ontario The Mothers' Allowance Act, R.S.O., 1937 Chapter 313 and amendments, 1938.	Maximum allowance mother and one child—in cities $35 month—in towns $30 month—in rural areas $25 per month, and $5 per month for each additional child. Orphan children in approved foster homes may benefit in cities—one foster child, $20 month—2 children $10, each additional child in same foster family $5 month. In rural areas rate is $15 per month for each of the first two children—$5 each additional child.	a. *General*—This may be taken into consideration where amount of allowance is set. Amount is at discretion of the Mothers' Allowance Commission. b. *Contributions from Earning Children, etc.* Contributions cannot be required from children not living at home.	Medical services provided to recipients under agreement between provincial govt. and Ontario Medical Association, March, 1942.	No provision: allowance not based on cost-of-living budget.
Quebec Needy Mothers' Assistance Act—S.Q. 1938, chapter 81 and amended by S.Q. 1940, Chapter 43.	Maximum allowance for mother and one child—in cities—$25 per month, in towns, $20 per month, in rural areas $15 per month and $5 for each additional child. Maximum allowance paid any family—$50 per month. If mother is unable to work because of mental or physical disability, she may receive an additional $5 per month up to a maximum of $50 per month. Payment for an invalid father in the family may be made at $5 per month. — Allowance for each additional child recently (March 1912) increased from $2.50 to $5. Payment of $5 per month for invalid husband in the home and maximum allowance increased to $50 per month	a. *General*—Mother is allowed to earn up to $300 year without her allowance being reduced. b. *Contributions from Earning Children, etc.* Quebec Civil Code makes children and children-in-law liable for maintenance of parents. Applicant must satisfy Bureau that there is no responsible relative who can support her and her children.	No provision........	No provision.

Nova Scotia			
Mothers Allowance Act, R.S.N.S., 1930, Chapter 4.	Maximum allowance $60 per month. Minimum allowance $15 per month. Amount of allowance is set by the Commission on a cost-of-living budget in every individual case. *January, 1942.* Maximum allowance has not been increased but average amount to each family has been increased. Families whose income exceeds $72 are not eligible for any supplementary income by way of mothers' allowances.*	a. *General*—Other income in family is taken into consideration where amount of allowance is set. Allowance is set where possible to give family the average family income for the district and having regard to their scale of living prior to death or disability of husband. b. *Contributions from Earning Children, etc.* No hard and fast rule. Considered as part of family income when budget shrunk.	No provision......	Part of family expenses and included in budget.

* Indicates changes have been instituted since January, 1943.

APPENDIX IVa

DOMINION EMPLOYMENT SERVICE POLICY

(Statement of employment policy to be carried out by the local Employment and Claims Offices across Canada, as adopted by the Unemployment Insurance Commission. From *First Report of the Unemployment Insurance Commission*, March 31st, 1942, pp. 13-15. Original text rearranged, and sub-headings added.)

The Employment and Claims Offices of the Commission will:

(a) endeavour to refer to suitable employment any employable resident of Canada, either male or female, of whatever occupation or calling;

(b) endeavour to secure suitable applicants to fill any vacancy notified by an employer;

(c) In a general way assist wherever and however possible in alleviating an unemployment situation, or in suggesting means for the alleviation of such a condition.

In registering applicants and in accepting notification of vacancies, and in referring applicants to vacancies, Employment and Claims Offices will not charge any fee, either to an employer or to an employee.

The Employment and Claims Offices will co-operate to the fullest possible extent with other branches of the Federal Government, with the governments of the several provinces, and with the councils of municipal corporations, for the purpose of assisting in the solution of employment problems within their particular jurisdiction. These offices will also co-operate with any non-commercial private or quasi-public agencies or trade unions or employers' organizations interested in finding employment for workers, to assist residents of Canada, wherever may be possible, in securing available work.

Coverage: Persons

In effecting placements, Employment and Claims Offices will endeavour to refer the most competent applicants registered and available for the employment offering, and where several persons of like competence are available for the same employment, a preference shall be given to the person or persons whose application or applications, as the case may be, show the longest period of continuous registration immediately before the date of placement; provided, however, that nothing herein contained shall prevent the sending of a number of persons to an employer for selection purposes, nor the sending of a particular person who may be asked for by an employer.

No applicant seeking work will be discriminated in favour of, nor against, by reason:

(a) of his or her racial origin, religious belief, or political affiliation.

(b) of whether or not he or she was engaged previously in insured employment.

The Employment and Claims Offices will not fail to endeavour to secure employees for an employer by reason of the employer inserting in his request for employees particular specifications as to the type of employees required, where such specifications are reasonable.

Reasonable steps will be taken to verify the qualifications of applicants who are unknown, and the *bona fides* of vacancies listed by employers who are unknown to the Employment and Claims Offices.

Without restricting the generality of the service

to be provided to employees of whatever occupation, and without prejudice to the employment rights of other persons, special attention will be given to the placement of veterans of the Armed Forces, of young persons who have not become established in industrial life, of competent applicants who suffer from physical handicaps, of professionally and technically trained applicants, of young persons wishing to undertake apprenticeship or training courses, of middle-aged workers desirous of entering on training courses, and of other similar special categories of applicants.

Coverage: Area

Each Office will endeavour to give placement service to the entire area assigned to it, and in no case will the activities of an Office be restricted to the particular municipality in which it is located.

The Employment and Claims Offices will attempt to induce unemployed persons to move from their present place of residence to points where their services are necessary, provided, however, that care will be taken to avoid encouragement of the movement of workers into any district where unemployed persons are already seeking employment of the type involved.

On request, an employer or applicant will be given available information regarding employment conditions, including wage rates current in the district for a particular occupation, but the Employment and Claims Offices will not seek to influence the fixing of wage rates or other employment conditions, either in general or in particular instances, nor will any information on wages or other working conditions be given out which might affect adversely the interests of any employer patronizing the Offices.

Every effort will be made to bring to the notice of employers and employees the facilities provided by the Employment and Claims Offices for making references to any placements in employment.

Conditions of Acceptance of Jobs

No applicant will be prejudiced in his right to be referred to future employment by reason of refusal to accept a position offered because: *(a)* the wage rate offered may reasonably be claimed to be less than the rate current for the occupation in the district; or *(b)* his right to membership or non-membership in a trade union or like association would be impaired thereby; or *(c)* the employment is affected by an industrial dispute.

In referring workers to employment, the Employment and Claims Offices will advise the applicant of the wage rate offered by the prospective employer, and while the Offices will have no financial responsibility if a subsequent dispute as to the rate of pay develops between employer and employee, the Offices will state the wage rates and other conditions notified by the employer, if later requested to do so by the employees concerned, or by competent authority.

The Employment and Claims Offices will accept no financial responsibility for the payment of wages by an employer where the contract of employment was entered into as a result of a reference to employment by one of the Offices.

When orders are listed with any office by an employer, and when such orders do not offer the minimum wages or working conditions specifically required by Dominion statute or regulation, or by provincial statute or regulation, any variation from prescribed conditions will be brought to the attention of the employer in order that he may have opportunity to make a correction. If the employer fails or refuses to make such correction in the conditions offered, the Employment and Claims Office will not refer applicants to the vacancies offered.

Where vacancies notified are in employment at which a cessation of work is reported to have occurred through an industrial dispute, the Offices will take such measures as may be possible to learn definitely whether a strike or lockout really exists. If it be determined that a strike or lockout does exist, applicants, on being advised of any employment vacancies so affected, will be informed that the employment is affected by a strike or lockout, as the case may be, and any form of notification to an applicant to apply for the said employment which may be given to an applicant by any Employment and Claims Office will be marked to indicate that there is a strike or lockout at the employment in question.

APPENDIX IVb

1. DISTRIBUTION AND PLACEMENT FACILITIES.[1]

Having examined and considered that part of its terms of reference relating to the proper distribution of labour, the Subcommittee has reached the following conclusions:—

1. Whatever success may be achieved toward providing full employment in the post-war period, facilities for the most equitable and most efficient distribution of labour, relating available workers to available jobs, are the essential basis to any programme, and must receive prime attention.

Dominion Employment Service

2. Employment office machinery, comprehensively developed and capably administered as a Dominion Employment Service under the Unemployment Insurance Commission is the most suitable medium through which these functions can be performed.

3. To accomplish satisfactory and effective results placement work should be operated by, or channelled through, the Dominion Employment Service. The Committee recommends that exclusive jurisdiction should be secured for the Dominion Employment Service; if necessary, by appropriate amendment to the British North America Act. (At the present time, there is no authority to prevent provinces from operating dual employment services or granting privileges to private fee-charging agencies.)

4. If exclusive powers are not established, care should be taken not to impose on the Dominion Employment Service any restrictions or special

---

[1] Second Report of the Subcommittee on Post-war Employment Opportunities, April 13, 1942.

duties which would place it in an unequal position
with employment offices left under provincial jurisdiction. (This may be especially important with
regard to demobilized members of the armed
forces.)

Information Services

5. For the securance of statistical information on
demand and supply conditions, on which alone
broad planning to meet present and future labour
requirements of industry and agriculture can be
based, a properly staffed, and adequately financed
Dominion Employment Service is essential. The
present urgent stage of manpower mobilization
makes this clear today. For meeting the post-war
transition, it will be necessary to develop information
as effectively as possible in advance, so that the
magnitude and the direction of necessary labour
transfers can be reasonably anticipated.

Advisory Councils

6. A national advisory council with regional and
local advisory counsils should be maintained as an
integral part of the employment exchange system.
These councils should include equal representation
of workers and employers, and representatives of
such other groups as can aid in relating community
needs to the Employment Service, and in making
the Employment Service known to the community.
While much of their work will have to be devoted
to building up co-operation in the development of
the Service, as soon as possible they should be
utilized as a medium for study and organization of
plans for meeting post-war dislocations.

War Industries

7. Joint councils of employees and management,
which are or may be formed in industries for the

improvement of production, should be encouraged and assisted. They provide a valuable means of bringing special information to the Employment Service from industries employing large bodies of workers who may have to be transferred, retrained or otherwise re-employed at the end of the war. It is recommended that the closest liaison should be developed between such committees and the Employment Service; and also that they should be utilized as agencies in each industry to devote some time in surveying their probable post-war position, more particularly with regard to the numbers and qualifications of workers for whom new employment may have to be found.

APPENDIX IVb

2. TRAINING FACILITIES.[1]

In its second report, the Subcommittee recorded its recommendations on post-war placement facilities. The organization of training and retraining facilities is the most closely related phase of its terms of reference; and on these the Subcommittee has arrived, after consideration, at the following conclusions:

1. Fundamental to the realization of full employment is an adequate and properly proportioned supply of skilled and semi-skilled workers, on which the further employment of unskilled workers depends. It is therefore imperative that, as far as possible, the supply of skilled and semi-skilled workers should be harmonized with the actual and potential requirements of post-war industry and agriculture in Canada. Existing training plans should be kept constantly under appraisal with this consideration in mind.

2. For this appraisal of training needs, it is essential

(a) that close co-operation be accorded to the Employment Service in developing it as the clearing-house for information on supply and demand conditions for particular occupations; and

(b) that every endeavour should be made to establish a high level of accuracy in the recording of the skill, qualifications and past experience of workers registered with the Service.

This information should be available in appropriate form for the authorities concerned with

---

[1] Third Report of the Subcommittee on Post-war Employment Opportunities, June 14, 1942.

training plans, and all others concerned in the matter.

Dominion-Provincial Training Programme:
  Employment Courses –

3. The organization of pre-employment training, developed first under the pressure of the depression period and subsequently for wartime emergencies, is still capable of extension and improvement. To be adequate for the post-war period, this machinery should be strengthened to cope with the severe adjustments which industry and agriculture will have to make at that time. Its long-range planning must envisage it as part of the permanent facilities through which the working forces of the nation, particularly the younger age-groups, will be fitted for useful employment and occupations suited to their capacities.

4. The pre-employment programme is at present being operated to meet the emergency requirements of wartime production, and is therefore, largely confined to acquainting workers with the minimum of initial skill necessary to enable trainees to undertake specific industrial operations. Resulting from this, there will exist at the end of the war a large supply of partially trained workers, which will probably be more than ample to meet the demands of peacetime industry.

These wartime training schemes of the pre-employment type are of little value in equipping workers with the more complete skills necessary for them to find permanent employment in post-war occupations. At an early stage, therefore, even during the continuance of the war, consideration must be given to adapting the existing training facilities to

  (a) providing more adequate vocational guidance service; and

(*b*) improving and completing skills through
properly regulated training and apprenticeship systems, devised and operated in co-
operation with employers and employees or
their representatives.

Supplementary Training and Apprenticeship

5. Pre-employment schemes are only a first step
in the proper organization of industrial training;
they must be followed up through supplementary
plans which provide actual job experience. Apprenticeship organization designed for post-war
conditions should cover:

(*a*) persons needing apprenticeship who are fitted
for it by age and other considerations; and

(*b*) persons with partial training or experience but
needing further training, or the development
of skill in an occupation related to that they
have previously followed.

6. Technical and vocational schools and pre-
employment classes should be utilized to the full in
co-ordination with apprenticeship training.

7. Attention should be directed now to the need
for considering the best ways of selecting from the
working forces of present wartime plants, those
employees who are most likely to be suited for supplementary training or special retraining for peacetime occupations. Advance study should be given
also to the nature of the skills and occupations
kindred to those now being developed for wartime
production which are most likely to be required in
the peacetime economy. In any plans based on
this type of information, proper allowance must be
made for men in the armed forces who are also
receiving training which may raise similar problems
of adaptation on their return to civil life.

In this connection, the provision in the proposed
Vocational Education Act (Bill 64) for "research

work pertaining to vocational training" and "dissemination of information relating to such training" is welcomed; and it is recommended that the new orientation of training facilities which will be necessary to meet post-war conditions be given consideration under this head.

Vocational Training

8. Vocational training forges the essential links between the period of general school education and that of wage-earning employment. The committee welcomes the Vocational Training Act (Bill 64, brought before the present Parliament), as a statutory recognition of the importance of these links, and as a means of bringing into effective co-ordination the different types of training already developed or projected for the future. . . .

9. It is noted that . . . the Dominion Government is authorized to institute training schemes itself, as well as . . . to assist the provincial governments in instituting or developing schemes on a provincial basis. In view of the large scale and heavy financial responsibility which must be envisaged for training facilities in the years of post-war adjustment, this provision is considered of highest importance.

10. The Committee has given consideration to the experience of the Technical Education Act of 1919 and the Vocational Education Act of 1931, and is emphatically of the opinion that the policy embodied in these Acts of providing a long-term budget for their financing, rather than annual appropriations, is essential for effective planning. . . It is recommended that in any regulations, . . . preference for projects planned for a substantial period should be clearly expressed. Early discouragement should be given to any idea that post-war vocational adjustment will be satisfactorily achieved by merely

temporary or emergency measures.

11. With regard to the Vocational Training Advisory Council, it is recommended that this Council should not be confined only to the consideration of such questions as are brought before it but should have reasonable powers of initiating enquiries and making recommendations to the Minister.

12. In the formulation of Dominion-provincial agreements, it is of great importance that standards should be set and recommended by the Dominion authorities. Every effort should be made to ensure a maximum degree of uniformity in the training facilities of each province.

APPENDIX IVb

3. THE TRAINING AND RECRUITMENT
OF BUILDING LABOUR.[1]

The Subcommittee is concerned with training facilities and recruitment conditions affecting workers of all classes in the post-war period. But it has given separate attention to the building and construction trades, for special reasons. One of these is the importance of activity in the construction industry as a means of stimulating the economy generally. Another is the virtual certainty that a construction programme will have to be put into operation more or less immediately in the transition period, once the changeover from war production to peacetime industrial pattern has begun. A third reason is that a substantial proportion of construction labour is mobile: since the war, numbers of actual or potential building workers have entered munitions fields or the armed services; after the war, there will be a corresponding transference of recruitment if conditions warrant.

In view of the clear prospect of these factors being operative in the post-war period, the Subcommittee strongly recommends that attention be paid now to the needs outlined below. But it wishes also to emphasize strongly the necessary condition on which proposals for ensuring proper recruitment of building labour must depend, if these provisions are not to work to the detriment of the industry. It is that works and buildings programmes must be planned and operated on a long-term basis, and not as a temporary or relief measure.

1. A long-term programme is the first requisite for the satisfactory reform and development of

[1] Fifth Report of the Subcommittee on Post-war Employment Opportunities, October, 1942.

training and recruitment practices in the building industry. It must be on a scale adequate enough to give reasonable assurance of continuous employment to prospective entrants and apprentices. But it is necessary also in order to secure the co-operation of employers and contractors, who will otherwise be apprehensive that the post-war works programme will be merely a short-term stopgap measure, inflating the building industry for a short time and then leaving it stranded later as other forms of industry achieve recovery to a peacetime pattern.

Apprenticeship

2. Where no facilities already exist, encouragement should be given in each province to the working out of an apprenticeship scheme in the building industry as a whole. Two important principles on which these schemes should be based are: (i) co-operative arrangements between employers, workers and the Department of Labour, and (ii) the provision of training in technical schools or special classes. It is not enough for the schemes to involve merely the giving of legal sanctions to indenture arrangements and reliance on "learning on the job" as the only form of training In this connection, the Subcommittee approves the experience of building trades development under the Apprenticeship Act of Ontario, and recommends it as a basis for similar development elsewhere.

3. It is highly important that every means should be sought to make possible the apprenticeship of youths to the trade as a whole, rather than to one firm or one master tradesman. The freedom of the apprentice to move from one employer to another is necessary, not only to enable him on occasion to secure more continuous employment, but so that he may get a broader training and experience from working for firms specializing in different lines of construction. The apprenticeship agreement, there-

fore, should relate, on the employers' side, to a pool of firms, not to a single employer. Similarly, the industry as a whole should agree to give standard recognition to training satisfactorily completed in the technical schools (or other approved institutions).

4. Provision should be worked out, in advance of the termination of the war, for making appropriate adjustments for young workers with some building experience whose apprenticeship was interrupted as a result of their entering a war industry of the armed services. If undertakings on this account can be secured from employers now, it will be easier to plan the necessary arrangements for this section of the new recruits and trainees who will be needed in the post-war period.

5. Appropriate adjustment should also be worked out to permit shortened apprenticeships for boys with some past history of work in the building industry, who should be particularly eligible for training in skilled crafts.

6. The need for special arrangements for adult apprenticeship should be seriously considered. A good many adult labourers, and workers who have transferred from other fields in later life, could be upgraded and retained as more useful and better remunerated tradesmen, if special supplementary training arrangements were made for them.

Schools and Courses

7. The fullest possible use should be made of all available technical schools; and early consideration should be given to the furnishing of an adequate supply of instructors for the enlarged training programme.

8. In the post-war development both of general public education, and of schemes developed under the Vocational Training Coordination Act, a due

share of attention should be given to improving the facilities for vocational specialization in building and kindred techniques.

Other Requirements

9. It is highly important that all parties concerned with both the apprenticeship arrangements and the training facilities of the future should be fully alive to recent technological developments in construction. New crafts and new industrial processes will have to be taught as well as the traditional building crafts. They will not be properly recognized or given their place in training programmes without the co-operation and goodwill of employers and of trade unions. Nor will the building industry be able to play its fullest role in the post-war economy unless its craft demarcations are rendered more flexible, and its techniques more adaptable, than in the past.

10. Serious consideration must be given to all measures making possible more continuous employment and better annual earnings in building trades, as the necessary inducement for an expansion of the skilled labour force in the industry. This includes not only measures for the overcoming of seasonal obstacles and more general provision for winter work, but reasonable guarantees against intermittent unemployment in the more active seasons.

APPENDIX V

INDUSTRIAL RETIREMENT PLANS IN CANADA.[1]

(a) Extent of Coverage in Canadian Industry

[The Queen's University survey covered 120 companies known to have retirement plans of one form or another. The report compares the coverage thus indicated with that which was brought to light by the survey made by the National Employment Commission a year before. It suggests that a generous estimate of the extent of coverage at that date would be 30 per cent of all wage and salary earners.

It must be remembered that today hundreds of thousands of new workers have been added to Canadian industrial payrolls. Some of the workers already covered by retirement plans are now war workers (where the plants have shifted their production); but the net probability is that only a fraction of the industries most likely to be involved in postwar shutdowns have adequate provisions for retirement compensation.

The provisions for retirement as defined in this survey are of course not the same as those which might govern dismissal-wages payable at any age.]

The National Employment Commission survey reported 722 firms (establishments), with 386,677 employees, making provision for retirement. The report was based on replies to a questionnaire sent to over 10,000 employers each employing 15 or more workers, in all industries except banking, agriculture, hunting, fishing, and domestic service. The smaller establishments and the excluded industries, with the exception of banking, are not likely to have made

---

[1] Extracts from study, published under this title, by Industrial Relations Section, Queen's University; Bulletin No. 1, 1938. (Interpolated matter in square brackets).

special retirement provisions. There seem to have been, in April 1937, approximately 400,000 employees (including employees in banks) in Canada working for firms which operated some form of retirement plan.

The present study, made in April 1938, analyses 120 retirement plans maintained by companies (including banks) estimated to employ approximately 265,000 employees in Canada. The great discrepancy between the 722 establishments reported by the National Employment Commission and the 120 plans included in this study is largely explained by the inclusion of all subsidiaries, branch plants, and district offices under the basic company plan in the latter study. The total number of employees of the establishments reported gives a better basis for comparison. The present study covers approximately 265,000 employees, roughly two-thirds of the 400,000 employees (allowing for banking employees) reported by the National Employment Commission. The difference is explained in part by the exclusion of governmental activities of an industrial nature

TABLE IV

INDUSTRIAL RETIREMENT PLANS IN
CANADA—COMPARISON OF COVERAGE

As Reported to The National Employment Commission, April, 1937		
Type of Plan	No. of Firms (Establish-ments)	No. of Employees
Formal...............................	593	349,521
Office Staff only.......................	22	6,733
Informal.............................	107	30,423
Total.............................	722	386,677

[1]Including one plan covering 51 municipalities. [2]Partly estimated.

(except public utilities operated by special commissions); in part by the effect of a more detailed questionnaire in eliminating firms which occasionally retire employees on pension but have no definite plan; and in part by the inclusion of only a sample of the informal plans known to be in operation.

From Table IV, which indicates the comparative coverage secured under the two studies, it may be noted that the plans have been grouped under different headings in each case. In the present study, only plans which lay down some definite standard provisions as to the conditions on which employees are to be retired, and the determination of the retirement allowance, and which, in general, make these provisions known to the employees, have been classified as formal.

The extent of the protection for Canadian employees afforded by industrial retirement plans can only be estimated indirectly. According to the 1931 Census there were 2,570,097 wage and salary earners in Canada. Approximately 15 per cent seem to have been employed in industrial and

As Included in Industrial Relations Section Survey,
April, 1938

Type of Plan	No. of Plans (Companies)	No. of Employees[2]
'ormal:		
Contributory[1]	63	107,000
Composite	2	77,000
Non-contributory	33	66,000
nformal	22	15,000
TOTAL	120	265,000

financial establishments with formal retirement
plans. The present study does not include the
numerous superannuation plans for government and
civic employees, teachers, clergymen, etc. Even
assuming such superannuation provisions to cover
a number equal to those employed by industrial
and financial establishments with formal pension
plans, at least 70 per cent of the wage and salary
earners of Canada would seem to be working in
establishments which make no definite formal provision for the retirement of their employees. Since
existing retirement plans sometimes exclude certain
classes of employees, or provide for voluntary
participation, or provide for age and service requirements which few employees are likely to fulfil,
the total number of employees in establishments
operating retirement plans is likely to be in excess
of the number actually enjoying protection against
old age dependency through the retirement provisions. Moreover, the adequacy of the actual
provisions varies greatly under the different plans.[1]

*(b) Significance of the Private Retirement Plan
Movement*

Potential economic gains and employee pressure
for retirement provision are both unlikely to be important in industries where employees are rarely
retained to old age, where labour is migratory,
where most of the workers are women, where the
firms are financially unstable, and where the need
for retirement provision occurs infrequently because
of the small scale of the business. Moreover, the
movement is unlikely to advance rapidly in any
industry where wages are relatively low and where
employees feel that present needs are more pressing
than provision for an uncertain future which may
never arrive, and which, in any case, may be
provided for by the state.

---

[1] Pp. 8-10 of the Queen's University study.

Since industrial retirement plans will probably never be extended to even the majority of employees, and since, in any case, they cannot protect the important group of aging persons working on their own account or not engaged in industry, they cannot be regarded as an alternative to an inclusive state-operated plan.

Although, with the passing of the United States Social Security Act, state provision for old-age insecurity has become a practical programme on this continent, even after the introduction of a contributory state plan in Canada there would still be a place for private retirement plans. In the first place, the amount of the retirement income under a state plan is usually small, and industrial retirement plans might be maintained to supplement the state benefits. In the second place, the retirement age under a universal plan is likely to be higher than the appropriate age for retirement from certain industries. In time, social pressure may compel each industry to accept responsibility for caring for those of its own employees who are retired before they become eligible under the state plan. Retirement plans provide for the period between actual retirement from industry and the time of eligibility for the state benefits would produce the same economic advantages as are claimed for present plans, and might prove acceptable to employees, especially in those industries in which wages are relatively high.

Although it seems probable that voluntary retirement plans will never become universal throughout industry, it is likely that a large number of companies in Canada will, for a considerable time, feel the need to maintain plans offering complete retirement protection or plans supplementing a state scheme. As long as such plans are in operation, it is desirable that they should be framed in the best interests of industry and of society.[2]

(c) Trends in Industrial Retirement Plans

1. The majority of the new plans confine the retirement plan to provision for *dependent old age,* and to the protection of the rights of the individual employees to the funds accumulated on their behalf. Many of the re-insured retirement plans have associated with them provisions for group life insurance, or group sickness and non-occupational disability insurance, or both. In order to ensure that too large a proportion of the income of employees is not devoted to one form of protection at the expense of more urgent needs, it is desirable:

   (a) to separate out the risks requiring insurance protection, and to provide for them, preferably under separate sections of a "package plan";

   (b) to arrange the contributions and benefits for these types of insurance in relation to each other, and to the level of money wages prevailing in the company.

2. With very few exceptions, the plans examined provide that all *permanent employees* shall be eligible for membership. A short waiting period for eligibility, its length depending upon special circumstances in the industry is frequently imposed in order to reduce administrative costs by excluding casual employees.

3. For employees hired after the inauguration of the plan, membership is *frequently compulsory.* For employees already in the service it is usually optional, but accompanied by a strong inducement to participate. The most effective inducements seem to be the limitation of benefits for past service to employees joining the plan within a short time of its adoption, and the grouping of two or more forms of insurance

[2] *Ibid.*, pp. 108-9.

under a "package plan". If complete coverage and uniform working conditions for all employees are to be attained, compulsory membership seems to be necessary.

4. The newer plans provide for compulsory retirement at a *definite age* (present experience indicates no later than age sixty-five). Later retirement is sometimes permitted under special circumstances, but usually only on the application of the employee and with the consent of the employer. Earlier retirement, with an immediate annuity actuarially adjusted, is almost invariably permitted at the discretion of the employer, on the request of the employee. Such flexibility appears to be desirable, provided that the annuity payable is adequate.

5. *No conditions for determining eligibility* for annuity other than attainment of the normal retirement age are imposed under the majority of recent plans. It has been found that service requirements operate to postpone desirable retirements, and limit the effective protection to a relatively small proportion of the employees. Moreover, since they are related to the conception of a pension as a reward for long and faithful service, they are inappropriate if retirement allowances are regarded as a form of wage payment.

6. Practically every new plan which has been adopted since 1929 has provided for *direct employee contributions,* and a number of previously noncontributory plans have been revised on the same basis. Direct employee contributions have been found desirable to ensure that the employees will take an active interest in the plan, and that they will be granted legal rights. Experience has shown such rights to be associated only with contributory plans, although the provision for direct employee contributions does not always, or in itself, guarantee them.

7. Usually, direct employee contributions and *company contributions* are so arranged that each provides approximately one-half the total funds necessary. Together they are designed to result in each individual employee having to his credit at retirement a total amount, from contributions and accumulated interest, sufficient to provide benefits roughly related to his aggregate pay and service. Contributions usually cease at the normal retirement age.

8. For convenience in administration, it has been found desirable, under the newer re-insured plans, to *group employees according to their salaries*, and to arrange for the same rate of contributions and benefits for employees in the same salary group. This method necessarily introduces some inequalities between individual employees. The salary-class limits require careful consideration in order to minimize these inequalities. If the upper limit of the lowest class is not low enough, the small-income employees may be devoting an undue proportion of their income to retirement protection. If the sub-divisions are not so arranged that the majority of employees within each group are near the mid-points of their groups, inequalities will arise between individuals. The portion of any salary above a relatively low maximum is frequently disregarded, since the number of individuals who would benefit by high retirement annuities is limited, and such individuals may reasonably be expected to provide for themselves such extra protection as they require.

Usually the salary-class method of calculating contributions and benefits is associated with level rates for all individuals in the salary group. This method introduces further inequalities between individual employees because their contributions are made at different ages. Because of accumulating interest, a $1.00 contribution made, for example, at age twenty-five produces a larger retirement reserve at age sixty-five than a similar $1.00 contribution made ten or twenty years later. If the final retirement annuity payable is, say, $1.00 a month for each year of service, it is evident that, for any one year, the direct contribution of a young employee will buy a larger proportion of the retirement annuity in respect to that year of service than the equal direct contribution of an older employee in the same salary class. Various methods have been suggested for arranging payments so that employees of different ages will, through their own direct contributions, pay approximately equivalent proportions of the cost of their final benefits, but all these methods introduce administrative difficulties.

9. Employees are commonly not asked to contribute during periods when their income is reduced because of *lay-off or illness*. Provision is sometimes made for making up such contributions voluntarily on the employee's return to work, so that the final retirement annuity need not be reduced. Ordinarily, employees definitely leaving the service of the company are refunded their own direct contributions (sometimes with interest) but forfeit the company contributions on their behalf. On re-entering the company, they have the same status as new employees. Under plans which annually vest in the individual employees complete rights to the company contributions on their behalf, any requirement of continuous service is obviously inappropriate.

10. The new plans provide a retirement allowance in the form of a *life annuity*, payable at the normal age of retirement, equivalent in value to the total contributions made on behalf of the individual employee, with the accumulated interest on these contributions. The relation of this benefit to the amount of salary during active service will vary between individuals because of different rates of salary increase during service. When direct employee contributions are based on salary, and the

balance of the scheduled benefits is made up from company contributions, the proportion of the annuity purchased by company contributions will vary as between individuals. If retirement benefits are looked upon as a form of wage payment, it is evident that this variation in company contributions on behalf of individuals in effect constitutes a concealed difference in wages.

11. Any immediate annuity payable to an employee retired before the normal retirement age is usually, under the new plans, equivalent in value to the deferred annuity, payable at the normal date, to which his accumulated reserves would entitle him.

12. The annuity payable to an employee retiring later than the normal age sometimes begins at the normal age; sometimes it begins at actual retirement and is increased to allow for the further accumulations of interest and for the reduced life expectancy.

13. Under a new plan, past service benefits of an adequate amount have usually been found necessary to . make retirements possible, both immediately and until the accumulations under the contributory plan provide adequate benefits. When the new plan is a revision of a non-contributory plan, it has been considered desirable to provide benefits for past service in accordance with expectations under the former plan.

14. A *maximum limit* for the benefits payable is provided under the majority of recent plans. Usually, this maximum is automatically provided by grouping all salaries over a specified amount into one salary class, with the same monthly contribution and benefit for all members of that class. This limitation on the amount of benefit payable has been found desirable in order to permit the company contribution to be spread over a large number of the lower-paid employees, and to prevent its allocation to a small number of high-paid employees. Minimum

annuities are less frequently provided, although they seem desirable in the interests of social security.

15. Employees are usually given the option of selecting the form of annuity most suited to their individual needs, so that they may make provision to protect their dependents against the risk of death shortly after retirement. The *optional annuity* is of the same actuarial value as the life annuity otherwise payable.

16. All the contributory retirement plans provide for a *refund* of the employee's own direct contributions, usually with interest at a guaranteed rate (but sometimes only in part, or without interest), *if the employee withdraws* from the company before retirement for any reason, or if he dies before reaching the retirement age. Companies have tended to look upon their contributions as funds especially set aside for retirement purposes, and to confine their benefits to employees remaining with the company until retirement. In order to ensure retirement protection to the individual employees, a number of recent plans have made provision for vesting rights to a paid-up deferred annuity, purchased with the appropriate share of company contributions, in withdrawing employees who agree to accept the refund of their direct contributions in the same form. This provision appears to be an important step towards guaranteeing employees full contractual rights to all contributions made on their behalf. Under a few plans, the extension of contractual rights has gone even further, and withdrawing employees, with as low as five years service, are given the right to withdraw all the funds to their credit without restrictions.

17. Recent retirement plans afford employees *legal safeguards* in the form of guarantees that the retirement annuity will be awarded to all persons who attain the normal retirement age while in the

service of the company, and that, once benefits are granted, they will be continued for the duration of the specified period. The further legal safeguard sometimes recommended, of a guarantee that no employee within ten years of the normal retirement age should be dismissed from the service without receiving an immediate annuity purchased with the funds to his credit, is not yet included in any of the Canadian plans. Since the benefits of the retirement plan are one form in which employees receive their wage payments, ultimately it seems desirable that the employees should be assured of full contractual rights, both to their own direct contributions and to the company contributions on their behalf (including accumulated interest, but deducting the appropriate share of administration expense), and that such rights should be vested in the individual employees regularly. Under re-insured plans, the employees are given individual certificates as evidence of their contractual status.

18. The provisions of the plans recently adopted or revised indicate that increasing attention is being paid to the problem of *sound finance*. It is becoming recognized that the liabilities accrue currently and that they should be measured accurately and provided for as they accrue.

If the company finds it expedient to pay past service benefits, an unfunded liability is created. The least expensive way of funding the liability, that is, the one which involves the smallest charge to operating expenses, is to make a lump-sum payment. Most companies find this too heavy an outlay to make all at one time, but undoubtedly sound practice dictates that it should be met as soon as possible. No company is justified in establishing a retirement plan unless it is prepared to set aside sufficient funds to meet future service liabilities as they accrue. If the company assumes responsibility for past service credits, it ought to be prepared to forgo profits of such amounts as will fund the assumed liability promptly.

19. Under practically all the retirement plans recently adopted, the liabilities of the plan are *underwritten by a life insurance company*. Re-insurance involves regular payments and complete funding of the liability. It also provides guarantees that the principal of the reserve fund will be secure, and that the assumed rate of interest will be earned. Moreover, the administration of the plan is likely to be more efficient and less expensive than under any but the largest self-administered plans.

20. The majority of recent plans, whether re-insured or self-administered, are recognizing the need to provide guarantees that the funds which are at once set aside for retirement purposes will not, under any circumstances, be recaptured by the company and used for other purposes. All re-insured plans provide this guarantee.

21. Recent retirement plans reveal a tendency to limit company discretion and assure impartial administration of the plan, by setting out more definite and simple rules, by placing control of the granting, determination, and payments of benefits in the hands of a life insurance company, or by providing for employee representation on the Pension Board administering the plan.

22. A number of the most recent plans make provision, so that, in case a state scheme of retirement protection is established, the company plan may be revised to supplement the state plan.[3]

---
[3] *Ibid.*, pp. 109-114.

APPENDIX VI

RENTAL VARIATIONS AND
THE MINIMUM STANDARD

Substantial variations in both the costs and the levels of living between one part of the country and another are realities which have to be faced in any consideration of standards for Canada. Several types of figures are available on a provincial basis which show these variations clearly: some of them are assembled in the accompanying table (Table V). Almost all figures, however, call for careful interpretation, for two reasons in particular. There is, first, the difficulty of determining which is cause and which is effect. Secondly, provincial boundaries are misleading, for the real differences of standards are frequently those between particular regions or districts, and most of all between cities on the one hand, and remote rural or frontier areas on the other.

Even if data for sufficiently small areas were available, important qualifications would have to be made before a cost-of-living-budget index could be accepted as sufficient for the local adjustment of a minimum benefit rate. In any case, the lower the national minimum is scaled, the less justifiable and less desirable it is to attempt to pare it down where regional living standards are exceptionally low. Moreover, as argued elsewhere (Section 20), in assessing the scales of social insurance benefits, there is an important distinction between the benefits which are of a short-run or transitional nature and those which are more continuous or permanent. The former are scaled automatically if prevailing wage rates are low; the latter apply to cases (e.g., of disability) where fortuitously high purchasing-power, if it should exist, is not likely to be socially harmful.

With these qualifications in mind, it is still true

that the one variable in a cost-of-living budget which has tangible cause, and may be reasonably singled out, is that of house rent. If adequate information were available it would appear to offer the best probability of providing an index on which graduation could be based. Some figures are therefore brought together in this section to throw further light on this factor; though they also reveal the difficulties of application.

Urban-Rural Variations

There is no question about the difference in the rental levels characteristic of large cities, small and medium cities, and rural areas, respectively. This is clearly demonstrated in Table VI, which shows the distribution of all tenant householders in Canada, not merely by province but by size of city. Practically universally, rents are thirty to fifty per cent lower in the medium-sized towns (5,000–15,000 population) than in the larger cities. In villages and in rural areas they are much lower still, rents of $11 to $12 a month being particularly common. (It should be noted that the figures for rural areas in Ontario, and to a lesser degree in Manitoba and British Columbia are misleading because the areas immediately adjacent to Toronto, Winnipeg and Vancouver which raise the average considerably, are really urban areas in all but name). It is important to note that the degree of uniformity really outstanding in this table is in the rents prevalent in cities and town of the same size, irrespective of provincial boundaries.

These facts are presented in a different and informative way in Table VII, which shows the proportion of the population in all the main cities of Canada who live in low-rent houses. The most significant feature is that low rents are much more common in the smaller urban centres than in the

TABLE V.—SOME INDEXES OF VARIATIONS IN COSTS AND STANDARDS OF LIVING

(a) Amounts ($)

Provinces	Public Welfare Expenditures (per capita)		Average Weekly Earnings		Cost of Living (Staple Budget)		Rents (Workmen's Houses)		Rents (All Tenants: Cities) Housing Census, 1941
	Welfare	Education	All Industry	Manufactures	All Items	Food	Class A	Class B	
	(a)	(b)	(c)	(d)	(e)	(f)	(g)	(h)	(i)
	$	$	$	$	$	$	$	$	$
Prince Edward Island	2.96	5.90	22.81	21.24	81.82	44.84	......	......	......
Nova Scotia	6.30	7.70	25.91	29.07	81.87	46.98	21.42	15.41	27.00
New Brunswick	4.42	6.08	24.35	25.19	86.83	47.15	24.13	17.38	18.00
Quebec	5.56	7.24	27.87	28.14	84.78	43.54	24.71	18.25	16.00
Ontario	8.63	12.01	30.76	31.37	90.96	46.24	27.31	20.27	30.00
Manitoba	7.47	9.63	29.30	28.48	86.30	43.20	26.75	19.50	30.00
Saskatchewan	7.18	8.72	28.14	29.87	82.78	42.41	27.88	20.00	27.00
Alberta	7.11	12.14	30.56	30.04	78.95	43.54	26.13	18.63	26.00
British Columbia	10.47	12.47	32.77	33.79	86.61	48.76	23.31	17.69	24.00
CANADA	7.26	9.78	29.49	30.15	87.61	45.63	25.61	18.84	27.00

(b) PERCENTAGES

Provinces	Public Welfare Expenditures (per capita)		Average Weekly Earnings		Cost of Living (Staple Budget)		Rents (Workmen's Houses)		Rents (All Tenants: Cities) Housing Census, 1941
	Welfare	Education	All Industry	Manu-factures	All Items	Food	Class A	Class B	
	(a)	(b)	(c)	(d)	(e)	(f)	(g)	(h)	(i)
	$	$	$	$	$	$	$	$	$
Prince Edward Island	41	60	77	71	93	98	....	....	....
Nova Scotia	87	79	88	96	93	103	84	82	100
New Brunswick	61	62	83	84	99	103	94	92	67
Quebec	77	74	95	93	97	95	96	97	59
Ontario	119	123	104	104	104	101	107	108	111
Manitoba	103	98	99	94	99	95	104	104	111
Saskatchewan	99	89	95	99	94	93	109	106	100
Alberta	98	124	104	100	90	95	102	99	96
British Columbia	144	127	111	112	99	107	91	94	89
CANADA	100	100	100	100	100	100	100	100	100

(a), (b). Provincial and municipal expenditures only; (a) on public welfare, excluding relief and (b), education. Based on figures compiled for the Royal Commission on Dominion-Provincial Relations, summarized in H. M. Cassidy, *Social Security and Reconstruction*, Chapter II. Figures relate to 1937.

(c), (d). Average earnings are for the bulk of non-agricultural employment as reported by the Dominion Bureau of Statistics, *The Employment Situation*, October, 1942, p. 6. The coverage at this source is of employees in firms with 15 or more on payrolls. Figures relate to October, 1942.

(e), (f). Cost of a staple budget, per month, by estimation from last published figures on this budget (*Labour Gazette*, June, 1941, p. 708). The method of estimation is to apply the D.B.S. Cost of Living Indexes to the appropriate budgets. Figures relate to March, 1942.

(g), (h). Class A are "six-roomed houses with modern conveniences." Class B,—"six-roomed houses with incomplete modern conveniences." These are monthly rents from a large sample of workingmen's houses in 69 cities. As explained in the *Labour Gazette*, (e.g., p. 1213, issue of October, 1942), they are "the prevailing rates for six-roomed houses of two classes extensively occupied by workingmen. The first class is of houses in good condition, favourably located in such districts with good modern conveniences. The second class is of houses in fair condition, less desirably located but still fairly central, without modern conveniences." Figures relate to October, 1942.

(i). Rents for all types of tenants; from a sample count taken in the 27 largest cities (population of greater areas over 30,000). The figures given are medians. Dominion Bureau of Statistics, Housing Census (June, 1941).

TABLE VI.—AVERAGE MONTHLY RENTS IN URBAN CENTRES CLASSIFIED ACCORDING
TO SIZE, AND IN RURAL AREAS (1941)

Provinces	Cities 30,000 and Over	Cities 15,000–30,000	Cities 5,000–15,000	Towns 1,000–5,000	Under 1,000	Rural Areas (Other than Farms)
	$	$	$	$	$	$
Prince Edward Island	......	......	21	16	8	9
Nova Scotia	32	19	17	15	17	11
New Brunswick	22	29	23	16	13	11
Quebec	26	29	19	19	12	11
Ontario	33	25	24	17	11	(20)*
Manitoba	28	24	18	12	12	(15)*
Saskatchewan	27	24	21	15	9	8
Alberta	27	......	22	16	12	12
British Columbia	26	20	23	18	12	(15)*

SOURCE:—Specially compiled, Housing Census, Dominion Bureau of Statistics, Medians of all tenant households, 1941.
* See note in text.

TABLE VII.—COMPARATIVE DISTRIBUTION OF RENTALS, TWENTY MAIN CITIES

(Proportion of the population living in rented houses paying up to certain monthly amounts, 1931)

City	Proportion of Tenants Paying	
	Up to $20	Up to $25
	%	%
Saint John	53·1	67·3
Halifax	36·8	48·9
Trois-Rivières	47·3	71·9
Montreal	34·9	55·8
Verdun	27·0	55·4
Quebec	33·4	53·2
Brantford	43·5	63·6
Kitchener	34·6	47·0
Hamilton	27·4	44·4
London	23·1	39·1
Ottawa	17·9	29·1
Toronto	15·2	25·3
Windsor	11·0	18·8
Regina	28·7	35·4
Winnipeg	25·7	33·7
Saskatoon	25·8	33·4
Edmonton	23·7	33·4
Calgary	21·9	33·0
Victoria	38·8	55·1
Vancouver	25·7	38·8
Larger Urban Centres (30,000 and over)	28·2	44·0
Smaller Urban Centres (Under 30,000)	58·8	69·1
All Urban Centres	40·1	53·4

Source:—Census Monograph No. 8, *Housing in Canada, 1941*, page 171.

TABLE VIII.—COMPARATIVE PROPORTION OF POPULATIO
LIVING IN LOW-RENTAL HOUSES, TWENTY MAIN CITIES,
1931 AND 1941

City	Proportion of Tenants Paying $15 or Less	
	1931	1941
	%	%
Saint John............................	32·4	33·7
Halifax...............................	22·2	15·4
Trois-Rivières........................	22·2	16·9
Montreal..............................	14·6	18·7
Verdun...............................	4·8	9·5
Quebec...............................	14·0	12·9
Brantford............................	21·6	12·7
Kitchener............................	20·6	14·1
Hamilton.............................	12·1	8·0
London...............................	8·5	10·9

Source:—Census Monograph No. 8, *Housing in Canada*, 1941, page 171, and
Preliminary Bulletin on *Housing Census of Canada, 1941*, Dominion Bureau
of Statistics, page 5.

larger towns and cities.   In 1931, fifty-nine per cent
of the tenants in the smaller urban centres paid $20
a month or less, as compared with twenty-eight per
cent of the tenants in cities of 30,000 population and
over.   If the dividing line is placed at $25, the
corresponding proportions are nearly seventy per
cent as against forty-four per cent.   It is also
evident from this table, however, that city conditions
differ in different areas.   There is a close degree of
similarity among the Prairie cities, but a wide
divergence among Ontario cities.   Taking all the
cities as a group the range is remarkably great.   In
Windsor, for example, fewer than twenty per cent
of persons living in rented houses pay less than $25 a
month, whereas in Trois-Rivières more than seventy
per cent do so.

Another approach to these figures counsels the
warning that an index based on rent, if it could be
devised, might be considerably variable over time.
Comparable data from the 1941 housing census
enable the differences in the proportion of low-rental
tenants occurring over a decade, to be shown.   The

City	Proportion of Tenants Paying $15 or Less	
	1931	1941
	%	%
Ottawa.............................	8·2	6·9
Toronto.............................	6·6	4·0
Windsor.............................	5·0	9·7
Regina.............................	18·7	17·2
Winnipeg.............................	16·0	14·4
Saskatoon.............................	16·2	29·0
Edmonton.............................	11·5	22·9
Calgary.............................	11·2	14·8
Victoria.............................	20·6	24·5
Vancouver.............................	12·9	20·5

broad geographical differences remain, but substantial changes have taken place in the ten-year period. The trend was not, as might have been expected, universally towards a larger number living in cheaper dwellings: in some cities the proportion moved downwards, for reasons which would not be clear without special investigation. Unquestionably, local building programs, or lack of them, would be among the causal factors, as well as changes in general prosperity and wage-earner incomes in particular.

Relationship to Incomes

One of the most revealing computations is that of Table IX. As the result of a special compilation made by courtesy of the Housing Branch of the Dominion Bureau of Statistics, the rents which are typical of tenant family accommodation throughout Canada are here related to the incomes of the principal householders. Clearly, differences in rental levels are not merely a regional phenomenon, but a matter of the family budget and the amount which can be afforded for rent. The range is very pronounced, rents of $17 to $21 a month being typical of families, probably of semi-skilled and unskilled workers, with incomes of less than $1,000 a year; whereas among families typical of white-collar groups, rentals between $32 and $38 a month are most common.   On the whole, however, there is less variation in the rents paid by low-wage-earners than might be expected.   In other words, for families at or below the minimum standard, a fixed rate of benefit need not create impossible differences in the ability to secure housing accommodation.[1]

It might be thought that practices evolved and established for the payment of rental allowances to families on unemployment relief would show a definite approach to a basic minimum; or at least might offer enough data to show what limits of variation need to be involved.   Thanks to the careful records assembled by the Canadian Welfare

---

[1] The relatively high figures for Ontario appear as an exception to this. On the other hand, it is definitely known that a considerable amount of "doubling-up," by which families actually pay lower rents than those which appear statistically, is prevalent among all these low-income groups.

TABLE IX.—RENTS PAID BY FAMILIES OF DIFFERENT INCOME GROUPS

(All tenant families: urban centres of 30,000 and over; 1941)

Family Earnings (Annual)	Canada
	$
Less than $500	19
$500-$1,000	21
$1,000-$1,500	24
$1,500-$2,000	29
$2,000- 3,000	35
$3,000 and over	48

Source:—Special compilation, Housing Census (1941), Dominion Bureau of Statistics. Family earnings listed as those of the principal tenant; i.e. rent may be shared with other families in some cases (particularly in lowest income group).

Council, it was possible to examine the total picture
of all the relief rent scales adopted throughout the
country in a particular year (1937). The main
result, however, was to show that no consistent
principles were applied to this important matter,
and the material was too diverse to warrant repro-
duction. In a few provinces some measure of
standardization was effected. In Manitoba, for
example, shelter allowances for two persons were
scaled at between $8 and $10; for four persons,
between $12 and $14. In Ontario, the common
practice was to pay 100 per cent to 150 per cent of
taxes as a rental allowance to home owners, and 150
per cent to 200 per cent taxes as a rental allowance
to tenants, with a maximum set at $15. In other
provinces, however, no similarly clear pattern is
discernible at all. While the data in general confirm
the fact that rentals in small towns and rural areas
are very much lower, it would seem vain to hope for
much guidance from past relief administration in
setting up a logical structure for variation in benefit
standards.

Maritimes	Quebec	Ontario	Prairies	British Columbia
$	$	$	$	$
16	18	26	17	19
17	19	26	21	20
22	22	28	26	24
29	26	31	33	28
38	32	37	38	33
51	46	50	51	45

Range and Determinants of Variation

A final factor in the consideration of a rental-variant for application to insurance benefits is the degree of complexity which would be involved. Since the Dominion Bureau of Statistics regularly collects data on working-class rents for a large number of Canadian towns and cities, it is possible to indicate roughly what a benefit-rate scaled to local variations would involve.

The material assembled in Table X is simplified in various ways. It relates to the lowest grades of housing accommodation in the urban areas concerned, evaluated as the prevalent rates by the Department of Labour's correspondents throughout the country. (a) Since variation is wide even at the poorest levels of housing, it is necessary to specify a range rather than a single figure: Table X, however, adopts the mid-points of the ranges reported. (June, 1940, is chosen as an average month in a year not likely to be widely divergent from post-war conditions). (b) The rent taken as standard ($19.00 monthly) is roughly one-fifth of the assistance minimum income cited in Section 4 ($94.54), this proportion being generally accepted as that which rent payments should not exceed at this income level. (c) It is assumed that reductions or increases in the standard benefit would not be put into force unless the prevailing rent is at least five per cent higher or lower than the standard, or a multiple of five per cent either way. The end columns show respectively the actual variation on an index basis, and the percentages of reduction or increase which would have to be applied if this type of rent index were made applicable.

It is evident that at least some of these adjustments would appear arbitrary. A more refined scaling of benefits related to individual cases would probably resolve this problem, but it would call for much greater administrative effort and cost. It would also bring the whole procedure much nearer to means-test conditions, and lose the simplicity which is one of the great virtues of the single minimum. There would still remain the necessity of setting a rate or percentage for rural areas; though this might perhaps be provided for by specifying that it should not be lower than the rate of the lowest town included in the official list. This might raise problems of statistical adequacy as well as of equity; and the difficulty of defining rural areas would also have to be overcome.

Contemporary British Experience

Variations in rentals are by no means confined to countries such as Canada, in which great distances as well as differences in the economic basis of the component regions are predisposing factors. In spite of the standardization which has been brought about in Britain through rent control, the levelling up of wages through national collective bargaining and statutory regulations, and systematic adjustment of unemployment assistance in recent years, there are still enough disparities in expenditures on rents for the matter to have been given special attention in the framing of the Beveridge recommendations. Various suggestions were considered for relating benefit payments to rents in certain localities, before the final outlines of the British plan were decided. One suggestion was that benefit should vary directly with the rent paid in each individual case; the simpler version of this proposal being the establishment of a standard rent at a certain amount, and the granting of additional allowances to families paying more than this sum, up to a certain maximum. The objection to the proposal, which is hard to answer, is that it would discriminate in favour of families who have either

TABLE X.—SAMPLE INDEXES OF RENTAL VARIATION,
IN RELATION TO POSSIBLE ADJUSTMENTS OF STANDARD
BENEFIT SCALES

City or Town	Mid-point of Reported Range	Relation to Assistance Standard	Percentage Reduction or Increase
	$	($19 = 100)	%
MARITIME PROVINCES—			
Halifax	20.00	105·3	+ 5
Saint John	18.00	94·7	− 5
Fredericton	18.00	94·7	− 5
Moncton	17.50	92·1	−10
Sidney	16.50	86·8	−15
Windsor	16.00	84·2	−15
Truro	16.00	84·2	−15
Bathurst	16.00	84·2	−15
New Glasgow	14.00	73·7	−30
Charlottetown	12.50	65·7	− 35
Amherst	10.00	52·6	−50
QUEBEC—			
Sherbrooke	21.50	113·2	+10
Montreal	20.50	107·9	+ 5
Trois-Rivières	20.00	105·3	+ 5
St. Hyacinthe	18.00	94·7	− 5
St. Johns	16.00	84·2	−20
Hull	16.00	84·2	−20
Thetford Mines	14.50	76·3	−25
Sorel	11.50	60·5	−40
ONTARIO—			
Sudbury	27.50	144·7	+45
Toronto	24.00	126·3	+25
Windsor	24.00	126·3	+25
London	23.00	121·0	+20
St. Catharines	21.50	113·2	+10
Hamilton	21.00	110·5	+10
St. Thomas	21.00	110·5	+10
Kingston	20.00	105·3	+ 5
Kitchener	20.00	105·3	+ 5
Port Arthur	20.00	105·3	+ 5
Fort William	20.00	105·3	+ 5
Niagara Falls	19.50	102·6	0

Applied to June, 1940, rentals, six-roomed houses with incomplete modern
conveniences in working-class districts. (Department of Labour monthly
compilations).

City or Town	Mid-point of Reported Range	Relation to Assistance Standard	Percentage Reduction or Increase
	$	($19 = 100)	%
ONTARIO—*Continued*			
Ottawa..............	18.50	97·4	− 5
Brantford...........	18.50	97·4	− 5
Guelph..............	18.50	97·4	− 5
Peterborough........	18.00	94·7	− 5
Owen Sound.........	18.00	94·7	− 5
Oshawa.............	17.50	92·1	−10
Orillia.............	17.50	92·1	−10
Galt................	17.50	92·1	−10
Woodstock..........	17.50	92·1	−10
Stratford...........	17.50	92·1	−10
Sarnia..............	17.50	92·1	−10
Sault Ste. Marie......	17.50	92·1	−10
Chatham............	17.00	89·5	−10
Brockville...........	16.00	84·2	−20
Belleville...........	16.00	84·2	−20
Cobalt..............	15.00	78·9	−25
WESTERN PROVINCES—			
Regina..............	23.50	123·7	+20
Winnipeg...........	22.50	118·4	+15
Trail...............	22.50	118·4	+15
Calgary.............	20.00	105·3	+ 5
Vancouver..........	19.50	102·6	0
Nelson..............	19.00	100·0	0
Prince Rupert........	19.00	100·0	0
Edmonton...........	18.50	97·4	− 5
Brandon............	17.50	92·1	−10
Saskatoon...........	17.50	92·1	−10
Moose Jaw..........	17.50	92·1	−10
Lethbridge..........	17.50	92.1	−10
Medicine Hat........	17.00	89·5	−10
Victoria............	16.50	86·8	−15
Nanaimo............	16.00	84·2	−20
New Westminster......	16.00	84·2	−20
Fernie..............	14.00	73·7	−30

deliberately chosen or been fortunate in obtaining a relatively high standard of housing; while, on the other hand, it would encourage landlords to raise their rents. This objection would apply in much the same way in Canada. It has not been referred to heretofore, since this Appendix is concerned with the preliminary matter of establishing some of the facts of the situation.

Another and simpler proposal was that benefit might be adjusted to rent only for the temporary benefits (unemployment and sickness), and not for pensions and other long-term benefits. This has little or no applicability to the Canadian scheme, however, since this already proposes variable benefits for the transitional risks, whereas the Beveridge plan is entirely flat-rate. The significant point is that, after consideration of several other alternatives, the conclusion was reached that the simplicity of a standard minimum outweighs the administrative difficulties of applying a formula for adjustment.

It is important to add, however, that the most fundamental influence on the whole situation could be exerted by a national housing programme. The major problem is to provide additional accommodation in the areas where new housing is most urgently required; or in other words, to have a supply of housing which would ensure sufficiently low rents. A properly distributed housing programme which paid attention to the types of workers resident in particular areas could go far to establishing reasonably uniform rent levels. And the more deliberately a housing policy for the lowest income-groups was pursued, the more this would be true for the classes most dependent on social insurance benefits at minimum maintenance rates.

INDEX TO TABLES

SUMMARY SCHEDULES